WITHDRAWN

THE ORIENT IN BIBLE TIMES

OFF THE COAST AT JAFFA, PALESTINE. SHIPS MUST STAND FAR FROM SHORE

BIBLE LANDS AND PEOPLES—HISTORICAL
BEING A COMPANION VOLUME TO "THE PEOPLE OF PALESTINE"

THE ORIENT IN BIBLE TIMES

BY

ELIHU GRANT

PROFESSOR OF BIBLICAL LITERATURE IN HAVERFORD COLLEGE

PHILADELPHIA AND LONDON
J. B. LIPPINCOTT COMPANY

TO PROFESSOR
IRVING FRANCIS WOOD
SMITH COLLEGE

PREFACE

We seek to fasten the attention of the reader upon the main points in the story of the Early East, to help people who are interested in the Bible to see the Hebrews among their neighbors and to give a rapid, unified impression of the course of events in the biblical world.

The background and presuppositions of that world differed in so many ways from ours that we need frequently to picture in imagination the world situation as people in Bible Times knew it. Ordinarily it takes much material and many books to help one do this. We have suggested some of these aids in the Book Lists at the close of the chapters. They will help those who wish to follow the subjects further. It is our hope by this survey of the available information to leave certain definite impressions of oriental civilizations with busy people of to-day. It will be possible to appraise the civilization of the Western World better when we know more of the buried East. So we draw attention to the leading cultures, those of Egypt, Babylonia, Assyria and Palestine. We have noted the triumphs of the Persians, the eastward trend of Greek influence, the conquest and organization of Western Asia by Rome. We see the rise and fall of the great powers and the fate of the smaller nations. Trade, politics, war, social institutions and international relations develop during these centuries. Our own age is seeking to recover all that humanity ever knew or cared for and to give a vivid introduction to life, customs and thought of the early peoples in their own right and also as they influenced the Hebrews either directly or indirectly.

Throughout Bible Times the Orient was an ever-expanding world of interest, including the civilized portions of Asia, Africa and Europe where they approached each other most nearly. Of those luxuriant millennia and fertile seats of customs and ideas the mightiest fell away in the thought of mankind. Their faiths yielded to the dominance of what may be called in certain aspects the Hebraic religions, Judaism, Christianity and Islam. Horus, Marduk, Asshur, Ormazd, Zeus and the sciences and philosophies associated with them have been absorbed or forgotten.

The writer acknowledges with gratitude his debt to the works which have been named in the Book Lists and to other great names in Oriental study, also to several friends who have provided the pictures used as illustrations. These last will remind us of the connection between the ancient and the present times.

THE AUTHOR.

NOVEMBER, 1919.

CONTENTS

ILLUSTRATIONS

THE ORIENT IN BIBLE TIMES

CHAPTER I

The oldest civilizations known are oriental. So remote are they to our gaze that they seem to blend into one, but study reveals many distinct ideas and cultures. To speak of only two of these, there were such different civilizations as the Egyptian and the Babylonian. Upon the two countries represented by those names there falls the strongest light of discovery. But that light, diffused by the widening of exploration and made clearer by the interpreters of the results, is showing a large ancient world instead of a small one. There were, in fact, many oriental peoples, each contributing to the richly diversified intellectual and material development of the early oriental world. They worked at life's problems and had wrought out many principles of civilization centuries before the peoples came into historical view. Certain of their institutions still serve us to this day.

As to the question, which of the countries or peoples reached a matured civilization first, we shall have to confess that there is no exact knowledge with which to answer. The conditions favorable to rapid growth were similarly present in several regions. The gains of several races, before history begins, must have been great. The probability is high that

1

there was considerable intercommunication between the different peoples of the early oriental world. They were too much alive to be insensible to the advantages which each could in turn suggest to others. The beginnings of Egyptian historical information may be dated about 4000 B.C., and of Babylonian a few centuries later, but our historical knowledge of either country may be increased by the explorers at any moment. If the debate as to the priority of either of these two civilizations ever comes nearer decision, it may be that the archæologists will then have data from the islands of the Mediterranean which will draw attention thither for the verdict. It is difficult for moderns to realize how far away in time these early orientals lived, for they were as ancient to Homer as he is to our times.

Many questions suggest themselves about these early peoples. Who were they and how did they look? That is to ask with what races were they related. Where did they live and under what natural conditions? What languages were spoken, what culture did they possess, what were their thoughts about themselves and the rest of the world? We possess the remains of their habitations, their tombs, and many of their implements. There are pictures showing persons, divinities, costumes and employment. We can say something about their material comforts and their spiritual satisfactions. Their writings are only a part of the tale of their very thoughts, emotions and aspirations.

These questions will be treated more or less fully as this story unfolds. It can be said concerning the appearance of the people in most of the eastern countries that, in the six thousand years of known history, they have changed very little. This is most notably true in such a country as Egypt. Many natives may be seen in that country to-day who would make good models for the portraiture of ancient Egyptians. A similar statement could be made concerning certain types in present-day Palestine, Asia Minor, Armenia and Persia. Perhaps in the region of ancient Babylonia the present population is least like the ancient. There were doubtless many varieties of face and form in the old populations as there are now. The dominant caste in a given country will be quite different to-day from the one which ruled four thousand years ago, but most of the types of ancient times can be illustrated within the great body of the people who now live in the region. The ancient statues and portraits give the likenesses not only of eminent persons, but also of captives, serfs and ordinary subjects. Even the pictures of dignitaries vary sufficiently to illustrate the above statements. In the portraiture of the very early Babylonians and Egyptians there are many instances of a heavy, thick-set figure as well as the slimmer, more athletic type.

One of the explorers has told an amusing story of finding a large wooden statue, about forty-seven centuries old, belonging to the period of the Fourth Dynasty of Egypt. The native Egyptian workmen immediately characterized it as a good likeness of the neighboring town mayor.

Relationships Between the Ancient World and Later Times.—There is a remarkable degree of relationship between the modern tongues and the ancient languages of the East, for example, the bond between modern and ancient Greek, Coptic and old Egyptian and between the vernaculars in Syriac, Hebrew and Arabic and the ancient speech of Bible times.

Observations of the races and customs in the modern Orient may be made very valuable as aids to a sympathetic knowledge of the Orient in Bible times. Not only has there been a degree of persistence of races and languages, but religious ideas, and customs of the present day are full of valuable suggestions. The social customs, the habits of mind, the instinctive reactions of the people of the present day provide a living museum of antiquity, while over all is the same sky and all about are the scores of other natural features that provide the setting which helps us to reproduce the Biblical life and interests.

It is only in modern times that the wealth and variety of these resources have been appreciated. Formerly, ancient culture was supposed to begin with the Greeks and Romans. That which was more ancient was buried, except for the precious narratives of the classical writers, chief among them Herodotus. To the Greeks, as to us, there was a peculiar interest in things oriental. Their lively minds felt the lure of the East. Perhaps it would be hard to define or account for the charm of the Orient. Is it found in the contrasts with our own spirit and life, in the apparent ease and dreaminess of the oriental life, or in the mysterious wisdom of the olden lore? Without doubt, it has often arisen in the relief to be found in change and novelty. Sometimes the sense of finish in art and of finality in authority have gratified the cravings of our varying moods.

Facilities for the exploration and study of the Orient have increased. Tourist travel had increased greatly in the years before the war. Steamship and railway lines, consulates, mission stations and archæological schools were among the means by which the West showed a quickened interest in the Near East. Very little of this approach to oriental fields had been made when the earlier explorers unearthed the buried cities of Western Asia or collated the monuments along the Nile. Their trials, their heroic labors and the almost incredible intellectual feats of the early decipherers of the inscriptions fill one of the noble chapters in the book of fame. Much less is known popularly of the half-century of consecrated toil that has systematized and published the treasures of oriental learning. The scholars in these fields evince the keenest interest and sharp rivalries have existed. Civilization has suddenly become aware of numerous unsuspected ancestors. The study of origins, always interesting, has been carried into more remote times. The horizon has widened. The empire of the ages is shown to be more extensive than we thought. We gain a deeper perspective and one more corrective of provincialism is offered us, one more challenge to the imagination.

The Peoples of the Early Orient.—The light which comes to us through historical information about the Egyptians, Babylonians, Assyrians and Hebrews has revealed the earliest known movements and some-

thing of the features of other races. On the western
border of the Egyptian Delta were the Libyans, eastward were the Arabians. Both of these peoples contributed elements to the Egyptian population. The
Hyksos came as invaders from the north and were
eventually driven back through Palestine. Many
believe that they were a Semitic people. At the
southern extreme of the Nile country were the Ethio-
pians. Canaanite is a name for the mixed population
of Palestine during the times of the Egyptian empire
and is often used in the Bible.

The most aggressive neighbors of Babylonia were
Elamites and Kassites, who dwelt in the eastern
mountains. The eastern enemies of Babylonia frequently made their way into the land by a conquest
of the South near the head of the Persian Gulf,
whence they overran the rest of the country.

In Asia Minor and Syria were the Hittite peoples.
Between them and the Euphrates the Arameans settled. The wars of Assyria disclosed many other
peoples on the eastern and northern frontiers of that
country. Among such were the forerunners of the
later Medes, Persians and Armenians. The world
was already too small to permit of unrelated movements among these peoples.

The Ways of Studying the Orient in Bible Times.—
A picture of the Orient in Bible times may be given
either by presenting the features of these peoples
separately, each for its own sake, or by showing what
these lands and peoples meant for Palestine and the
Hebrews. It is well to use first one method and
then the other, for there are advantages and disad-

vantages in either. All the peoples who have been named knew about each other. The maps which the Greek geographers made show us how much more was included in their world, the shores of the Mediterranean and an indefinite extent of Asia eastward to India and probably China. This shrunken bit of earth, as it seems to us, was believed to be surrounded by the world ocean. The lands of the Far North and the Far South were the unexplored homes of barbarians and savages. The line of civilization ran east and west from the Mediterranean to the Euphratean world. The special centres of culture were Babylonia, Egypt, Crete with the Ægean islands, Asia Minor and Syria. In naming these, one describes a circle which includes the Levant and Western Asia. It is an interesting fact that while Jeremiah was prophesying in Judah an Egyptian pharaoh sent an exploring party of Phenician sailors who circumnavigated Africa. What an addition to knowledge and what a stimulus to the imagination that must have provided! Babylonian and Assyrian traders and punitive expeditions had, long before that, gathered knowledge of interior Asia from the Caspian Sea to India and from Media to the Mediterranean.

More important than a list of items of their knowledge about the earth would be the early oriental feeling of the world of their day, its social organization and ideals. For while the political history of the countries of the East will be necessary for an intelligent grasp of the ancient world, the life of the Orient will be more fully known if we look frequently upon its social pictures and seek to appreciate its thoughts, words and racial achievements. These afford bases for understanding the present world better.

Different Ways of Looking at Life.—In every great age of world history there has been a leading world view. Any portion of the earth that fell outside the range of those views and feelings might just as well be considered as belonging to another age or circle of interests. One of the interesting facts about the modern world is that the different circles of life are intersecting each other. We were accustomed to think that Europe and America were somewhat distinct, but Asia was certainly separate from both. Of course, there were specialists in learning, diplomacy and trade who cultivated oriental interests. While we were sometimes drawn by the mysteries of the Orient, we were more often repelled by the strange forms which human evil could take among oriental peoples. Now the sense of distance and strangeness is diminishing rapidly. Even interior Arabia, which possesses one of the types of life most remote from our experience, is being drawn into quickened relationship with the rest of the world by recent events. Interior Africa and other once proverbially distant peoples are becoming parts of a unified world.

However, there is at this moment a great Christian world, a great Moslem world, a great Confucian and a great Hindu world, not to speak of other spheres within which typical methods of thought obtain. Each of these is modified by the others. The very consciousness of difference and separation has been a common bond and a testimony of the essential solidarity of humanity. While there is pleasure in learning of the career of human beings anywhere, there is peculiar satisfaction in tracing the cultural origins of peoples from whom our own language, religion, art and social institutions are derived. This knowledge helps us to understand ourselves better. We have a right to know whether we are in line with a reasonable past or whether we are the random products of eccentricity and chance. If our impulses and aims have a meaning, if there is such a thing as progress, surely history must be able to advise us. Sometimes a pessimistic comparison of ancient and modern achievements has been made. Certain have claimed that we have surpassed the ancients merely in a formal, material way. They base their comparison upon the substantial civilizations of the past, the artistic, philosophical, religious and legal triumphs of the Greeks, Romans and Orientals or even the prehistoric Americans. Even if we do not agree with this point of view, we must feel the weight of the testimony from ancient times. Surely in an intellectual sense there were "giants in those days."

Where Does the East Begin?—The countries around the eastern end of the Mediterranean, the so-called Levant, are often referred to as the Near East. Sometimes all Eastern Europe, Russia, the Balkan States, Greece and particularly the regions in which Constantinople is central are included. Migratory tribes from East-European lands spread their movements into the countries which are mentioned most often in the Bible. The earliest Greek civilizations were developed in Asia Minor and the nearby islands.

The greater part of Western Asia has been under the political control of the Turkish empire for several hundred years. The official religion of Turkey is Islam, the faith of Muhammad, the Arabian prophet. The groups of Christian peoples here and there in the empire were supposed to be tolerated, but they were frequently subjected to persecution and even to massacre. Turks and Arabs belong to different races. Their languages are very different. Turkish politicians have been most adroit. Usually they have been able to divide the opposition to the government whether within the empire or abroad among the nations. Thus they have often kept discontented groups at home from combining against the throne and jealous foreign powers from uniting in policies that would abolish Turkish rule. In spite of delay, however, the process of disintegration has been steady. The empire has shrunk amazingly in the last century, losing all of North Africa and most of the small states of Southeastern Europe. The nations within the empire have spoken decisively. Several languages are dominant in the different parts of this great domain. Along the coasts of Asia Minor, Greek is commonly heard; in the interior, Turkish; to the north-east, Armenian; while in Syria, Palestine and Arabia the language is Arabic, as indeed it is throughout most of Northern Africa.

Western Interest in the Near East.—For many years Americans have joined in the effort to ameliorate

RUIN OF CRUSADERS' CHURCH AT BEEROTH

RUINED GREEK ALTAR AT RAM ALLAH

conditions in the Near East and have pursued religious and educational missions there. These have frequently been supplemented, most graciously, by medical services to the needy populations. Beginning a century ago, the work has been continued by several religious bodies in Syria, Asia Minor, Persia and Arabia. But the most notable American effort during recent decades has been in connection with a chain of higher schools and colleges. Such are found at Constantinople, Smyrna, Tarsus, Harpoot and Beirut, as well as in Egypt. All the larger countries of Europe have maintained missions in the Near East. In Syria and Palestine many fine buildings arose to house and centralize the educational and medical activities.

Jewish agricultural colonies flourished at several points in Palestine. Consular stations were met with in the larger cities and occasional exploring parties of Europeans or Americans were granted permits to excavate for antiquities. Until a few years ago most of the greater powers maintained postal service under their own control at certain strategic points in the empire. Turkey defended itself not only by the policies already referred to, but by an almost inconceivable slowness to grant any privilege that would advance civilization, education or what the West calls progress. The old Turkish régime appreciated the fact that Western ideas and the Ottoman dynasty were incompatibles. The fear of insurrection and revolution was the spectre that troubled the days and nights of Abdul Hamid.

In these and many other ways we are helped to a

more realistic grasp of ancient history in those lands. On the other hand, the deep vistas of ancient life give indications of much that may yet ensue in the Levant. We must make allowances for traits which are peculiar either to the ancient or the modern peoples and the technical advance of later times, but we have always to deal with certain fundamental oriental facts of geography, social methods and religious spirit.

History Records the Social Life of Humanity.—It takes up the subject of human society at the point where the social organization has passed beyond the merely family or tribal life to an administrative group of tribes which has developed sufficient self-consciousness to make a record of its activities. The record may be a list of events and their leaders. Proper history begins with such an attempt to make a record or memoir. Before that time the archæologist may gather together the relics which a society has dropped, such as implements, articles of daily use, or burial remains. There may be people to-day who have not yet entered the stream of history. Such a people may form a rich field of observation for the ethnologist, archæologist and psychologist who make sketches and observations of them. Such studies of a people who do not themselves feel the desirability of recording their interests are comparable with the natural histories which are written about the life of the lower animals.

History in its broadest conception would include also the record of human achievements in every field of science and art. It has usually sought to under-

stand, as well as to chronicle, human advance. The
best results are not the mere accumulation of dates
and statistics, interesting and valuable as that is, but
are found in a philosophy or interpretation of humanity. Are there laws of human action and reaction
through long courses of the historic movements?
What part does geography, climate, soil and waterways have in forming a people? What are the significant religious, political and industrial institutions of
a given society? What have been the occasions of the
downfall of nations? Is there a world-history which
includes the histories of the separate peoples, that is
to say, a true history of human kind? History might
be looked upon as a sociological study, except that
history is more interested in society as a complex
organism of institutions, while sociology is biologi-
cal in its temper.

We ought to gain by these investigations a greater
power to grasp the essential truth of times and circumstances not our own and so reach a saner adjustment to our own times. We ought to acquire what is
known as historical perspective, that mental vision
of things in their true proportions and in truthful
relation to the whole of human experience.

SUGGESTIONS FOR STUDY

1. Compare the two accounts of origins in Genesis 1 and 2 with
each other; compare either of them with the Babylonian story
of origins.

2. What are the essentials for any civilization?

3. What is meant by the term "oriental" whether in art,
thought, or custom.

4. How account for the superiorities of the Greek mentality?

5. How long has knowledge of Egyptian and Assyrian writings been possessed? Which scripts remain unread?

6. Plan a campaign of exploration in some oriental country, including specifications of travel, living and digging.

BOOK LIST

H. D. B., I, 500 (*i.e.*, Hastings' Dictionary of the Bible, 5 vols.).

J. L. MYRES: The Dawn of History.

BARTON: Archæology and the Bible.

JOHN P. PETERS: Nippur.

BURROWS: Discoveries in Crete.

E. J. BANKS: Bismya.

SERGI: The Mediterranean Race.

PETRIE: Ten Years Digging in Egypt.

MASPERO: Manual of Egyptian Archæology.

NOTE.—The design of these suggestions is to supplement the chapters for those who care to go farther in the subjects. Ordinarily the books mentioned in the lists will not be repeated, although they will frequently be found useful again for later chapters.

ABBREVIATIONS FOR TITLES OF PERIODICALS

(B. W.) Biblical World, University of Chicago Press.

(J. A. O. S.) Journal of the American Oriental Society.

(A. J. S. L. & L.) American Journal of Semitic Languages and Literatures.

(J. B. L.) Journal of Biblical Literature.

f or *ff* = pages or verses following.

CHAPTER II

The Union of Three Continents.—Europe, Asia and Africa were joined continents in ancient times. At their junction lies the region of our interest. The deltas of the Nile and the Euphrates are a thousand miles apart. The roads from the one to the other circle the sterile desert which lies in the direct line between them. Life was more generously provided for in those favored river valleys than in the neighboring countries. In general it seems that primitive races of men were inclined to settle in fertile river lands and upon coastal plains near the sea where it was possible to acquire the means of livelihood continuously without nomadism. They would desire to stop the encroachments of envious marauders, and the superior productiveness of their chosen sites equipped them to resist outsiders. The inhabitants of a river valley have a richer and more easily defended home than coastal populations. Those open to the sea have not only to fear an enemy from the mountains but also piracy from the water. Nomadic savages live too nearly a hand-to-mouth existence to sustain long battle, while advanced peoples in the rich country have the sinews of defence. Fortified towns, supplies of food, and better weapons give them the advantage over brute force.

As one looks along the axis of the three-fold continent, the parallel of thirty degrees north latitude, one notices a succession of mountains, deserts,

and waterways, and particularly the desert plateau
of Arabia flanked by fertile regions towards the Nile
valley and towards the Euphrates. It is entirely
probable that the Arabian peninsula furnished an
influential portion of the population which the early
historical picture allows us to see in the two river
valleys. On the other hand, certain scholars believe
that traces are discernible of an African origin of
even the primitive Arabian peoples. In that case
the migratory movement would have been from the
north coast of Africa across the Nile Valley, where
it left the Egyptian aborigines, then on to Arabia.
Thence by outspreading and reflex movements from
Arabia it would affect Asia and, again, Africa. The
most serious debate as to origins in the Euphrates
Valley is upon the question of the Semitic or pre-
Semitic authorship of the Babylonian culture. Many
now agree that when the Semitic invaders reached
the valley they found a civilization which had been
produced by a non-Semitic people.

The Comparative Isolation of the Early Egyptians.—
For a long time life in the Nile Valley was very
exclusive. The dominant race felt that everything
outside their fertile strip was barbarian and threatening. Reduction of restless marauding tribes to
submission was a frequent necessity. Moreover, the
Nile Valley was the rich prize for ambitious rivalries
within Egypt. Occasional journeys were made to
the Arabian mines for treasure or to remote parts
of Africa whence ivory, feathers, slaves, etc., could
be secured. The nature of the Nile Valley encouraged an up-and-down river direction of travel.

Except in lower Egypt, where the Delta invites intercourse with the Mediterranean world, the country was shut in by inhospitable desert and mountainous regions.

The Greater Openness of Early Babylonia.—Babylonia in its river valley was far more open to the outside world and extended the influence of its culture westward to Syria earlier than did Egypt. The different methods and results of Babylonian influence in Asia may be ascribed to causes a few of which we may surmise. The geographical contrasts with Egypt already suggested are apparent. It is possible that the migrations which went forth from Arabia spread in a fan-like movement of Semites and made it easier for descendants of the emigrants to permeate the Asiatic regions at will. Similarities of language, cultural feeling, religious instincts, and the continual roaming of tribes of not too remote kindred, caravans, the habit of land-travel in itself combined to effect a Babylonization of Western Asia. In Egypt, with its African surroundings, where habits of travel were by water and where the heart of Africa would always be the inviting mystery, it is not strange that the people had so little to do with Asia. Except for the position of the Delta they would have had far less. Every suggestion of nature led upper Egypt toward the tropics. To it Asia was indeed a foreign country. The strong Semitic influences which were brought to bear upon Egypt were almost wholly assimilated to the native standards. Outside powers have affected the country for long periods but have eventually been rejected and the country has

2

in every instance retreated to Africa for the national expression.

The Early Assyrians.—We may consider the Assyrians as derived from the same lineage as the Semitic Babylonians. These colonists of the north missed the Sumerian and Kassite contributions to the racial stock. Whether they were, on the other hand, affected by the Hittite element may be debated. At any rate, they faced very different problems in their hilly regions, and in comparison with the Babylonians wrought out what appears to have been a more nearly characteristic Semitic civilization.

The Leading Peoples of the Early World.—A study of the three great nations, the Egyptians, the Babylonians, and the Assyrians, will furnish a good basis for understanding the early East. The other continental civilizations seem so plainly derived as to render them less important in the very early periods. The one possible exception, the Hittite, may or may not prove to be such. That is a problem for the immediate future. The Hittites developed centres of power in Asia Minor, the authority of which reached well into Syria. These peoples come into our historical view chiefly as opponents of the nations already mentioned. (See page 78.)

The question of mere priority in time between Babylonia and Egypt is of small interest as compared with the question of influence upon the ancient world through which the cultural line of descent reaches us. "The culture of Greece owed much to Babylonia and European civilization became, in turn, heir to her achievements through the Greeks." (Craig's edition of Winckler, H. B. & A.) Our division of the day into hours is a reminder of the Babylonian measure of time. While we divide the day into twenty-four periods of one hour each the Babylonians used a double-hour period called the kasbu. The duodecimal system seems to have been theirs and is ever before us in the modern clock-face.

Ancient Egypt Up to the Time of the Expulsion of the Hyksos.—The Nile has always been credited with being the key to the situation in Egypt. Were it not for that river the Sahara might prevail over all northeastern Africa and a great salt bay a hundred miles deep would exist where now is the Delta. But the noble river flowing from Africa's equatorial lakes and receiving two large tributaries from the direction of Abyssinia passes over six precarious stumbling places known as the cataracts of the Nile after which it flows gently into the Mediterranean at the northeastern corner of Africa. Its great length of about four thousand miles is owing partly to the winding course in the middle third of the way where it describes a letter S. It traverses a little over thirty-four degrees of latitude, from three degrees south to thirty-one and one-half degrees north.

The Land of the Nile.—In describing the Nile Valley everything is mentioned in the order of Egyptian discovery and expansion, that is from the north towards the south, up the river. The cataract nearest the mouth of the Nile is referred to as the first cataract and represented during most of the ancient period of Egyptian history as the southernmost boundary of the country. The ancient town of Syene, modern Assuan, is situated at this point. It is referred to in Ezekiel, chapters 29 and 30, as Seveneh. At the Delta the river spreads into several channels and reaches the sea through two main outlets, the so-called Rosetta and Damiette mouths. The rest of the valley is very narrow, the cultivable parts being only a few miles wide at points and never exceeding thirty. In the Nile Valley there is very little rain, but the river has an annual rise and overflow that dresses the bordering fields with a rich sediment. The black deposits of river mud make an annual farm of the entire valley region. By careful mechanical husbanding the receding waters are so retarded as to provide ample moisture for heavy crops.

The map of the fertile Nile borders presents a peculiar appearance, something like a kite with a long tail. This valuable agricultural area would measure somewhat less than the total area of the state of Massachusetts. It is bordered on either side by low hills. On the eastern side these rise into mountains between the Nile and the Red Sea. The Nile was not only the annual fertilizer of the land but the main highway for travel and commerce which was carried on by means of boats and rafts. Boats continued to be the chief carriers of the country until the construction of the modern railroad which runs along the bank. This all but universal custom of the early Egyptians, of traveling by Nile-boat, led them to conceive of their solar deities as traversing the heavens in boats. The ancient Egyptians fished and hunted in the waters and marshes of the river and they have left pictures of the fish, the fowl and the wild beasts on their monuments. Trees were scarce, though there were the palm, acacia and sycamore. But the country is a natural vegetable garden and is good soil for the fig, orange, lemon and pomegranate.

The People of Egypt, Classes and Customs.—From the pharaoh and his family down to the lowliest slave the Egyptians were a practical, orderly, peace-loving folk. From the stiff convention and precision of certain of their monuments an idea has obtained that the Egyptians led an angular life too much given to the contemplation of funerary interests. But we have reason to believe that this is a wrong impression. They may not have been very different from other people but they lived in an extraordinary country for long ages. The mixture of races in the valley of the Nile was accomplished with peculiar thoroughness. One of the rarest climates in the world descended from a perfect sky upon the dwellers on the most fertile of soils. The regularity of the two seasons and the river's overflow with the light and shade of day and evening were educational in themselves. The winters are salubrious, the summers very warm. Thus along the majestic river there has developed one of the most permanent of earth's peoples, Africa's greatest folk, in continuous line from before the dawn of history. Their known history began three thousand years before the time of David. Beauty, majesty, sublimity characterize their art. Scientific precision and orientation mark their gigantic works while exquisite grace and fineness are seen in their smaller products. A true sense of law runs through their conventions. They could draw with vivid realism when they chose, but ordinarily they yielded to the ancient canons of art.

The three superior classes were the nobles, priests and soldiers. In the cities there were free-men who formed a class of traders and merchants. The majority of the population was a subject class divided into serfs and slaves. The very richness of the agricultural lands imposed a heavy burden of work on the people, but they seem to have been as cheerful and happy a folk as lived anywhere in the great countries of the East. The rulers were probably the only Egyptians who departed from the rule of monogamy. Women had rather larger place perhaps in the esteem of the Egyptian people than in other countries. The wife and mother occupied a position of dignity and of right.

Primitive Life.—The earliest Egyptians of whom we have any remains lived on the edge of the desert or the highlands where their stone implements and shallow burials have been found. They hunted in the marshes of the Nile. Their earliest fabricated huts were made of reeds and boughs interwoven and plastered with mud. Over these they might hang skins or plaited mats. The next type of dwelling was made of brick, dried in the powerful sunshine, with a roof of boughs and mud as before. The household utensils were made of bone, wood, stone and clay. From hunting and fishing the people went on to agriculture, wooed by rich alluvium. This meant more food and also more regular living. In the course of time it meant less freedom for the masses of the people. The huts of the gardeners were built

CAMELS BEARING LOADS OF BRUSH AND DRAWING PLOW
(Photograph by A. Edward Kelsey, Ram Allah, Jerusalem)

in groups which were surrounded often by a protecting wall. In these settlements bazaars or markets developed and the growing business of barter encouraged the arts and crafts which had already achieved beautiful and useful results. The old stone age had passed, the new stone age had come into its own. The most beautiful objects in polished stone were produced, arrow points, knives, dishes, vases, jewelry. Metal was soon used along with stone and clay. Glass brought its fascinating possibilities to the aid of adornment. Beautiful fabrics were woven from flax. One may trace the pride and delight as well as the drudgery of the ancient workers in the abundant remains found in the graves. The dead man's weapons were placed near him. His tomb simulated a room. Jars and bowls stood near.

In very early times a man's servants may have been slain at his burial so that their spirits might accompany him and serve him. But this custom was, if ever common, commuted to the provision of little clay images of attendants who should serve the purpose. Imitations of household furnishings were provided in many cases. Pictures of the departing or returning soul in the form of a bird are shown in the paintings. This phantom soul could be aided by magical formulæ to enjoy its funereal treasures. The tomb-paintings and carvings are often lively descriptions of the industries and occupations of the people. There is a particularly bright and enthusiastic touch to the Egyptian's memoirs. Toys, beads, necklaces, rings, scarabs, combs, metal mirrors, fans, knives, miniature boats, a checker-board, boxes of ivory and ebony, couches, chairs, vases of clay, stone and metal which have been found are merely a suggestion of the variety of his lighter interests and possessions. Mining expeditions were conducted in Sinai at a very early time. There copper and turquoise were secured by the miners under protection of Egyptian soldiers who kept off the bedawin. Many paintings and reliefs in Egypt depict lively scenes of hunting, war and domestic interests. When we remember that the hieroglyphic inscriptions which abound are often the drawings of birds and other creatures as well as many familiar objects finely cut in stone we can imagine that Egyptian remains are the most pleasingly picturesque in the world.

Decorative design drew upon animate and inanimate objects for its motives, the reeds and branches, birds, crocodiles, elephants, giraffes, deer, and human folk in its various activities. The hardest stone was attacked by workers with stone and bronze tools, sand rubbing and all but infinite patience. In all these branches of art some of the finest products are those of the very earliest times. The stiffer conventions came with the beginnings of the dynastic age. In the household much use was made of linen, wool and straw.

The Egyptian placed his dead at first in shallow graves scooped in the sand, then at a later time in deeper holes round or rectangular. The bodies were placed in skins, or linen wrapping, and finally in clay coffins. The body lay in a sleeping position. Up on the plateaus the primitive dead were apt to be cramped in a position that brought the knees up to the chin, but later the form was laid out straight. The very early corpses were mummified by nature, the warm dry sand absorbing the moisture and preserving the frame. It has been suggested that the dynastic Egyptians took this hint from nature and thus learned to improve the methods of preserving bodies by art. The rich made a house for the dead in the rock beneath the sand; this surrounded by a platform with a core of sand and stone led them on as explained on page 34 to the great monumental tomb. Memoirs and even biographies of the dead were inscribed on the walls of the large tombs.

Roads ran between the villages over which donkeys were the usual beasts of burden. On the river, the great thoroughfare, the earliest boat was probably a bundle of papyrus stalks propelled by a pole. Large boats with hollow interiors, flat keels, high sterns and cabins were developed. These were driven by oars and sail.

Religion of the Egyptians.—We ought to speak of the religious ideas of the people. These gave form and credentials to the political government. There were two distinct kingdoms in pre-dynastic times which were the descendants of more numerous lesser states. But the religion of the days of the two kingdoms had already become officially the cult of the god Horus. So when the union of the two kingdoms was effected and the dynasties of the pharaohs began, the official Horus worship continued to dominate the lesser faiths of primitive localities.

Horus was the god of light, the opponent of darkness. The king was looked upon as a superman, an embodiment of the great god. The symbol of Horus was the falcon. The religion of historic Egypt continued in one form or another and under varying names and symbols to be practically the worship of the sun-god down to Christian times. Horus, Rā, Atum, Khepera, Amon-Rā were some of these names.

It took many centuries to reach this simplicity and such an organization of the cult as would be comparable with the centralized monarchy. Time was when every locality had its god or gods. But in the course of time the numerous gods yielded their place to certain orthodox groups, triads very commonly, or enneads, groups of nine. The priesthoods were devoted to these theological studies. The priests of Heliopolis had great fame for learning. The temple foundations were the ancient counterparts of our colleges and universities. There the arts and sciences were developed. Medicine, anatomy, surgery achieved distinction. A religious philosophy was developed to account for the natural world and for the faiths of men. Thence arose the beautiful myths of later Egypt which subordinated and organized the welter of divinities until they issued as divine families, as, for example, the group of which Osiris was the head. Osiris had a wicked brother Set, a devoted wife Isis and a glorious son Horus. Back of this family group were the ancestors, Keb the earth divinity, and Nut the heavenly god, Shu and Tefnut the atmospheric forces and the original egg of being produced in the primeval ocean. Other great gods were Ptah of Memphis, embodied in the

sacred Apis bull, Sebek the crocodile god of the
Fayum district, Thoth the god of letters, Amon,
Khnum, Min, Mentu, goddesses such as Hathor, Neit,
and Bast, all three of whom came to represent the
one female principle of the goddess of the sky. There
was a second sacred bull, the Mnevis bull of Heliopolis, embodiment of the sun-god of that city.

It may appear that Babylonia and Assyria offer
us more contemporary and immediately available
Biblical information, but Egypt, the nearest great
neighbor to Palestine, gives us the earliest detailed
knowledge of the geography, races, and customs of
the country of the Bible before the Hebrews came to
live there. If one will patiently follow the history of
Egypt, at least in outline, one will gain a sense of
familiarity with the ancient orient which will always
stand one in good stead in Biblical reading.

SUGGESTIONS FOR STUDY

1. Make a map of the Arabian land-mass, showing the seats of
civilization around it.
2. Characteristics of the Semitic peoples and theories of
their origin.
3. Describe the Nile Valley and bordering lands.
4. Compare and contrast the Nile and Euphrates Valleys.
5. The more important references to Egypt in the Bible.
6. What early races flourished near the eastern end of
the Mediterranean?
7. Early Egyptian art and handicraft. What objects are
drawn in hieroglyphics?

BOOK LIST

H. D. B. Extra Vol. p. 368 and p. 72.
G. A. BARTON: A Sketch of Semitic Origins.
J. H. BREASTED: A History of Egypt.

J. H. Breasted: A History of the Ancient Egyptians.

J. H. Breasted: (Underwood and Underwood, N. Y.) Stereoscopic Views of Egypt.

Erman: Life in Ancient Egypt.

Maspero: The Dawn of Civilization.

H. R. Hall: The Ancient History of the Near East.

Garstang: The Land of the Hittites.

King and Hall: Egypt and Western Asia.

Ratzel: History of Mankind.

Petrie: The Arts and Crafts of Ancient Egypt.

Cormack: Egypt in Asia.

Amelia B. Edwards: Pharaohs, Fellahs, and Explorers.

CHAPTER III

The Story of the Development of a Nation.—For a minute and thoroughgoing study of Egyptian history no better scheme of division has been proposed than that of Manetho, the native historian of the country, who lived about three centuries B.C. He divided the reigns of Egyptian kings into dynasties. If about thirty of these are taken the total known material can be handled with intelligent appreciation. Much criticism of this method is possible, but it is still the most convenient. On the basis of it, we should suggest the following divisions which will give a more rapid single impression of the course of development of Egyptian life:

I. The Archaic Age   A. The Persian Period
II. The Memphite Age   B. The Greek Period
III. The Thebaic Age   C. The Roman Period
IV. The Imperial Age
V. The Saite Age

The five ages designated stand out clearly as summits of distinctively Egyptian achievement. In between them as valleys were interregna of decay, oblivion, anarchy, or invasion. These divisions will serve our purpose very well if we do not forget that they do not follow immediately, each upon the other, but in every instance follow upon periods of disaster from which each of these ages were revivals of Egyptian prosperity and civilization. Thus, for

example, between II and III was Egypt's great
Dark Age, during which, no doubt, the foundations
for future glory were being made possible and secure
but of which we know little. Between III and IV was
the Hyksos invasion and usurpation, after which a
great patriotic movement ushered in the Empire.
Between IV and V was the saddest decadence of
Egyptian power, while age V marked the· reappear-
ance of the ancient culture in a new world.

After the five ages of native government there
came the successive periods of foreign domination
when Asiatic or European powers conquered and
administered the country.

The Archaic Age.—Primitive Egypt was a land to
be conquered by assiduous toil. Small sections of
country rewarded agricultural labor in proportion
as that labor was intelligently adapted to the peculiar
conditions of the land, prominent among which was
the regular overflow and subsidence of the Nile. Thus
the early Egyptians were spurred on to reap larger
and surer benefits in crops, to reclaim the many
marshy regions, to drive out the noxious creatures
and to introduce such useful animals as the buffalo,
ass and goat. Such conquest of a country, naturally
rich but demanding painstaking development, re-
quires intensive farming which yields its largest
benefits to numerous small holders. We may think
of the early tribes in Egypt as being won from less
remunerative pursuits, such as hunting, fishing and
the rearing of flocks, by the exceeding fertility of the
soil. And as the influence of agriculture is to develop
the tribe, so these aborigines would add to the func-

tions of their organization until each considerable group became a principality. Originally there were, probably, many little kingdoms or principalities. In later Egypt there were still preserved the distinctions of an earlier time in what the Greeks called "nomes." We should call them districts or counties. Over each Egyptian nome was an officer called in Greek the nomarch, or chief of the nome. Whenever the central government tended to break up, in time of decentralization and disintegration, these local nomes became more important and even at times independent. They seemed to be the natural rallying centres in periods of federal weakness. Thus the nome in historic Egypt seems to point to the local governments in prehistoric times.

Upper and Lower Egypt.—We feel assured that these many local powers became merged into two strong neighboring kingdoms, the North and the South. One of the persistent titles of the known kings of all Egypt was "Uniter of Both Lands" and the historical kingdom of Egypt was known as "Both Lands" or "The Two Lands." The two capitals of primitive times were Nechbet and Buto. Both cities were divided by the river into two towns. One-half of a capital city was considered the home of the special divinity of the kingdom while the other half in each case was assigned to the god Horus, who was honored in both kingdoms. For instance, at Nechbet (modern El Kab) the town on the eastern bank of the Nile pertained to Nechbet the vulture goddess and the town on the west bank was known as Nechen (Hierakonpolis of the Greeks) where the god Horus, in the form of a sitting falcon, was specially worshipped. The union of the two kingdoms is dated by Breasted about 3400 B.C. The same authority claims as the earliest known date in all history the time when the calendar was introduced in Egypt, the astronomically fixed date of 4241 B.C.

Even before the two kingdoms came together they must have exhibited many similarities of ideas and customs. Each bequeathed to united Egypt the styles and conceptions which had been peculiar to them, so that titles, officials, court usage and regalia preserved memories of the early states. In later Egypt the royal head-dress was a combination made by placing the white hat of the south or upper country within the red one of lower Egypt or the Delta.

Professor Eduard Meyer thinks that the indications of cultural similarity throughout the country suggest the entrance into the Nile Valley of a race which founded the two related states by conquering the little kingdoms. These kindred masters of the North and South worshipped Horus but cultivated besides the native divinities whom their gods had subjugated. The union of the two kingdoms brought about the government of the Pharaohs and the line of dynasties referred to by Manetho. The honors of the consolidation are confused in the legends, but seem properly divided between the kings Narmer and Menes. It is to Menes that later tradition has always assigned the rôle of uniter of Egypt, but it now seems clear that he but completed in a notable manner the work of Narmer. H. R. Hall develops an explanation of the early royal names somewhat different from this. (See "The Ancient History of The Near East," 104 *ff.*)

The ancient Egyptian referred to his sovereign as "Great House," that is Pharaoh, very much as we refer to the administration at Washington and to the president as The White House. The title Pharaoh became the customary word in referring to an Egyptian king. In modern times it was customary to refer to the government of Turkey as The Sublime Porte, referring to the Bab Ali or High Portal at the government house in Constantinople.

The First Capital of the Pharaohs.—Thinis or This, the site of which is not exactly known but which must have been near Abydos, was the home of Menes and the Pharaohs who ruled united Egypt for four hundred years. Their tombs have been found at Abydos. In their lifetime they warred with the wild tribesmen or Bedawin of neighboring Asia and with the Libyans. They sent their mining expeditions to the Sinaitic peninsula. They constructed stone buildings and employed the useful device known to us as the arch. It was customary to sketch in outline the events of a year on tablets of ivory or ebony. Many of these have been found and tell of buildings, expeditions and feasts. Scanty as such references may seem, they have the great value of being contemporaneous documents, and as in Babylonian date lists they may have selected what was considered by the ancients as their most notable endeavors. To us the events thus pinnacled have often a whimsical disproportion to the vast ages over which word of them has come.

3

There seem to be indications of a temporary
breaking of the bond which held the two kingdoms
in a united Egypt. We are not fully assured that
this was so. It may have been but a threatened dis-
solution of the unity. When we come to the close
of the age the capital of the united country is found
in the ancient city of Memphis.

The Memphite Age.—Beginning with the third
dynasty it has been customary with certain writers
to speak of the "Old Kingdom." The capital was
at first in the city of Memphis and the spirit of the
rulers of that city is the characteristic genius of
the age. The third dynasty which certainly ruled at
Memphis is opened with the name of King Zoser
and probably closed by King Snefru (2980–2900).
Zoser was interested in mining in Sinai. He either
built or usurped the pyramid of Sakkara. The practice of seizing upon the monuments of ancients for
one's own funerary and building honors began early.
The great tomb at Sakkara, the oldest known specimen of its kind, was a terraced pyramid. This form
preceded the pyramid proper or standard type which
was introduced by King Snefru.

The Development of the Pyramid.—The building
of these artificial mountains of rock was the chief
ambition of kings during several hundred years. But
the time came when weakness and revolt prevented
kings from employing a nation's sinews in such selfish enterprises. During this dynasty one of the
earlier forms of tomb was used as well as the pyramidal forms. This was the so-called mastaba or platform tomb under which a shaft of masonry was sunk

in the ground to receive the body. This type was
in turn a development of the earliest ordinary shaft
tombs which were excavated in the earth. Such
shafts, originally but a hole in the soil, were at a
later time lined with brick or stone, then still later
surmounted by a platform with sloping sides. By
placing one or more platforms of masonry each
smaller than the last on the first mastaba, a terraced
tomb resulted which led to the type at Sakkara and
eventually to the true pyramidal shape. A curious
custom worth noting was the building of duplicate
tombs, one to protect the actual body of a king
and the second a sham tomb placed at the seat of
some divine cult to honor the god. Thus the limi-
tations of space were awkwardly recognized and
spiritual exigencies were met by increase of material
provision. A modern analogy is found in the shrine
of a Moslem saint which is occasionally situated in
some other place than that of actual burial. It is
thought in such cases that the spirit of the deceased
is able to visit the honorary tomb and indeed may be
attracted to it as a permanent abode.[1]

Early Invasion.—A legendary tradition says that
in the times now reached a people called ''Amu''
from Asia invaded Egypt. They may have been a
Bedawy tribe and their activity symptomatic of the
danger to which the country was exposed frequently.
The Egyptians in their monumental inscriptions
designated neighboring peoples by such national
names as Tehenu for the Libyans or Shasu for the
Bedawin, but in referring to themselves they used

---

[1] See " The People of Palestine," p. 111.

the term "men" (romet) as being the people of first
importance. This custom of calling oneselves "people" may be considered common practice with early
nations. The Egyptians called the earliest historical invaders from Asia "Amu." This may therefore
be the word which the invaders applied to themselves.
It reminds us of the Semitic word "Am" for people.

Snefru was the last king of the Third Dynasty.
His inscriptions have been found in distant Sinai,
where the mining operations in the copper mines
needed the protection of his troops. The punitive
expeditions against nomadic raiders are described
at Sarbût el-Kadîm and Wady Maghâra.

The Pyramid-building Age.—The Fourth Dynasty
is famous because of the largest of the pyramids,
three of which were built by Kings Khufu, Khafre,
and Menkure, commonly called Cheops, Chephren
and Mykerinus. The first of these three discontin-
ued the custom of building duplicate tombs which
seems not to have been taken up again by his successors. Instead, the energy of the sovereign was con-
centrated on the erection of one massive sepulchral
structure, at once the most gigantic piece of masonry
and in the most immovable pattern that architecture
can conceive. One does not wonder that the Egyptian
architect named Meri who lived in the days of Usertesen I (Sesostris) called a pyramid "an eternal
dwelling " or "seat." Khufu's reign lasted twenty-
three years. His pyramid stood 480 feet high and
spread over thirteen acres of ground, being 755 feet
on each side. By walking twice around it one goes
somewhat over a mile. It is built of limestone and

contains three grave-chambers. The uppermost of these chambers is near the heart of the mass. It is finished in granite and contained the sarcophagus covered with heavy granite slabs. Around the great pyramid lay three small ones for members of the royal family. In front of his own stood, according to custom, the funerary temple where the cult of the dead king was observed. A tiny statuette in ivory found at Abydos' is in contrast with the huge pyramid of Khufu, but it can tell us with life-like portraiture how the great king looked to his contemporaries, nearly five thousand years ago. The quarries which the pyramid builders used are found in the Mokattam mountains opposite Memphis. It is sometimes maintained, and with strong probability, that a comparatively small number of expert stone masons, who would be members of the priestly fraternity in the Ptah temple at Memphis, worked continuously on the pyramid, but that during the season of high-Nile when farm work ceased the entire peasant population of Egypt was conscripted for the work. A completed pyramid was built in steps which were filled in with blocks cut so as to give the sloping sides a perfectly smooth surface. This increased the difficulty of discovering the opening to the royal tomb-chamber. The passages leading to the chamber were intricately arranged so as to mislead and obstruct the way of the meddler seeking to penetrate to the resting place of the royal sarcophagus. Connected with each great pyramid was a special temple, while all about, simulating the courtly fashion of life, stood the tombs of the nobility.

Tetefre, the immediate successor of Khufu, reigned but eight years, too short a time to suffice for the completion of a pyramid. Khafre, son of Khufu, was next in succession. His pyramid was nearly as large as Khufu's. In a structure near by, probably the funerary temple, nine statues of the king, cut in different kinds of hard stone, were found. One of them was in nearly perfect condition. The others were more or less broken. Statues of his contemporaries were found as well. Menkure, son of Khafre, followed, and his pyramid is the third of the great Gizeh group. It was only 218 feet high. But this king held a fame in Egyptian tradition for exemplary piety. Is it barely possible that lessened resources and authority are not alone accountable for the smaller structure but that ethical compunctions may have led to the erection of a smaller monument of stone than his predecessor? He left a larger monument in the reverence of his country people.

A Portrait in Stone.—The statue known as the Sphinx is as famous in its way as the pyramids. It stands in front of the pyramid of Khafre. The head still retains certain of the features of that king whose portrait it bore.

A severe political shaking was experienced by this Fourth Dynasty, which was the last assuredly Memphite family. The new house to rule over Egypt was Heliopolitan. This is the Fifth Dynasty, 2750 B.C. Evidently the storms that rent the previous administration had subsided and the Fifth Dynasty entered into power peacefully, lived near Memphis and followed lines of activity indicated by former

pharaohs. One of the kings of this new family introduced the practice of adopting a special royal name
upon accession to the throne. The divine name Rā
was used in making up the new title. This followed
upon the doctrine that the king was begotten of Rā,
who came in person to earth. Thus the throne-name
of this pharaoh who introduced the practice was
Userenrā. His own princely name was An. The
Sinaitic mines continued to be worked during this
age. Trading expeditions were sent out; one went
along the coasts of the Red Sea. The pyramids of
all but the last king are at Abusir. But that of Unis
the last king is at Sakkara. It is inscribed with
valuable Egyptian texts. The noble houses of this
time were able to secure considerable power and
threatened the absolute rule of the sovereign. Their
efforts prepared the way for feudal times which followed upon the passing of the stronger pharaohs.
The factional strife of the nobles hastened the downfall of the Fifth Dynasty. One sign of the decentralization of power is the small size of the pyramids
of the Fifth Dynasty kings. But a high culture may
develop under a growing feudalism. This was the
case in that age. There was a greater distribution
and equalization of resources which extended the
ability of lesser rulers to encourage progress
throughout the provinces. A few decades ago there
was discovered an interesting will, of Nekonekh,
who lived in the reign of Userkaf. It was on his
tomb in Tehneh and shows how a favored noble had
been enriched by the king, probably at the expense
of some other family then in disfavor, and how he

planned for his heirs. His wealth was in the form
of landed endowments, the enjoyment of which
demanded that the beneficiary be allowed to occupy
two priesthoods at once. Nekonekh bequeathed these
emoluments to his thirteen children by appointing
each to serve as priest for short terms, in turn. All
the incomes from the land were parcelled out in similar manner. It would seem that the veneration of
certain classes of sacred animals in Egypt dates from
about this time.

The Classic Age of Early Feudalism.—Teti was the
first king of the Sixth Dynasty, about 2625 B.C. This
was a succession of active rulers who busied themselves with schemes at home and abroad. Their
inscriptions have been found in many regions of
upper and lower Egypt and in Sinai. Battles were
fought with the Syrians and with the Nubians. Feudalism had triumphed and was able to exhibit its
best fruits. The comparative weakening of the
power of the kings of the Fourth Dynasty was due
probably to the influence of the priests of Heliopolis.
Another invasion of the supreme prerogatives had
been made by the noble houses of the land who made
themselves prosperous by weakening the power of the
pharaohs of the Fifth Dynasty. It was this further
encroachment on dynastic absolutism made by lords,
nobles, and local governors that brought the Sixth
Dynasty into power. During these times it is
observable that the pyramids of nobles and provincial rulers which used to be grouped around the
great one of their sovereign in the royal cemetery
were more commonly found in the provincial capital

or at the seat of the princely house. .As the bonds
that held the submission of the nobles to the king
gradually loosened, some strong noble might make
an effort to usurp actual sovereignty. If he succeeded, or in the measure of his gains, he would try
to centralize his own authority and domain.

Statesmanship in Early Egypt.—The great name of
the era is that of Pepy I, who exerted large influence
over the nobles and, even though his state was a
feudal one, dominated the times by his personality.
He followed a vigorous foreign policy which, if successfully handled, is always a political advantage
to a feudal lord. One of the king's trusted officials,
Uni, has left a biography which includes descriptions
of two expeditions, one against the nomadic Arabs
eastward from the Delta and the other by sea up
the Palestinian coast where the inhabitants were
made to suffer the loss of vines and fig orchards.
It is one of Pepy's titles to praise that he was able
to tolerate so great a man as Uni near him. This is
one of the earliest instances of a great subordinate
official in the service of royalty and the state, or as
we designate him, a statesman. He entered the service of his country under Teti, was advanced by
Pepy I and by his successor. He flourished during
three reigns, successful as a judge, a provincial governor in Nubia, and as a military commander. His
inscription is a valuable document for the understanding of the three reigns of which he was so
thoroughly cognizant. It was the name of Pepy's
pyramid Mennefer, or Memphis, which was at this
time transferred to the ancient city which had been

known formerly as White Wall but from henceforth was called Memphis, in common usage.

The Longest Reign in History.—One reign during this period, that of Pepy II, is remarkable as being the longest in history. It lasted ninety years. Probably the kingdom did not profit by such an unusual duration of one man's incumbency, as the succeeding rule lasted but one year, after which a cloud rests over affairs. The end of the dynasty may have come violently. When a clear view of Egyptian history is again afforded, three centuries have elapsed. Memphis fallen from its early importance has been succeeded as a capital by Heracleopolis. During the last years of the power of Memphis various provincial capitals had vied with it in importance— Akmum, Abydos, Thebes, Elephantine, etc. The receding tide of authority left the boundaries of the nomes more apparent than ever. A nomarch became a kinglet with his own court. The passage had been made from strongly centralized absolutism to a weakened monarchy, thence to a flourishing feudalism, followed by the woes of further decentralization and the disintegration of authority. Thus the Old Kingdom went down in the surging waves of an iconoclastic revolt. The agents and immediate causes are not discernible now. The destruction wrought was almost barbaric. Priceless works of old Egyptian art with the temples that contained them were demolished. It is frequently the case when such thorough demolition of the monuments of rivals ensues upon their subjugation that the embittering spirit of religious hatred has entered.

The Thebaic Age.—The period between Manetho's Sixth and Eleventh Dynasties was one of the most obscure in Egyptian history. According to Manetho the capital may have remained at Memphis during what he calls the Seventh and Eighth Dynasties. Thence it went to Heracleopolis for the Ninth and Tenth and to Thebes for the Eleventh. But the entire period is one of especial darkness for the historian. It is at least possible and interesting to compare the activities and affiliations of three noble families within this period, namely, those of Heracleopolis, Siut, and Thebes, disposed in this order from north to south. The first and last cherished the desire for royal dignity to which they succeeded in turn. The second was content with being the faithful ally of the first.

Heracleopolis is assigned eighteen rulers and 285 years of power. It is not credited with any great or very significant undertakings, though its rule marks the upward trend of Egyptian affairs after the collapse of the old régime. Its career was in difficult times, and it must have had merit to have secured allies so faithful and creditable as the princes of Siut.

The House of Thebes, whose princes held the responsible post of "Doorkeeper of the South," aspired to royalty. Its vigorous leaders were able to overthrow in their own favor all rival claims and found the line of Intefs and Mentuhoteps which history knows as the Eleventh Dynasty. Thebes, from being a place of little significance, came to the station of one of the mightiest cities of the ancient world.

It was the true successor of Memphis and its princes
and priests had very great influence in shaping the
Egypt of the Middle or Theban Period and of the
Empire. The wars necessary to seat these Thebans
in supremacy were waged against Heracleopolis and
its faithful ally the House of Siut, which lay between
Thebes and Heracleopolis.

The Theban line resumed the activities of Egyptian kings of the Sixth Dynasty both at home and
abroad. It is noteworthy that, while they built pyramids, these were not the ambitious affairs of the
early dynasties, which indeed could only be con=
structed by despotic, centralized power and great
wealth wholly at the pharaoh's disposal. It has been
suggested that the hopelessness of hiding the royal
tombs from robbers may have been another cause for
the discontinuance of the great pyramid. Such. despotic conditions as had obtained during the early
dynasties had ceased, but other activities engaged
the powers of these Eleventh Dynasty kings. They
organized the state admirably and developed the
country's economic resources.

The Theban Feudalism.—The Twelfth Dynasty is
also to be counted with this Theban Age, although
its members held court, not at Thebes, but in the
north, near modern Lisht, and in the Fayum. The
new capital was named Ithtowe, which means "Cap-
tor of the Two Lands." Six mighty kings of this
line stand out in history because of the solid achievements of their lengthy reigns during which Egypt
enjoyed her classic age. Unfortunately the buildings
of the time were ruined by the vandalism of later

ages, especially by Ramses II of the Nineteenth
Dynasty. But scattered over Egypt extant inscrip-
tional materials, as in the tombs of Beni-hassan and
Bersheh, furnish the historians with data. The kings
of the Twelfth Dynasty reached their goal by conquest of the former dynasty. Amenemhet I sup-
planted his rivals about 2000 B.C. Again and again
in Egyptian history is illustrated the fact that there
are two powerful aids to ambitious politicians, the
one being a movement back to an old condition, a
former capital, an aggrieved priesthood, or a discon-
tinued policy, the other being a new movement, the
promise of reform or the service of discontent.

Amenemhet I may be viewed as the logical finisher
of the work of the Heracleopolitan kings of the
Ninth and Tenth Dynasties and of the Intefs and
Mentuhoteps of the Eleventh, that is the redemption and unification of Egypt which had so sadly
disintegrated after the decay of the Old Kingdom.
The successors of Amenemhet I continued the weakening of local feudatories in favor of the authority
of the crown. But Egypt of the Twelfth Dynasty
continued to be a feudalism.

There was revived with the Twelfth Dynasty the
ambition for foreign enterprise, conquest, and expansion, pretty well forgotten since Pepy I. The southern boundary was pushed to a point forty miles
beyond the Second Cataract where fortified posts
were established on both sides of the river. This
accomplishment came with the energetic Usertesen
III (Sesostris). He sent an expedition into Syria,
the precedent of later conquests in Asia, in the days

of Ramses. During this period there is clear evidence of commercial relations with Asia Minor, the Ægean and southern Europe. Thus the early Mykenean civilization came into contact with mature Egypt. We notice also the beginning of the custom of appointing the crown prince as co-regent with the ruling pharaoh and thus insuring the succession of a well-trained ruler. The prince so named conducted wars in pursuance of the policy of expansion.

Amenemhet III, one of the greatest kings of Egypt, built the gigantic reservoir in the Fayum by which the waters at the season of high Nile could be stored to be released as needed during the subsidence of the river. By this device 27,000 acres of land were reclaimed to agriculture.

The Hyksos Invasion.—There is evidence on the monuments of the day that all through those decades Asiatic wanderers penetrated the Delta country. But at the close of the period came the most serious known invasion of ancient Egypt. A people of unknown origin who are generally called Hyksos, formerly referred to as Shepherd Kings, pressed into the Delta seeking homes and crowding insistently into the best agricultural country. For a century they struggled with the native population for the supremacy in lower Egypt and then went on to dominate the upper valley politically. They sought to establish themselves permanently in Egypt and to force their religion upon the Egyptians. Who they were has been so variously answered as merely to exhibit the poverty of the data for determining that question. Driven from Asia or in the van of some great migra-

IN OLD CAIRO

ON THE NILE

tion, Semites or Hittites, these are the questions and surmises. We know that the Hittites invaded Babylonia and probably held the seats of power in Mesopotamia for a considerable period. Could these Hyksos have belonged to a kindred movement branching more directly southward while the Hittite conquerors went east and south?

Josephus (contra Apion 1:14 *ff*) discusses the origins and occupations of the Hyksos and gives names of some of their kings. Their frontier fortress was at Avaris in the Delta. Native Egyptians continued to rule and sustain courts but as tributaries of the foreigner. Had the Hyksos been less iconoclastic they might have been absorbed in the native race, but they kept their hateful identity, hostile to native ideals, a foreign substance to be ejected at the first possible moment of sufficient patriotism.

The Imperial Age.—Just as the disorders of a former period had been ended by the energy and fortunate position of the Theban nomarchs, so now resistance to the Hyksos centred at Thebes, which must itself have suffered from the oppressors since traces of them have been found even farther south. The expulsion of the Hyksos necessitated a long struggle and they probably quitted the Delta many years later than the upper country. The Seventeenth Dynasty which began the war of liberation was for some time contemporary with the Hyksos kings. But only of those later members who were successful in crippling the enemy do we have knowledge. There is preserved from that age the autobiography of an Egyptian officer, Amosis, who took part in the war, and from it we learn that, Avaris having been captured, the foes were not simply expelled from Egypt but were pursued into South Palestine, where Sharuhen, which was either a temporary station in the retreat or an ancient stronghold, was captured. Probably, as is usually the case after so long occupation, it was the ruling caste of the Hyksos that was expelled while their humbler kindred became a permanent element in the Delta population.

The decisive stroke against the Hyksos was given by the first king of the Eighteenth Dynasty Amosis, 1580 B.C. He appears to have been in the royal line of succession. With his subsequent successes against foes in Asia began the period of Egypt's most ambitious relations with that continent. Experienced troops at the disposal of war-like pharaohs suggested campaign after campaign with the peoples of Palestine, Syria, and Mesopotamia. Egypt's peculiar genius like that of Babylonia was for peace, but the war spirit was forced into the political system by barbaric incursions and the patriotic fervor of resistance. Then followed the seductive charm of military conquest. The Theban gods Amon and Mentu were now looked upon as inspirers of war. Professional campaigners lusting for booty formed a class of consistent supporters of an aggressive foreign policy. The Egyptian chariotry, made possible by the growing use of the horse, was a formidable instrument of battle which became symbolic of might. It is thought that the Hyksos brought the use of horses into Egypt. They were animals for the use of the nobility who employed them in hunting and war. All military matters were made subjects of more specialized and expensive treatment than had formerly been customary.

An important political effect of the campaigns against the Hyksos was the centralization of power in native Egypt which led to absolute monarchy and empire. The standing army was one of the results of the wars and became a powerful factor in supporting the unique position of the new kings. All culture must henceforth consult the military.

Amosis was a great restorer and builder of sacred edifices. Thebes, the capital city, was especially adorned. The temple of Amon at Karnak begun by kings of the Twelfth Dynasty was enlarged and perfected by Amosis. Thebes became one of the famous cities of the world. In its rise and decline we may write most of the history of ancient Egypt.

Amosis ruled over twenty-two years and was buried in the ancient cemetery on the west bank of the Nile across from Thebes. His mummy has been found at Dâyr-al-Bahâri. The age which began with him was the most splendid that Egypt had known. From an oppressed country Egypt arose, upon the expulsion of its conquerors, to develop its inner resources and to dominate the affairs of western Asia. Syria was raided as well as other border countries. The captive became an empire.

Amosis' son was Amenhotep I, who, though of no great political strength or importance, was revered by his people and honored to the extra degree of being deified after his death.

There followed three Thothmes and Queen Hat-

4

shepsut a very influential ruler. Thothmes III was active as a warrior and a builder. After him was Amenhotep II who had a long but not remarkable reign. Then came Thothmes IV with a short and uneventful rule. Amenhotep III with his foreign wives introduced influences into Egyptian history which were very significant, leading as they did to the disruption of the empire.

Thothmes I had to quell rebellions and uprisings in Ethiopia and Syria. In Ethiopia the restless inhabitants sought to shake off the Egyptian overlordship which had been imposed during the earlier years of the dynasty. Thothmes I went farther with his punitive campaigns than most expeditions and reorganized the government of the disaffected country. A number of districts were formed with a governor, and a crown representative supervised all. Colonizing and building were also resorted to as likely to cement the bonds of union between Egypt and Ethiopia.

The Foreign Policy.—All the ancient nations sought after a successful method of administering provinces abroad. Like many modern nations their natural impulse was to exploit a dependency for material treasure, slaves, etc. But so much trouble attended the management of even a rich province on so purely selfish a basis that the ability of the ancient politicians was sorely taxed to plan for the harmonious maintenance of imperial sovereignty. Conquest, captives, tribute, and rule by a proxy were the usual steps of Egyptian foreign administration. So it was in Thothmes' campaign in Asia. There was no such device employed as in Ethiopia. The pharaoh marched into Asia, won battles, secured booty, set a partisan in authority and left for home. Again and again costly campaigns were conducted for glory and for immediate advantages, but not with any far-seeing, time-saving policy of organizing the province so that its own interests should prevent it from going to war with its master. A foreign people was an opportunity for military robbery. The prime object was the largest possible yield most speedily gathered. It would be interesting to know when the ancients reached the point of considering the problem as to whether other races were capable of assimilation to one's own standards or could, in lieu of that, be made congenial neighbors by any means. We should probably find that commerce and the arts afforded the earliest bases for a truly humanizing intercourse of foreign peoples.

The campaigns of Thothmes I took him as far as the Euphrates, where he placed two stelæ commemorative of victory. We may pass quickly over Thothmes II in order to discuss the significance of his sister and wife, Hatshepsut. She acted with him as co-regent. She was a forceful politician, probably the real ruler as long as she lived, which was well into the reign of Thothmes III, with whom also she was co-regent. These relations are in dispute.

Hatshepsut sent a famous trading expedition by water down the Red Sea Coast to Punt. It was customary in those days of infant commerce to call the goods which were brought back from an expedition the tribute of the country visited. It was, clearly,

an elaborate barter between the sovereigns of two
countries. Parihu, the king of Punt, received the
travelers hospitably and sent them back to their
royal mistress with incense, ebony, ivory, gold and
skins. Such royal undertakings were the forerunners
of trading expeditions by lesser personages or groups
of merchants who provided the capital for the ven-
ture. On the walls of the funeral temple of Hatshepsut at Dayr el-Bahari are pictures of incidents of
the famous expedition.

Thothmes III, Egypt's mightiest soldier-king, succeeded to the full title of ruler upon the death of
his half-sister the co-regent. He showed a vindictive
spite, not uncommon with kings of ancient Egypt, in
despoiling monumental mention of his predecessor
the great queen. Indeed she had shown the same
spirit towards the monuments of her former consort
Thothmes II. Asia was the field of Thothmes III's
most celebrated activities. The provinces in South
Palestine and Syria seized the opportunity offered by
a change in rulers to rebel. The pharaoh quickly took
the field with his armies. The final test came at
Megiddo. This was the name of a city-fortress com-
manding a pass in the hills, twenty miles southeast
of the Carmel promontory. The Egyptian troops
won the victory over all the confederates in the field
and then captured the city. Megiddo or Har-
Megiddo, sometimes pronounced Armageddon, was a
strategic military position in Palestine, where the
opposing forces of Asia and Egypt were very apt to
meet in conflict. The Egyptian won another decisive
battle there in the days of Josiah, king of Judah,

by which that king lost his life and Palestine became subject to Egypt. That was 870 years later, in the days of Pharaoh Necho (see II Kings xxiii: 29). Thus at both battles of Megiddo, Palestine was reclaimed to Egyptian suzerainty. Thothmes took immense booty to Egypt. The suppliant rulers brought tribute. Many prisoners of war had been taken and numerous hostages of royal blood were accepted. The fame of Thothmes the conqueror spread everywhere. Even the king of Assyria was said to have sent a gift. In all fifteen arduous campaigns were fought. Each time, a city was captured, tribute taken and a similar course of rebellions and reprisals followed. Manifestly, here was something analogous to the royal "hunt" rather than anything comparable with provincial administration. The pharaoh was uniformly successful. Doubtless discomfitures were minimized and the chronicler in his handling of the story of the campaigns did not allow the regal glory to dim. Famous cities of later history fall under our notice in the list of this pharaoh's conquests—Karkhemish, Aradus, Tyre, Kadesh on the Orontes.

SUGGESTIONS FOR STUDY

1. What has Herodotus to say about Egypt?
2. Compare the rôles of Menes, Minos, Manu and Moses.
3. Read the stories of Joseph in Genesis 39 to 50.
4. Styles of costume in early Egypt.
5. Make drawings of the various types of pyramids.
6. How did the Nile teach engineering and science to the Egyptians?
7. What points of historical interest are in the vicinity of Cairo?

THE ORIENT IN BIBLE TIMES

BOOK LIST

H. D. B. I, 653.

J. H. BREASTED: Ancient Records of Egypt. 5 vols.

G. A. BARTON: Archæology and the Bible.

BUDGE: The Mummy.

BAEDEKER: Guide Book for Egypt.

H. G. MITCHELL: Genesis. (The Bible for Home and School.)

WADE: Old Testament History.

WENDALL: A Primer of Egyptian History.

DRIVER: Modern Research. (Schweich Lectures.)

Encyclopædia Britannica: Articles on Menes, Minos, Moses, Indian Law, Pyramids, Nile.

CHAPTER IV

Egypt and Palestine.—The survey up to this point gives one the general background for the Ancient World around the eastern end of the Mediterranean. But from this time on actual information concerning Palestine is more often obtainable. This change is made possible very largely through the discovery, a generation ago, of a large number of letters written from Palestine in the period of Amenhotep III and IV. With the first of those reigns began the participation of Egypt in the famous correspondence known to us from the Tell el-Amarna letters. The name given to the collection is taken from the ruined site in Egypt where they were found by peasants. They contain the diplomatic notes and state correspondence of governors and kings in Asia who wrote to the Egyptian pharaohs. They were written on clay tablets in the Babylonian language and the cuneiform character. They testify to the dominant position established by Thothmes in Asia. They give just as clear evidence of the cultural influence of the Babylonians in the age immediately preceding the Egyptian sway. The most intimate knowledge of ancient oriental politics is afforded by the documents. International and provincial complications, ambitions and motives are revealed with life-like faithfulness. Most of the letter-writers were local rulers of Syria and Palestine more or less submissive to the court of Egypt, but a small number is from foreign potentates. Burnaburiash, the Kassite king of Babylon, and Dushratta of Mitanni land are repre-

sented. In the letters from the provinces one can
mark the decline of Egyptian prestige from the reign
of Amenhotep III to that of his son, the fourth of
the name. The Amarna letters make archæologists
curious to know what became of the corresponding
letters from Egypt to foreign parts. What we
have remaining is but one side of a prolonged
diplomatic conversation. Dushratta, king of Mitanni, writes as the father-in-law of Amenhotep
III, since one of the Mitannian princesses Kirkipa
had been given to the Egyptian king in marriage.
This is but an instance of the large Asian influence
which came into Egypt after the wars of Thothmes.
The life-blood, the language, the art and the religion
of the country of the Nile were profoundly affected
by the wave of internationalism.

Amenhotep III built the temple of Amon-Rā at
Luxor and is credited with the two statues of Memnon on the west side of the Nile opposite Thebes.
These stood before the pylon of the king's funereal
temple. The name of the architect and sculptor was
Amenhotep the son of Hapi. The material of the
statues is a hard sandstone. A fracture in one of
them resulted in so delicate an adjustment of the
sides of the fissure that the change of temperature
occasioned by the morning sun caused a musical
sound to issue from the rubbing of the tiny particles.
This was the one called the vocal Memnon.

It is possible that the religious movement of the
succeeding reign had already been felt in this one
and that in building the temple of Amon-Rā at Luxor,
the king revealed a desire to harmonize theological

polemics. At any rate, the home policies and problems were so engrossing that less and less attention was paid to the foreign domain. The letter referred to from Burnaburiash of Babylon was sent to Amenhotep IV to complain of outrages suffered by Babylonians in passing through the acknowledged sphere of Egyptian influence in Canaan. Merchants had been robbed and killed. Up in the lands of Syria and Palestine where anarchy was threatening, the great unrest was brought on by invasions of tribes who acknowledged no pharaoh and who made it exceedingly difficult for the vassals of Egypt to maintain a loyal stand. Rib-Adda, the king of Gebal north of Beirut, complained of the Khabiri folk who were overrunning the land. Ebed-Khepa wrote in similar strain from Jerusalem concerning the raids of the Khabiri who have detached town after town from the pharaoh's service and who will take away the whole province unless the pharaoh sends troops at once. Evidently no significant help came up from Egypt for the letters cease near the line of despair and one is led to ask two great questions, Who were those successful Khabiri who were conquering Palestine and Southern Syria and why was Egypt so silent to the appeal of its hard-pressed officials in the north?

The Khabiri were invaders of Palestine in the Fourteenth Century B.C. It seems probable from all that we know now that they came from the east and southeast and that they were Semitic tribesmen (see pages 206 and 209).

An Early Attempt to Unify Religious Thought and Practice.—To realize why Egypt was so silent to the appeals of its northern vassals one must read of the character and interests of King Amenhotep IV, or, as he was later known, Ikhnaton. The idiosyncrasies of this king have been attributed to various causes, to the influence of his mother, or of his wife, or both. We do not know the facts concerning the origin of his system of thought. He departed from the orthodoxy of his day and founded the cult of the solar disk. He was a youth of lofty intellectual ambition, idealistic and rigorously logical. He came to the throne at the height of the empire and ruled seventeen years. He lacked political acumen or any adequate interest in the practical side of government. He was enamored of speculation. A propensity to closet philosophy led him to become an academic theologian. He was probably impatient with the diverse interpretations of the sun-worship which were current in that age and sought to establish concepts that would unify devotion to the supreme deity and incidentally perhaps symbolize Egypt's world position and empire. Of course he ran counter to all popular thought which was very pluralistic when he insisted upon a monotheistic interpretation of life. Priests may have held similar monotheistic notions previous to that reign, but the king tried to enforce his ideas universally and exclusively. Ikhnaton found that the priests would oppose him bitterly. Their attitude may have been due either to fear of popular failure or because of danger to their dignity and the prestige of their established cults.

The dominating conception of the new system was that the sun itself is the life-giver and embracer of all lands and peoples. Distinctions of our day, such as materialist, spiritualist, deist, etc., could hardly be applied to the thought of that age. It was the actual material sun and its heat and force which Ikhnaton adored. To that extent he would seem comparable with a materialist, but he was the most advanced idealist of history to that time. We do not know that he held any idea of the omnipresence of the deity but simply believed that the sun's rays, that is, its power, went everywhere throughout the daytime. At night the sun was absent from the world. Had Ikhnaton lived in our age we might say that he was a deist at night. Logically perhaps he ought to have personalized the night or darkness and the foes within them or to refer all to a hostile force, but we do not know that he did this.*

The reforming king invaded the time-honored art of Egypt and made it conform to his ideas. Names were changed to fit the nomenclature of the reformed cult. His own name became Ikhnaton or Khuenaten, which means, according to some, "Spirit of the Solar Disc" or "Pleasing to Aten." His new capital was called Akhetaton. This town was at the site of modern Tell el-Amarna where the archives of the reign were found. The letters already mentioned give much detail concerning the domestic and foreign relations of Egypt. They show that the high respect in which Egyptian authority was regarded abroad during the reign of Amenhotep III had declined during the reign of his son and that the Syrian vassals were slipping the bonds that held them to Egypt.

* But see Hall, A. H. N. E. 300.

Amenhotep IV was too much engrossed at home with his propaganda to cultivate the foreign possessions.

Why the Reform Failed.—Ikhnaton effected his revolution and did not scruple at last to use drastic measures to enforce conformity to the royal will. In January, 1907, Professor Breasted discovered one of the temples which was erected to the new faith. It was a despoiled temple of Gem-Aton, at Sesebi, just below the Third Cataract.

Life in the royal family would seem to have been exemplary. The king accorded signal honor to wife and daughters. He worked incessantly but broke down finally under the strain of his illuministic program, probably because he did not see the desired conformity of the facts of life to his ideas. He was a zealot, iconoclast and partisan afflicted with eyes that speculated rather than observed. He seemed to yearn for a triumph of ideas. What he needed was a substratum of popular loyalty. He engendered hate, lost the confidence of his people and the provinces of his fatherland. He became odious to those who did not know him and was referred to as "the criminal of Akhet-aton." That very fact may perhaps be charged against him. The extenuating circumstances are that he was a pharaoh, not used to conciliating the crowd, a young idealist educated to the notion that things would continue at about their present level of excellence, a man too fine and too one-sided to grasp the whole problem of his age, an Egyptian without military aptitude, a priest and an artist without an adequate idea of the necessity of securing means for his ends.

It is likely that on the death of the reforming king his body was placed within the tomb which he had provided at his capital. Only a few of his courtiers who had planned to be buried about their lord were thus interred. The reform wave soon receded and the schism which had depended on the energy of the royal innovator was obliterated in a return to the ancient faith. The two sons-in-law who succeeded Ikhnaton were not the men to resist the reaction successfully. Within twenty years the change to the old order of things was complete and the capital was established again at Thebes.

An Estimate of a Famous Dynasty.—The comparative abundance of remains augmented by the Tell el-Amarna records give the age of the Eighteenth Dynasty unique literary significance. When one adds to this the religious activities of King Amenhotep IV one rounds out the period with ascriptions of a peculiar versatility. Yet in net results the age accomplished little. It seems as if Egypt had been lifted and then dropped back again into the very place where the Eighteenth Dynasty found it. This was literally true of the site of the capital. The dynasty began and ended at Thebes. It was an age of great significance for Syria and Palestine. Movements of Amorite peoples, of Khabiri tribesmen and Hittite folk were preparing the ground for the state of affairs familiar to the readers of the earliest portions of the Old Testament. The reactions upon Egypt were notable. The king had become an emperor and levied directly upon his subjects for the imperial army. The collapse of foreign prestige was followed by vigorous attention to Asiatic interests so that the resultant impression of the age of the Eighteenth and Nineteenth Dynasties is not permanently affected by Ikhnaton's interlude. The gradual extinction of the nomarchs may have resulted from the civil wars. In any case the crown was exalted in authority and enriched by the lands which had formerly belonged to the nomarchs. Foreign conquest enhanced the prestige of the new monarchy. Wealth to prosecute the wars was secured in the campaigns. The Asiatic provinces were governed chiefly by native viceroys whom the Egyptian court controlled by means of envoys. Thus with strongly centralized power, personally controlled troops, ample munitions of war, and growing prestige the more military pharaohs found little to hinder their victorious campaigns. It must have seemed to them as if the gods had specially provided the nearer Asiatic countries as fields for their campaigns and as foils for their royal prowess. Pride in their unchecked careers and a natural desire to emulate the deeds and fame of preceding conquerors led more than one king to the excess of self-laudation. The chariot and horse which had led to changes in the methods of warfare became to the Hebrew prophets and psalmists of a much later day symbols of Egypt and of worldly power (Psalm xx, 7).

The disturbances for which Amenhotep IV had been responsible could not be quieted without vigorous reorganization, and this was the main work of the ruler who was probably acting as regent when called by his patrons the Theban priests to the throne.

This was Harmhab, the man who initiated the new epoch. He was followed by the first of the famous Ramesside pharaohs who ruled Egypt during the following two centuries.

The New Dynasty and Its Problems.—In the Nineteenth Dynasty the great names are two Ramses, two Setys, and Merneptah. Of these Sety I appears to have been great in good qualities and Ramses II great in vanity. Sety I was a patriotic king, a vigorous administrator, reverent toward the memories of his ancestors and a conscientious builder. It was his task to begin the reclamation of Egypt's lost provinces in Asia. The foreign possessions had shrunk to a negligible remainder under the combined movements of Semitic invaders from the East and Hittite expansion from the North. Sety defeated the Bedawin of South Palestine and captured Semitic strongholds. The conquered regions were made to pay tribute. Farther north he captured Yenoam and Kadesh in Galilee. The country of the Lebanon was taken and supplies of lumber secured for Egypt. Still farther north he came into conflict with the Hittites, on whom he inflicted defeat. He was content, however, with Palestine and Phenicia, which he had definitely brought back under Egyptian control.

Ramses II appropriated the glory of his predecessor, and although doubtless an impetuous youth of considerable valor, he has left a reputation for vanity and selfish ambition. This is due to the long grandiose poem celebrating the Hittite campaign. Professor Breasted has given us a very clear and lifelike account of the Battle of Kadesh from this document. Ramses' army moving northward through Palestine in four divisions approached the head-waters of the Jordan north of Lake Galilee. The pharaoh pressed on towards Kadesh. When he reached Shabatuna he left two divisions south of that city and with the remaining divisions began to sift the country for the enemy. The Hittites were nearer than he supposed, in fact, they were lying in ambush on the opposite side of Kadesh as he came up to it. False reports brought by Bedawin misled the Egyptians. These nomads claimed to be de-serters from the Hittite army which they reported as a hundred miles away, to the north. Just at the critical moment, as they were about to fall into the ambuscade, the Egyptians captured two spies who, being severely beaten, confessed the startling knowl-edge that the Hittites were near. Ramses was in advance with one division. The enemy was able by clever maneuvering to attack the two divisions near Kadesh in turn and by hurling one upon the other to demoralize the troops for awhile. Ramses sent at once for the divisions near Shabatuna and put his personal troops into action. The full Hittite force was soon upon him. The king was in a precarious position, from which he extricated himself by a most energetic offensive. He was able to turn almost certain defeat into what he called a victory, but which may have been little more than a drawn battle. The foe took refuge within the city and a hasty peace was concluded, after which Ramses took his worn army back to Egypt. Conflicts with the Hittites continued with equally indecisive results for several

THE WINDING LITANI RIVER AT A POINT BETWEEN TYRE AND
ZAREPHATH (SAREPTA) IN PHENICIA

ROAD IN THE LEBANON MOUNTAINS

years, when a permanent treaty of peace between
the Egyptian and the Hittite nations was entered into
by Ramses II and Hattusil, ruler of the Hittites.

The Treaty Between Egyptians and Hittites.—This
treaty is a famous document and well worth studying.
The text was inscribed on silver. It had a protocol
which outlined former relations of the two countries.
The rest of the document dealt with the terms. Former treaties were confirmed, a defensive alliance was
arranged and other alliances deprecated. There was
a provision for the extradition of fugitives, an appeal
to the gods of both countries to witness the treaty
conditions, oaths, and the national seals completed
the ratification of the document. Some years later
Hattusil visited Egypt and gave his daughter in marriage to Ramses II. It was clearly understood that
Palestine pertained to Egypt. Southern Syria probably recognized the same suzerain. Ramses' visits
to the region north of Beirut were celebrated by an
inscription which may still be seen near the Nahr el-
Kelb. Most writers believe that Ramses II was the
pharaoh referred to by the Hebrew writings as the
oppressor of the Israelites. Nearly forty years ago
one of the explorers, Naville, excavated Pithom (Ex.
i, 11), a store city which Ramses built in the delta to
serve him in his Palestinian campaign. The reign
of Ramses II, glorious as it has been made to appear,
was an age of decay. It was a weakened state that
fell to the sway of Merneptah.

Invasion by Sea and Land.—During the last of
Ramses' reign and in the early years of Merneptah's,
western tribes pressed in upon Egyptian territory

5

even to the banks of the Nile, rendering agriculture and travel along the river precarious. They were Libyans and allies bearing names of uncertain identity whom some believe included peoples from southern Europe and Asia Minor. Merneptah made careful preparation to meet these intruders. In his fifth year the pharaoh routed the combined force in its raid upon the harvest of his subjects. His army included archers but the Libyans did not have that class of fighters. For six hours the terrific arrow shower of the Egyptians kept the Libyans off until their ranks were broken. Then at the closing-in for hand-to-hand fighting the chariots of the Egyptians put the enemy to flight. Records of the victory were found by Petrie in 1896 on the funeral temple of Merneptah at Thebes. The following is Professor W. M. F. Petrie's translation:

The wretched conquered prince of Libya fled, under the protection of the night, alone, without the plume on his head; his feet failed, his women were taken away before his face, the provisions of his store were plundered. He had no water-skin for his sustenance, his brothers plotted his murder, his officers fought with one another; their camp was burned to ashes, his whole property became a booty of the soldiers. Arriving in his country he lamented. Every one in his country was ashamed to receive him, "Punished prince, evil fate, feather," called him all the inhabitants of his city.

Come far out upon the roads; there is no fear in the heart of man; castles are abandoned, the walls are opened, the messengers return home; the battlements lie calm in the sun, until their guards awake the soldiers lie asleep; the cattle are let out on the pasture again, no one fears to go on the Nile; by night resounds not the cry, "stop," or "come," "come," in the mouth of the people; one goes with singing, there is no more the lament of sighing man; the villages are settled anew, he who has tilled his crop will eat it.

Devastated is Tehenu (Libya), Kheta (Hittite Land) is quieted; the Kanaan is seized with every evil; led away is Askelon, taken is Gezer, Yenuam is brought to naught, the people of Israel is laid waste, their crops are not. Kharu (Palestine) has become as a widow by Egypt.

This is evidence that the name Israel so famous in later Biblical literature had attained importance in Palestine as the name of a people among the powers of that region. A fair inference would be that a tribe or group of tribes dwelling chiefly in northern or western Palestine were already known by the name that denoted their kindred of some hundred years later. The northern kingdom of Israel in the days of the early prophets may well have included descendants of these and other tribes which were gradually joined with them. They would be predominantly Semitic in origin but not exclusively. Other stocks, perhaps Hittite and Mediterranean, were united with the desert races, and under the judges and Saul these were rough-hewn into a nation.

Social Conditions and the Hebrew Serfs.—In the comparative poverty of Egypt in the age of Merneptah art did not flourish. The remains are evidence of meagre undertakings built often at the expense of some earlier structure which was robbed to provide materials. Professor Petrie describes how Merneptah's funeral temple was built in the neighborhood of that of Amenhotep III apparently to enable the laborers to steal stone from the earlier structure. A time of anarchy followed the death of Merneptah. There were several rulers in quick succession. Civil strife among the landed nobles and plundering among the commoner folk went on, while for part of the time a Syrian made himself powerful in Egypt. Those who estimate that Ramses II was the Biblical pharaoh of "the oppression" are wont to name Merneptah as the pharaoh of the Exodus or else to place the event during this period of anarchy and usurpation. Setnakht was the new king who settled the disorder of the times. He drove out the Syrian usurper and died leaving the throne to his son Ramses III. The latter was the notable pharaoh of the period. During his rule the state of affairs reminds one of the palmiest days of the Eighteenth Dynasty. The task awaiting him was similar to that which had faced Merneptah, to drive back the encroaching western tribes, Libyans and others. After that accomplishment there was a serious attack from the north through Palestine which devastated that country and threatened the very existence of Egypt. The enemies have sometimes been thought of as pirates originally from the north African coast, but more probably they came from the islands and northern shores of the Mediterranean to find new homes. Perhaps they fled from unendurable conditions in their old habitations whence hunger and the pressure of other migratory peoples drove them. They were styled "Peoples of the Sea," Pulesti, Daanau, Shakalsha, Shardina and Washasha. By the time that these emigrating folk had reached Palestine in their descent from the north and west Ramses awakened to the peril and prepared both ships and troops to resist them. The enemy's fleet was trapped and destroyed by a well-planned naval attack which was timed to coöperate with land operations by the troops. The victory was decisive for the Egyptians. The battles by land were fought in Philistia and the remnants of the invading army which were not enslaved and carried off by the conquerors were refugees in the regions

near by. Ramses continued a defensive warfare,
including campaigns in Syria, after which the Hittites do not again appear as aggressors in the proper
Egyptian sphere of influence, and gained further
successes against Libyans. The latter half of the
reign was devoted to pursuits of peace. The king
undertook commercial adventures to the Red Sea
coasts and the land of Punt. His emissaries brought
back precious stones and metals. He sought to
replenish Egypt with trees, planting areas otherwise
waste and burning.

Socially, the age was decadent. The blight of
vicious living fell upon the whole country. A notable
and deplorable feature of the period was the opulence
of the ecclesiastical foundations which amassed over-
much of the country's resources and carried the economic centre far beyond the point where a balanced
commonweal was possible.

Diseases of the Body Politic.—A state within the
state, in fact, several such interests within the state,
were nourished by the policy of these late pharaohs
compelled doubtless by aggressions which they could
not resist. But the dominant force of all was the
cult of Amon with a scandalously large share of the
wealth and personal power of Egypt. As might be
expected, when the material resources and political
importance of Amon increased the moral power of
the cult declined. Thus two evils conspire against a
land whenever the spiritual power parades in material splendors. In Egypt the government succumbed
to the priesthood and the priesthood to the ruin
drawn down upon all by its own greedy policy. After

Ramses III there were nine other pharaohs of the name: The glory had departed and the magic of a name and of a religion little better than incantation became the hope of kings who were as incompetent as the Merovingians of Europe. These kings made the motions which accompanied royalty of that day when the priests were the real statesmen.

The kings of the Eighteenth and Nineteenth Dynasties made grievous mistakes, the brunt of which had to be borne by their less fortunate successors. In a few respects the Nineteenth Dynasty may be likened to the age of Louis XIV, or, perhaps nearer, to that of Solomon. Brilliant, astounding, apparently as such an age or reign may seem, it may, as in many historical instances, be an exhausting one, a time during which troubles are accumulated for some unfortunate heir. Great expenditures consume not only the wealth that has been laid up but the energy and patriotism of a people. Oppression crowds down the great productive classes among the people and by creating wealthy, luxurious upper classes who may be essentially unproductive brings about a state of affairs in which the virile stock of the peasantry is degraded below the level of life which is desirable for it to occupy. This leaves the upper classes politically suspended. The privileged class in Egypt at the opening of the Twentieth Dynasty was the priestly class. It was with them that one of the two great mistakes had been made. Concessions and favors had been heaped upon the priests of Amon-Ra already aggrandized by the reaction in their favor after the downfall of the Aten cult. The ecclesiastical administration of the Amon worship became immensely wealthy and as the high priesthood was now hereditary, it soon became a stronger dynasty than the one on the throne.

Competing Capitals United.—The Twenty-first Dynasty instead of focusing about one capital formed its life around two foci, Tanis and Thebes. The great name of the period was Herihor, who possessed advantages, social, military and priestly. He wielded great influence and finally assumed the name of king. He strove to legitimatize the royal position of his house. His son Payonekh married a royal princess of the pharaonic line. A competitor was on the throne at Tanis in the Delta. Eventually the two ruling families were united by marriage. The dates and order of succession are obscure. Scanty remains have been found at Dayr el-Bahri and in the tombs of the priests. The country was in a disordered state. Strenuous means were necessary to guard the royal cemeteries and the bodies of the ancient pharaohs. One remembers how Old Egypt had been formed by the union of two kingdoms, north and south. That line of cleavage reappeared in the disintegration of the country during these unhappy times. All these events brought on by moral decay and the aggrandizement of a single class led to further usurpation of the throne by that other foe of the empire, the mercenary soldier.

Saul, David and Solomon were contemporaries with the Twenty-first Dynasty and it would appear that Solomon married one of the Egyptian princesses of the age. ''And Solomon made affinity with Pharaoh,

King of Egypt, and took Pharaoh's daughter and brought her into the city of David . . . " (I Kings iii, 1). Solomon's new father-in-law campaigned in Philistia and captured the outpost Gezer. This town he turned over to Solomon (I Kings ix, 16). It is commonly thought that the pharaoh referred to was either the last or the next to the last member of the Twenty-first Dynasty. But Professor Breasted argues that no less vigorous king than Sheshonk I of the Twenty-second Dynasty would meet the historical terms of the situation. He is called Shishak in our version of I Kings xiv, 25, where it is said that he looted Jerusalem. These Palestinian triumphs are recorded at Karnak. Sheshonk the Libyan was the reuniter of Egypt. This new line of pharaohs belonged to the race which had been so severely defeated in the days of Ramses III and before that by Merneptah. These beaten foemen became the paid soldiery of the Egyptians. Libyans were enlisted in such great numbers that they formed the larger part of the army. This foreign force served Egypt until its officers found it practicable to serve themselves even to the extent of securing royal power. Of course one usurper had to meet another and no dynasty can remain stable when the disease of usurpation attacks the political system. Sheshonk was compelled to win his way against the ambitions of his former comrades in arms, the other powerful Libyan captains.

The beginning of the period of Egypt's submission to the Libyans marked the secession of the northern tribes of Israel from Jerusalem and the

A PORTION OF THE EASTERN WALL OF JERUSALEM SHOWING
STONES OF SEVERAL PERIODS FROM OLD JEWISH TO
LATE ARAB

LOOKING UP THE GORGE OF THE WADY KELT (BROOK CHERITH)
FROM THE JERICHO ROAD

dynasty of David. The vigorous Libyans ruled over
two hundred years. Four of their kings bore the
name Sheshonk. While the second one was on the
throne Ashurnazirpal III was terrorizing Western
Asia. Omri and Ahab had ruled Israel. During the
long reign of Sheshonk III Assyria was declining, the
house of Jehu had succeeded that of Omri in Israel
and the murderous Athaliah at Jerusalem was succeeded by Joash, king of Judah. Sheshonk IV closed
his reign almost synchronously with Jeroboam II of
Israel and the ministrations of Hosea the prophet.

The Ethiopian Control.—The next power to seize
upon disordered Egypt was a former province, Ethiopia, which had become independent toward the close
of the Twenty-first Dynasty. It increased in strength
until it was able to drive out the Libyan masters and
provide Ethiopian rulers for its old mistress. These
successive changes when rapidly sketched show as
plainly as possible the helplessness of native Egypt.
One of its ruling families is driven out of power by
the priests of Thebes. They in turn are expelled by
the Libyan mercenaries of the army and these are
overcome and followed by a former province of
Egypt. Could a country be more desperately con-
ditioned than to be in turn the prey of its priests, its
soldiers, and its provincials?

The Ethiopian who attacked Egypt and succeeded
to power was Piankhi. In his inscription describing
his expedition into Egypt he states that there were
twenty rulers in the country. He was successful over
them all and established himself as king. This was
near the date of the Fall of Samaria. (See page 243.)

Piankhi did not condescend to occupy an Egyptian capital but ruled Egypt as a dependency, from Ethiopia. Such a thing had not happened before in history. Even the hated Hyksos rulers dwelt, probably, in the country which they conquered. There was a brief period of Egyptian independence under a prince named Bekenrenf and then a resumption of Ethiopian control. Shabaka was the new Ethiopian ruler who put Bekenrenf to death and gained all the Nile country. He abetted the little Syrian states against Sargon of Assyria, without much success. In 701 the Egyptians were more fortunate in their opposition to the Syrian interests of Assyria. A strange misfortune overtook the army of Sennacherib after its early successes in Palestine and drove the Assyrian commander to retreat to his own country. (See page 246.)

The Fall of Thebes.—Esarhaddon of Assyria, who succeeded Sennacherib (see page 146), made earnest effort to reduce Egypt which had been the thorn in the side of Assyria, as it pursued a policy of expansion in Western Asia. The Egyptians had their partisans in the capitals of the small states of Palestine and by political activity sought to diminish' Assyrian prestige. It was a dubious battle for years between the Assyrian and the Ethiopian until the time of Asshurbanipal of Assyria, whose army sacked the glorious city of Thebes, an event which shook the world of that day (661 B.C., see page 250), much as the evil fate of Rome did a later world. Egypt must have suffered severely. Ethiopian influence came to an end in the country and the independent fortunes of the kingdom of Ethiopia are less and less observable, as that country became more typically African. Assyria, in the early days of its control in the Delta, had organized the government of Egypt and left certain native princes in charge. One of these was Necho of Sais. His house, known as The Saite or Saitic, became very influential. Necho's son Psamtik I, encouraged by Gyges of Lydia, threw off the Assyrian authority and set up as king of Egypt. Sais was the capital. The Greeks were encouraged to settle in Egypt where their influence became great.

The Greeks in Egypt.—The Greeks had established merchants in the Delta before the end of the Seventh Century in the persons of the Milesians. The Station of the Milesians and the capital Sais were in neighborly and harmonious relations with each other. Psamtik opened another station Daphnai, now the site Tell Dafnah. This was later dismantled and the main station, that near Sais, was named Naukratis. This became a self-governing city of Greeks, who came from different parts of the Hellenic world. Here they developed their part of that wonderful Grecian race consciousness which separated between Hellene and barbarian and set the standards of the world's culture. Shades of Merneptah! These settlers from Asia Minor and the islands who prospered under the favor of the Saite pharaohs were a new "Sea Folk" picking their way through the profitable enterprises of Egypt, hated as heartily as the olden Egyptians hated the Sea Peoples.

Babylonians Followed by Persians.—Under Necho

II, who vied with Babylon in the partition of the falling empire of Assyria, Palestine was reclaimed by the Egyptians for a few years, but in the ensuing contest the pharaoh's army suffered a severe defeat at the hands of Nebuchadrezzar in 605 at Carchemish. This decisive battle made Babylon under Nebuchadrezzar, dictator of Asia. The long reign of this Babylonian king did not close until the year 562. But a new world-power was looming in the East and Egypt, Babylonia, Lydia and Sparta were soon forced into an alliance against Cyrus the Persian. The busy eager preparation of the world to resist the great Persian may be reflected in the forty-first chapter of Isaiah. But the Hebrew seer believed that the preparation would avail nothing.

"Keep silence before me, O islands; and let the peoples renew their strength; let them come near; then let them speak; let us come near together to judgment. Who hath raised up one from the east, whom he calleth in righteousness to his foot? he giveth nations before him, and maketh him rule over kings; he giveth them as the dust to his sword, as the driven stubble to his bow. He pursueth them, and passeth on safely, even by a way that he had not gone with his feet. Who hath wrought and done it, calling the generations from the beginning? I Jehovah, the first, and with the last, I am he. The isles have seen, and fear; the ends of the earth tremble; they draw near, and come. They help every one his neighbor; and every one saith to his brother, Be of good courage. So the carpenter encourageth the goldsmith, and he that smootheth with the ham-

mer him that smiteth the anvil, saying of the solder-
ing, It is good: and he fasteneth it with nails, that it
should not be moved" (Isaiah xli, 1–7).

The familiar bustle and ring of preparation of
men and munitions runs through this stirring de-
spatch from Bible times. Self-preservation was the
object of the great coalition against Persia, but the
members were for the most part detached from the
plan of defense and conquered separately. Croesus,
king of Lydia, was defeated in 546; thereafter followed the subjugation of Babylonia, Syria and Palestine. The conquest of Egypt came in 525 by Cambyses, son of Cyrus.

A Dynasty with Antiquarian Interests.—The Twenty-
sixth Dynasty which was overthrown will always be
interesting because of its antiquarian sympathies and
its experiments in restoring an ancient cultural style
in the life and art of the people. The pharaohs
sought to realize the ideals of the kings of the Fifth
and Sixth Dynasties. Like them they sought burial
in Sakkara. It is interesting to note that while the
kings at Sais were modelling their institutions upon
those of antiquity a similar veneration of the old
was developing in Babylon where King Nabunaid
was more successful as an archæologist than as
a statesman.

Significance of Egypt for Readers of the Bible.—
When the vigorous Hebrew tribes were coming to
national consciousness Egypt was in decline. The
significance of Egypt's past was that Egyptian civilization had helped mold the ideas and methods of
the Orient. Together with Babylonia, Egypt was

responsible for that life in the greater settlements of
Palestine which set the fashion of ancient life. This
old Canaanite life was the teacher of the Hebrews
who learned of the people whom they conquered,
even as the barbarians of Europe learned of the
Romans whom they displaced. The organization and
methods of civilized life were held by the persistent
Canaanites until the Hebrews were able to assimilate
them. (See Judges i, 21, 27, 33, etc.) Compared with
the great countries about, the land of Palestine was
one of the poorest of the settled regions. But its
strategic social position in the ancient world made
it sensitive to all currents of thought. In a substantial degree it was suburban to the Delta. The impress
of Egypt upon the imagination of the writers of the
older documents of the Bible is very noticeable. To
know Egypt, therefore, in its modes of life and
thought, in its art and history, is to account for one
important element in the cultural consciousness of
the Biblical folk.

The Nations of the Hittites.—One of the most
important and one of the least understood peoples
of the ancient orient was the Hittite. They are men-
tioned in most of the historical books of the Old
Testament. Main centres of their power existed in
Asia Minor at the present Turkish sites of Boghaz-
Köi and Eyuk, east of the Halys, and on the
Euphrates rivers. Lesser kingdoms and outposts
were found in Syria. By certain investigators the
Hittites are thought to have been the forerunners
and even the ancestors substantially of the present
Armenians who live in a part of the Hittite sphere

of influence. Other scholars have seen Indo-European, still others Mongolian evidences in the Hittite remains of architecture, physiognomy, language, dress, religion, etc. There may have been partially federated alliances of kingdoms made up of the two racial stocks mentioned, with a ruling caste of one or the other.

The Hittite influence in the affairs of Western Asia was especially noticeable from 2000 to 1000 B.C., while princes of the Hittite name were active a few centuries later. In the early period of their domination they wrecked the Semitic power in Babylon which we call the First Dynasty and made easy its conquest by the eastern Kassites who became rulers of Babylonia. They may have been influential in some now unknown way in the disruption of ancient Egypt by the Hyksos. It is worth remembering that while the latter introduced the horse into military use in Egypt, the Hittite folk are credited with having brought that animal into Western Asia.

The Mitanni of Mesopotamia were one of the greater Hittite peoples and kingdoms. Dushratta, of Mitanni, in the fourteenth century B.C. was one of the foreign princes whose letters to Egypt were found among the Tell el-Amarna tablets. Both war and peace found the Hittite-Mitanni and Egyptian nations engaged with each other. Marriages were contracted and doubtless certain influences political and religious may be traced therefrom. Hittites and Mitannians, though kindred peoples, fought in bitter wars in which the former prevailed under their King Subbiluliuma, son of Hattusil I, who was a kind of Sulayman. Kings Arandas, Mursil and Mutallu followed, then Hattusil II, who made the famous treaty with Ramses II.

At the height of their power the Hittites controlled the lands afterwards made known to history by the Cappadocians, Phrygians, Lydians and Cilicians. The empire phase of Hittite development lasted about two centuries or less. Besides the better known foes of the Hittite confederates, such as Egyptians and Assyrians, there were the Aramean peoples from the East and the Sea Peoples from the West, and perhaps an Indo-European folk which helped in the general disintegration of Asiatic states about 1000 B.C.

SUGGESTIONS FOR STUDY

1. Prepare a paper on the Tell el-Amarna correspondence.
2. What relation was there between Khabiri and Hebrews?
3. Why were the letters from Palestine to Egypt written in a Mesopotamian language and character?
4. Describe the ruins at Luxor.
5. What influences will help to explain Ikhnaton?
6. How account for Ethiopian ability and success: may it be repeated?
7. The Biblical accounts of the Exodus.
8. Why did the Delta country increase in importance?
9. Recent discoveries in Hittite-land.

BOOK LIST

L. B. PATON: The Early History of Syria and Palestine.
PETRIE: History of Egypt.
PETRIE: Syria and Egypt from the Tell el-Amarna Letters.
MASPERO: The Struggle of the Nations.
HOGARTH: The Ancient East.
WINCKLER: The Tell el-Amarna Letters.
WEIGALL: The Treasury of Ancient Egypt.
NEWBERRY and GARSTANG: A Short History of Egypt.

CHAPTER V

The Continuing Importance of the Near East.—One of the remarkable disclosures of the World War was the fact that questions of world magnitude could not be dealt with or settled without calling into the field of current history again those lands which were the homes of the peoples of the Bible. In a sense geography never becomes ancient. To be sure rivers meander and deserts shift, climate varies and deltas fill, but new tracks must have regard to old ones. Moreover, those reasons which made the Levantine regions the sites of early culture continue to be influential and to make that part of the world central to many interests which have grown out of it. The geography of the Tigris-Euphrates country has been modified in some degree. The delta has spread farther south into the Persian Gulf so that the processes which add a mile in less than a century have since great Hammurabi's day extended the land southward sixty or seventy miles. Unfortunately this gain is largely in reedy, pestilential swamp, but it will yield to engineering treatment. The tragic campaign up the river from the gulf will be talked of long after the modern improvements have reclaimed to garden conditions the domain of the water-buffalo and the Affej tribesmen. The gardening possibilities of these rich lands will be developed again and the enthusiastic accounts of the ancients will be appreciated.

6

For years before the war, the members of the
Arabian Mission had been investigating the possibilities of relief in the lands of the Shatt-el-Arab and
north. An interesting change in the country has
resulted from the shifting of the course of the rivers
many times, so that the sites of old river cities are now
far from the streams while artificial canals and natural meanderings are intermixed. Ancient Babylonia
was made by the rivers even as Egypt was made by
the Nile. But the Tigris and Euphrates together
made a broader region. It is one of the most striking
contrasts of geography that puts Arabia and Babylonia so near to each other. As the surrounding
oceans lessen the sterility of the thirsty edges of the
Arabian peninsula, even more remarkably do the
noble rivers mellow the northeastern border of
Arabia and bring down the fertilizing soils.

Sumer and Akkad.—It was in the combined valleys
of these two rivers, the Euphrates and the Tigris,
that there arose and continued from the Fourth Millennium to about the middle of the First Millennium
B.C. a civilization which may be called the Babylonian-
Assyrian. We have our first historical view of the
country in the far south where the two rivers ran
nearer to each other and emptied into the Persian
Gulf. There were the richest lands, made fruitful by
the overflowing streams and the powerful sunshine.
It was naturally a deluge-country. The disadvan-
tages of the situation were overcome by the earliest
builders of cities who made platforms of brick on
which to place their settlements. It is hard for us to
imagine life without structures of timber, metal and

stone. All the more wonderful are the uses to which the clay or mud of old Babylonia was put. Out of this material were made dykes, towers, temples, forts and palaces. Stucco, glazed tile and even the tablets on which the writing was inscribed were of clay. Packages were sealed with lumps of it through which cords were drawn and on which impressions were stamped so that the lumps and strings served a purpose similar to that of modern lead-seals and wire. Agriculturally, architecturally and artistically the civilization was triumphant in the use of mud. So habituated to clay-working were the colonists of the more northern districts, toward Assyria, that even in a stony region they continued for a long time to follow the southern custom of using bricks. Man and his affairs were surely constituted of the dust of the ground in Babylonia.

Babylonian writing, stationery and books seem very cumbersome. When the writing was in pictures engraved on stone the results fall within the realm of monumental art. In old Shumer, however, stone was an imported article and too valuable to use for ordinary purposes. The genius of the primitive Babylonians evolved the writing tablet from the brick. By exercising care in the selection and treatment of various clays the scribes produced different textures and shades of fireproof stationery. In the early period, say down to about 2200 b.c., the tablets used for writing were well baked to a hardness comparable with stone. From that time to the Roman period only the unusual tablets were baked carefully in kilns, many were but partly baked and others merely sun-dried. Perhaps in the age of Hammurabi the high cost of living affected stationery and library materials or else the rapidity and volume of business outstripped the capacity and care of the scribes. The writing of that age reflects the increased pressure upon business methods as the fully written picturesque characters of the Sumerian changes to a depleted cursive or running hand. The script is more crowded and slanting. Professor Barton has made exhaustive studies in the subject of Babylonian and Assyrian writing in his "Origin and Development of the Babylonian Writing" (2 vols, 1913), in which he illustrates graphically the changes from the ancient hieroglyphic down through the Sumerian variations, the First Dynastic, the Kassite, the Assyrian standard and the New-Babylonian-Persian styles of writing.

As in so many countries, the world over, the early Babylonians drew pictures to represent ideas. This is what is meant by the term ideographic. At first they pictured the commonest objects and then their modifying thoughts about those objects. This led to the invention of a long list of signs. The list could be made shorter by an economical use of the most common signs. For illustration, if English writing had begun in the same way, we should have had a picture of a man and another of a duck or a drake among our signs. Now if we wished to write by these means the symbols of the plant called the mandrake, we might do so ideographically by drawing a picture of the plant, or, if we didn't wish to multiply signs, we might sometimes write mandrake by the two

signs "man" and "drake." The resultant word mandrake would in the latter case have nothing to do
with the original meanings of the signs man and
drake which came to be used simply as syllables or
sounds. A further economy was secured by letting
one sign stand for different syllables and meanings
in different contexts and combinations. For example,
suppose our sign for "drake" came to mean "age"
also, then the verb manage could be formed and the
skilful reader could tell quickly from the connection
in which the word was found whether the text was
talking about a plant or about handling the affairs
of business. There would be no more perplexity in
such cases than in the endeavors of a foreigner seeking to understand the many meanings which certain
English words of similar or identical sound have;
for instance, the word "fast" and its many meanings. The Babylonians were able by the methods
suggested to express abstract ideas, the different
parts of speech, conjugations, declensions, etc. The
number of signs reached many hundreds but in practice a few hundred usually sufficed.

The scribes were able to work with great rapidity
and skill. They made tablets and tablet-covers in
sizes to fit the amount of writing to be done. They
took pride often in giving a pleasing appearance to
the written surface by orderly arrangement of lines.
Ruling, spacing and tabulation were often calculated
to a nicety. Tablets from the size of the thumb-nail
to the folio have been found. Most business contracts
and letters of the classical period could be written
in a clear hand on tablets approximating the 24mo

size. Such a tablet as this from a half-inch to an inch in thickness, made of finely ground clay, with convex faces, would be held in the hand in order to write on the front side. Ordinarily it would then be laid on a hard surface while the back was inscribed. The finger-prints of the writer are frequently observable about the corners and edges. The writing began at the upper left-hand corner of the tablet and went straight across the face. Line after line continued to the foot of the tablet which was then turned endwise and the writing continued down the other face so that the last line was usually back of the first one unless it was necessary to write along the edges. Very rarely the scribe turned the tablet on its left edge when he wished to write on the second face, much as we should turn the leaf of a book. As with us, letters were often enclosed in an envelope. This was made by coating the completed letter in fresh clay and inscribing the name of the addressee on the outside which then looked like a larger tablet. If it were important a business contract would be wrapped with a coating of clay and in that case the wording of the inner tablet would be repeated substantially on the covering. For all practical purposes the outer writing would answer, but, if any legal dispute followed, the court could have the outer shell removed and the unspoiled original writing brought into the testimony. We have a reference to these double documents in Jeremiah (xxxii: 11–14). The open deed was the outside one and the sealed deed was on the tablet within.

Babylonian tablets have been found in different

regions of the ancient world, several hundred in
Egypt (page 55), a few in Palestine and more in
Asia Minor. The home-land on the Euphrates-Tigris
rivers has yielded tens of thousands. Doubtless the
mounds there hold hundreds of thousands more of
these valuable documents. They will reveal in intimate detail the affairs of the temples, streets, and
markets. Besides book-keeping accounts, law-tab-
lets, chronicles, leases, loans, labels, tags, legal decisions, pledges, inheritances, partnerships, letters,
arithmetical, medical and religious records there is
a literature including stories, myths, hymns, and
prayers. Lesson-tablets, grammatical aids and dictionaries exist revealing the fact of difficulties in the
way of the ancient learner of the Sumerian and
Semitic as they were written on the tablets. The
stylus may have been made from a reed with a corner
or angle at the end. The corner of the end of a square
match tip when pressed into modelling clay gives pre-
cisely the effect of the tailed wedges of the cuneiform
writing.

Fertility of Old Sumer.—The Babylonian lands produced abundant crops of grain and vegetables. Our
earliest knowledge of the people shows them enriched
by the bounteous nature about them, living in villages
and cities. The cities were the local centres of government. Religion was highly developed and the
early rulers were priest-kings equipped with honor
and wealth, consequently with power. Each city
was the home of a special cult. Inevitably the forces
that make for war, greed, lust for power and fame,
suspicious fear of what others may intend to do,

operated to subordinate one city to another and logically one god to another. It is more commonly believed that the race of people which laid the foundations of the ancient civilization in that region was a non-Semitic one now known as the Sumerian. This belief needs further investigation and specification. Certain eminent scholars contest the general impression stoutly and claim that Semites from Arabia moved into the fertile lands of the lower Euphrates before the Sumerians arrived, being earlier by some hundreds or even a thousand years. These nomads mingled their desert-and-oasis culture with the new arts of the alluvium, made city forts from which their chieftains vied with others for headship and introduced the worship of Semitic gods and goddesses. Later, when the Sumerians entered the country they drove the Semitic folk northward towards Agade, introduced further arts and religious conceptions and gradually developed a system of writing. Throughout these prehistoric centuries, as well as in historic times, the pictured representations of the deities were of a decidedly Semitic type.

Movements Towards Unity.—Fairly well-marked districts grew out of the amalgamation of city principalities. These were called in geographical order beginning at the river's mouth: (1) The Sea-Lands, (2) Kaldi, (3) Shumer or Sumer, Biblical Shinar, (4) Akkad. The latter two names were often combined and designated as one region and the two names were employed in the titles of rulers much as Upper and Lower Egypt or the Two Lands were used in the titles of pharaohs. Kings were known as "King of

Sumer and Akkad.'' The history of the country began in the south, expanded along the rivers northward and across the country to the west. The westward expansion of power began early and reached as far as the Mediterranean. The culture of old Sumer and Akkad spread with the march of traders and soldiers and like a succession of waves covered Mesopotamia, Syria, and Palestine.

The Openness of the Land to Invasion.—These lands and peoples in the valleys of the two rivers were accessible from every side. The racial character of the population and the style of government were subject now and again to modification because of incursions from the sea and its shores to the south, from the Elamite mountains to the east, from the Arabian desert and from Syria on the west, from the rivers, mountains and lands to the north. The Delta was the most open land in Egypt, but even it was not so accessible from every side as Babylonia. A strong Egyptian government or a strong native feeling kept the country of the Nile comparatively free from foreign elements up to the days of the Hyksos and for long periods thereafter. In Babylonia from the earliest times there was a succession of strong dominant races and a much more cosmopolitan influence radiated from that part of the world. Probably the blending of racial stocks was more constant and thorough in Babylonia than in any other seat of ancient culture.

Nippur, in the heart of the ancient country, was one of the earliest of its dominant cities. We surmise this from the religious prestige which the city enjoyed, or which was ascribed to its god En-Lil, long after other cities had outstripped Nippur economically and politically. When the great king of Ur, Ur-engur, who brought unity after anarchy in Babylonia, was able to add Nippur to his conquests, he took the significant title King of Sumer and Akkad. A notable event in the scientific efforts of the new world to uncover the secrets of the oldest was the exploration of Nippur. The expeditions, conceived and financed in Philadelphia, were able to do a remarkable piece of work in exhuming the buried story of Babylonia from so central a site.

Babylon was one of the younger of those ancient cities of the land. But it became the seat of power for a dynasty of Semitic rulers of the same blood as the Amorites of Biblical fame. These western Semites made Babylon the mistress of the Mesopotamian world and bequeathed the name Babylonia to the four southern districts named on page 88. The greatest king of the line was Hammurabi. He more than any other is to be credited with the notable achievements of his family which is called The First Dynasty. It was in power for three hundred years from 2225 to 1926 B.C. This, the classic age of Babylon, was roughly contemporaneous with the classic age of the Thebans, say the Eleventh and Twelfth Dynasties in Egypt.

The dynasty which has for a long time been called by historians the Second Dynasty of Babylon is now known to have been partly contemporaneous with the First and not strictly in succession to it as was formerly supposed. This discovery led to a substantial change in the dates once assigned and also to the treatment of the Third Dynasty soon after, if not practically in succession, to the First. Just what connection the Second Dynasty had with Babylon beyond the furnishing of a thorny problem to the successors of Hammurabi has not been thoroughly cleared up.

The Third Dynasty was The Kassite. The race came from the northeastern mountains, conquered the Sea-Land folk of the Second Dynasty and settled at a place called Karduniash, near the mouth of the rivers Euphrates and Tigris. From their southern vantage point the Kassites spread through the land until they captured Babylon which they made their capital. The period of the growing influence of the Kassites in the lower country marks the development of a people in the far north who were known to later history as the Assyrians.

Who Were the Assyrians?—Evidently they were connected racially with the Semitic elements of the Babylonian people, probably with those early Semitic Babylonians of the days of Sargon I (see page 106) rather than with the later Western Semites of the days of Hammurabi. There is a problem, among the many early oriental problems to be cleared up, which may yet be more satisfactorily dealt with and that concerns the participation of the Hittites in the racial stock which we call Assyrian as well as its influence on the Palestinian folk.

So far as the Assyrians were kindred with the Semitic Babylonians of the early period, say 3000 B.C., the relationship may have come by colonization from the south or by earlier branching off from the same parental stock. The home of the Assyrians was in the rougher mountainous country of the north where climate and the interests of life led to the development of a ruder folk. The Assyrian character developed fewer of the cultural gifts and more of the war-like activities than their southern neighbors. Until the last the life of Babylonia was marked by cultural considerations and that of Assyria by military enterprise. They remind us a little of Greece and Rome. One cannot say that Babylonia did not show military enterprise nor that Assyria lacked cultural interests, but Assyria's culture was essentially of Babylonian origin and the broad distinction made above is substantially true.

The course of Assyria, after securing the ascendency over Babylonia, was not an uninterrupted march to supreme greatness but a succession of expansions and contractions of power, certain reigns being more glorious than others, certain periods showing strange decline until a brilliant leader appeared to reclaim for Assyria her old prestige. In the first greatness of Assyria between 1300 and 1100 B.C. Shalmaneser I, Tukulti Ninib, Ashurdan, and Tiglath Pileser I were the heroes. There followed a hundred years of comparative impotence for Assyria which was about the time of David and Solomon in Palestine. Among the military Semites, and especially in Assyria, we notice the tendency to use famous royal names many times, until four or five have borne the same name.

The revival of Assyrian power began with Tiglath Pileser III. Ashurnazirpal III and Shalmaneser III were the other great kings of the period. There followed this another decline for about eighty years, which is synchronous with Elijah and Jehu in Israel. The next renewer of the empire was Tiglath Pileser IV, who was followed by Shalmaneser V and the great Sargon of Assyria when the empire was at its highest point of glory and power. At that time the kingdom of Israel, with its capital Samaria, fell before the Assyrian. Sennacherib, Esarhaddon and Ashurbanipal followed. The last named ruled his country at the zenith of Assyrian culture and during the widest expansion. The empire weakened steadily until in 606, with the capture and destruction of Nineveh, it fell never to rise again. It is through records of the expeditions of the Assyrian kings to the east, north and west that we first hear of many minor nations, peoples and tribes whose descendants became famous in history, Elamites, Medes, Persians, Armenians, etc.

Immediately upon the fall of Nineveh the Babylonian kingdom rose into new life under two vigorous kings, Nabopolassar and Nebuchadrezzar, and inherited most of Assyria's possessions. Babylon was the most persistent of capitals and cultural forces. Rome alone can vie with Babylon in duration of influential existence. After less than a century of Babylonian renaissance a new empire formed in the farther east called the Medo-Persian. Its great genius Cyrus took with ease the reins of power from the older civilizations and initiated a new turn in world politics with Persia as the dictator of Asiatic affairs.

We may for our own convenience, summarize the foregoing and the story to follow by dividing the history of the two kindred nations, Babylonia and Assyria, into five ages corresponding roughly to the chief phases of these ancient peoples:

I. The Archaic Age.
II. The Babylonian Age.
III. The Kassite Age.
IV. The Assyrian Age.
V. The New Babylonian Age.

If we continue the discussion to include the conquest by Cyrus the Persian we should add the Persian Period, which was followed by the conquests of Alexander, who ushered in the Greek Period. In a restricted sense we may mention also a Roman Period.

The Archaic Age would include the prehistoric civilization known to us by archæological discovery, the early Sumerian and Semitic period of city-states with their struggles for dominating influence down to the rise of the city of Babylon about 2225 B.C.

The Babylonian Age, from 2225 to 1926 B.C., is so called because of the leadership of the city of Babylon under the West Semitic kings of whom Hammurabi was the greatest. The other city-states were absorbed into the kingdom with Babylon as capital.

The Kassite Age, from 1926 to 1350 B.C., or, possibly the dates should be set a little later, began with the overthrow of Hammurabi's Dynasty in favor of these mountain folk from the East who were neither Semitic nor Sumerian. It is difficult to define their racial connections. The probabilities seem to indicate Indo-European.

The **Assyrian Age** does not include the entire life of Assyria as a vassal state in the north on the Tigris but begins with the successful resistance of the Assyrian kings to the Kassites when Assyria gained its independence of Babylon and proceeded to be an equal and then a dominant state, the most dreaded world power of the ancient orient. The age closes with the Fall of Nineveh in 606 B.C.

The **New Babylonian Age** was brought about by the weakness and Fall of Assyria and the revival of the old Babylonian State under Kaldean princes. It lasted until the conquest of Babylon by the Persians in 539 B.C.

SUGGESTIONS FOR STUDY

1. Why was Palestine prominent in the World War?
2. What were the lands of the Turk at the beginning of the nineteenth century.
3. Where are the leading oriental collections in America?
4. Main points in the Sumerian Controversy?
5. How are early chronologies reckoned? See article on Chronology in the Encyclopædia Biblica I, 773.
6. What were the trade routes from Babylonia to Egypt?

BOOK LIST

L. W. KING: Sumer and Accad.
BOSCAWEN: The First of Empires.
GOODSPEED: A History of the Babylonians and Assyrians.
HANDCOCK: Mesopotamian Archæology.
OLMSTEAD: The Am. Jour. of Semitic Languages, etc., Vol. xxxiii, 4; xxxv, 2.
R. W. ROGERS: History of the Babylonians and Assyrians, 6th ed.
JOHNS: Ancient Babylonia.
BALL: Light from the East.

CHAPTER VI

The Archaic Age.—The early inhabitants of southern Babylonia were encouraged by the wonderful fertility of the Delta to follow an agricultural life. As in Egypt, the river became a highway. The country was irrigated by many canals and a system of ditches kept the gardens moist. From the mud and slime the peasants built their huts. Our earliest historical impressions of these people is that they are far advanced in the arts of civilized life. What long stretches of time must have preceded the dawn of history and what creditable achievements must have been made to have brought them so far on the way. Little city states under their kings were warring with each other, art and writing helped the people to express themselves, and a great religious development had been attained when men begin to hear from the valley. So far exploration has made us better acquainted with the history of the early Sumerians of the southern half of the country than with the career of the early Semites of the northern half. How far back of the historical period the contests between Sumerians and Semites existed we cannot tell. Our earliest historical view shows them in the familiar attitude of Sumerian preponderance in the South and the threatening proximity of the Semites on the North. The Semites are thought to have come in successive waves through the ages from the general direction of the northwest. But it is also possible that a continuous seeping in of nomadic Semites from Arabia was the rule whenever the organization

of the country was relaxed. This continual encroachment of nomads from the Arabian deserts pressing
into all the countries which form the rim of Arabia
has been the tendency in times of political weakness.
It accounts for the Semitic admixture in northeastern
Africa, including Egypt, and the strong elements in
Palestine and Syria. From being wandering nomads
such emigrants became dwellers in cities and were
assimilated to the old civilizations. In order to continue their influence they must govern amidst traditional conditions of agriculture and trade. Hence
the new masters had to learn to use suitable institutions which had been perfected by their predecessors,
for novices have no genius for invention in so complicated a field. Thus desert tribes became citizens
of Babylonia and chieftains became city kings. The
moment they conquered civilized institutions they
must learn. They must acquire the art of administration or relinquish the prize, for there were other
hungry tribes to snatch what weak hands could not
hold. The feuds and covenants of former tribal
populations would often continue in their later village or city estate. An example of this is discernible
in modern times in the Syrian villages of Palestine
where tribal organization persists and where the
quarrels between such parties as Yemen and Kays
may reflect the divisions of olden, nomad days. A
great mixture of races took place in the Babylonian
region. Sumerian and Semite are but names disguis-
ing many different stocks which descended into the
valley and left their permanent impress upon the
blended racial result.

7

The Temple Towers and Early Worship.—Ziggurats, etc. The most striking object on the Babylonian plain must have been the temples with their towers. These houses of heaven or everlasting houses occupied spaces not unlike that left on top of Zion for the Holy House in Jerusalem. But in the hill-less and stoneless Babylonian country these shrines would seem even more prominent and with their stepped towers, simulating the terraces of a hill or mountain side, made of enormous masses of sun-dried brick, would remind the early inhabitants of their former mountainous homeland, while the later population, forgetting such symbolism, would think only of the great deity and of the strength of the state. The successive stages of the temple-tower numbered from three to seven. The general ground plan was rectangular, though in the evolution of the tower curved bases developed. The ascent to the holy shrine at the top was around the outside of the structure, probably by a ramp. The surface of the walls lent themselves to progressive treatment, for protection and adornment, with glazed brick and color effects. In Egypt one is amazed at the feats which piled mountains of rock in such precise manner to form pyramids, while in Babylonia we admire the industry which manufactured billions of mud-bricks to lift the life and worship of the ancients well above the flooded soil.

Centuries, perhaps millennia before we can call the people of the land Babylonians, the primitive folk felt that the forces of nature were animated with souls. Common sense suggested that the souls all about one be placated and a friendly relationship established. The forces which thus became deities to early thought were divided into powers of the sky, the earth and the waters. According to the organization of human society these were supposed to bear relationship to each other and to have their greater and lesser functions to perform. In the course of long ages certain notable deities, *i.e.*, functions, came to the front as the greater favorites, while the host of lesser deities played minor parts in the order of the world of experience. This distinction between gods must have arisen in the minds of the people much as the different ranks arose among men in public life, on the basis of testing and importance. Men would learn quickly where they found help more often and which dangers were the most to be dreaded. Gods acquired reputations of kindliness, resourcefulness, ferocity, and other personal traits. Just as among people so among gods the question had to be decided, according to various circumstances, whether to spend most of one's effort appeasing the difficult or cultivating the gracious personality. One can judge of the considerations which would lead a community to choose its supreme god. There were many competing agricultural settlements in the Babylonian plain. Each would feel that the head deity had chosen it, not remembering how in the process of ages each community had in reality elected its special deity to headship above the others in the people's esteem. In every city the people honored their special patron deity with a worship which centred in a temple devoted to the god. Thus in Eridu Ea, the god of the waters, was the city divinity. Less than a dozen miles away was Ur, where Sin the moon-god was the deity. At Larsa the sun-god, Shamash, was in authority. At Erech (Uruk) Ishtar was the favorite. Ishtar, under different forms and names, was afterward honored as the favorite female divinity in many countries and became one of the great influences of the ancient world.

In the merging of the economic and political interests of certain Babylonian cities pantheons had to be rearranged and the order of precedence of the gods within them settled. The priests busied themselves with the theological thought necessary for the settlement of such questions. The grouping of divinities in pairs, as father and son, husband and wife, or triads or double triads, etc., arose out of such mental effort to harmonize the divine order. One of the ancient deities was Anu the sky-god, later perhaps En-lil, the earth-deity, appeared and Ea, the god of the waters or the sea. These three were ranked as an early triad.

The Growing Complexity of Religious Ideas.—Our earliest strong impressions of history in Sumer come from the period when En-lil was the most revered name in the pantheon. This deity was a primitive storm-god descending from the mountains and may be compared with the conception in Judges (v, 4 *f*),

"Jehovah, when thou wentest forth out of Seir,
When thou marchedst out of the field of Edom,
The earth trembled, the heavens also dropped,
Yea the clouds dropped water.

DISTANT AND NEAR VIEWS OF THE FIELD OF ROCKS NORTH OF
BETHEL (GENESIS XXVIII)

The mountains quaked, at the presence of
    Jehovah,
Even yon Sinai at the presence of Jehovah,
    the God of Israel.''

But as a people's life develops, their thoughts of
their gods take on corresponding changes. The
primitive god of a primitive people becomes the
more developed deity of a civilized folk. Without
a change of name his character becomes enriched in
the thought of his devotees. By the time that the
two races Semitic and Sumerian became neighbors
their respective contributions of religious ideas were
large, and when they eventually mingled their pantheons there was much harmonization or subordi-
nation of beings and ideas to each other to be worked
out by the priests. It came about that their thought
of the nature and functions of En-lil changed under
the influence of the rich country which was making
of the Babylonians a well-organized agricultural and
commercial people. En-lil became the divine lord or
king of a civilized people. He was supplied with a
divine consort or queen who was called Nin-lil.

The early inhabitants identified certain of their
deities with the heavenly bodies and thus they were
able by a study of the stars to develop an art of reading heavenly influences. The purposes of such gods
could be conjectured from the map of the sky. Not
only did they think of sun, moon, stars, etc., as deities
but, somewhat as in Egypt, they conceived of different attributes and aspects of these as gods. The sun
as such was Shamash. The sun as peculiarly gra-

cious or beneficent was known as Ninib. The destructive, ferocious principle of the sun was Nergal. Sometimes it is hard to tell whether the words used in describing the deity are thought of as merely attributive or as indicating a separate deity. A recent compilation of the Babylonian divine names gives a list of more than three thousand. (Deimel, Pantheon Babylonicum, Rome, 1914.) Sin was the gracious moon-god, the god of desert-peoples, of travelers in tropical or subtropical regions who must go by night. He was likely to be replaced in a country of farmers by the god who would be more useful to them, the god of the sun. But Sin received considerable veneration and his name enters into the composition of many personal names of citizens of Babylonia.

With the march of politics the Babylonians "chose new gods" or had them chosen for them in some instances. The conquering First Dynasty of Babylon enforced the supremacy of the city god of Babylon, Marduk. The older lord or belu of the land En-lil, of Nippur, was succeeded by the younger belu, Marduk. Belu is the equivalent of the Canaanite word baal and we may see an analogy in Babylon of the victory of Jahweh in Palestine over the Tyrian Baal. (I Kings, 18.) In the syncretism of Babylon Marduk bade fair to outstrip, even to the point of absorbing, Anu, En-lil and Ea. Apparently this was not the first time that Marduk had won in a competition of cults, for it seems probable that as Borsippa, the companion town with Babylon, was absorbed as a suburb, so its god Nabu was subordinated to Marduk. Nabu was the custodian of wisdom and of destinies, holding the tablets whereon decisions are recorded and possessing the understanding that reads the sky where fates are displayed to the wise.

The appearance of the Sumerians can be learned from the statuary and reliefs which they have left behind. Many of the statues are headless, but separate heads have been found, so that all the features are illustrated. From the age of Gudea have come several standing or sitting figures of large size. Besides these there are a number of statuettes and reliefs. The Sumerian is shown by these to have had a short, stout figure. The skulls are broad with large rear process, ears midway of the head, forehead low, eyes large and full, eyebrows meeting. The nose is fairly straight, the cheeks broad and high. The mouth is full and the chin large. Either the glands or the muscles of the neck give the appearance of fulness under the jaws and ears. The Sumerian was clean-shaven in contrast to the bearded Semitic men. One of the favorite statues is a seated figure on a four-footed settle. On the head is a cap which looks like a heavy knitted woolen skating cap with doubled brim. On the lap is the plan of a building and a stylus. The figure represents the patesi Gudea of Lagash, about 2500 B.C., as an architect. His hands are clasped above the house-plan and he wears a simple garment draped over the left shoulder.

Early Strife.—It will be worth while to look rapidly over some of the knowledge that remains of these Sumerians who were in power before the rise of the city of Babylon. A great deal of our information concerning the early civilization of Sumer has come from the long-continued exploration of the ancient city of Lagash. For over fifty years the activities of such men as Loftus, Taylor, de Sarzec, and Heuzey brought out what was to be known of Lagash which was a very important centre. Its destinies were linked with those of Kish, Umma and other important towns, north and south. Moreover, Lagash was a typical Sumerian site. One of the most beautiful and valuable monuments of ancient times came from this exploration. It is called the Stele of Vultures and is a stone monument on which these birds are seen hovering over the slain on a battle-field. Seven fragments of the monument were found. Six went to the Louvre in Paris and the seventh to the British Museum in London. It was erected in the reign of Eannatum. From the inscription we learn that Umma was the most persistent rival of Lagash. Wars and treaties between the two cities are described from the viewpoint of Lagash. There is reference to a former suzerainty of Mesilim, king of the northern Semitic city of Kish. But Lagash had made steady gains since that time under Kings Ur-Nina, Akurgal and Eannatum. Ur-Nina enjoyed a reign of comparative peace and a reputation as a servant of the gods. He served faithfully the god Ningirsu of Lagash and the goddess Nina of the same city. He erected statues to several gods and he sought especially to conciliate the god Enki of the city of Eridu. An onyx bowl has been found which he dedicated to the divinity Bau, the consort of Ningirsu. Ur-Nina improved his home city and constructed canals. It was probably thought that the cultivation of the gods by royalties was one of the most valuable services which could be rendered to the state. In the days of Eannatum the people of Umma repudiated certain boundaries between Umma and Lagash, which had been agreed to since the days of Mesilim. Umma was punished severely by Lagash for raids upon the lands of the latter and the Stele of Vultures records the vengeance which Eannatum exacted. He set up the memorial stone with its elaborate justification of his campaign against Umma and a description of his success. Such galling reminders must have been odious to a defeated foe and we can hardly be surprised if in later times, when opportunity came, the people of Umma smashed the humiliating record against themselves. A later ruler of Lagash, Entemena, who called himself a patesi, won a victory over Umma and was even severer than his predecessor. Urlumma, the patesi of Umma, was captured and put to death, while the government of the city was entrusted to a faithful vassal of the victor named Ili. This man had been serving as a "sangu" or priest of another city under the power of Lagash. It is an early instance of promotion by transfer. Ili, who had been of a rank lower than patesi, was now made patesi of Umma. Just how much was included in the office of patesi is not perfectly clear. Something priestly and something regal attached to the title. Perhaps viceroy would be a good modern equivalent. If the god was considered the true sovereign the king himself might be called patesi. A patesi might be the viceroy of a deity, of a king or of a superior patesi. A prince might prefer to use the title patesi while he was in fact a king and so regarded by his subjects. Entemena and four succeeding rulers were called patesis. Urukagina the usurper called himself king. Troublous times for Lagash preceded and followed the rule of Urukagina. He claimed credit for a number of needed reforms. One of these led to the removal of many burdensome minor officials and another was the reduction of priestly fees. He attacked unreasonable exactions by the privileged classes and to that extent favored the working people. He complained bitterly of his foes, the people of Umma, who wrecked his city and under their great ruler Lugal-zaggisi destroyed the political importance of Lagash.

Lugal-zaggisi controlled Umma, Lagash, Ur and Erech. The latter was his capital. He may be called the first unifier and pacifier of all Sumer.

Lagash arose from its ashes to new glory at a later day after an era of decentralization among the Sumerian powers. This revival was under the great Gudea. He is the best remembered of the patesis. Two score of his monuments are in existence to-day, cones, cylinders and statues. (See page 103.) He was a great builder and administrator.

But the scene shifts to the north between the days of Lugal-zaggisi and Gudea. In the country of Akkad the first great Semitic power was established in the hands of Sargon I (Sharrukin), who was succeeded by Rimush, Manishtusu, Naram Sin and Shargali-sharri. Sargon has the greatest fame among early Babylonian rulers. This fame was elaborated by myth and legend and became the theme of an extensive religious and magical literature. Stories told of his humble origin and early experiences remind us of Moses. When full allowance is made for his legendary fame Sargon's name remains as that of a great conqueror and builder.

A Semitic invasion from Gutium overcame both the Sumerian and Semitic powers in Babylonia. We may think of the dynasties of Agade, Erech and Gutium as probably overlapping to a considerable extent, but yet in some degree in succession. Moreover, they were partly contemporaneous with the line of Sumerian patesis in control of affairs at Lagash.

Ur of the Chaldees was the next city to be prominent. Its king, Ur-engur, went a step in advance of all the other rulers and brought both the south and the north, Sumer and Akkad, together in one organic union. The political succession of these cities that vied with each other for commercial advantage is not the only interest remaining to us from those times. Every shrine, divine name and myth of old Sumer and Akkad was eloquent of sentiments dear to the people which kings also must heed if they would succeed in their political careers. The hymns, prayers and mythological texts reflect conceptions and values of olden times. Favorite themes of many parts of the world had their analogies here in the old seats of culture. Gods and monsters and combats between them, great nature myths, explanations of origins, and of sea, land and sky, the poetic science and philosophy of the day never far sundered from religion were given definite location in the sacred soil. Under the weakening of the control of Agade

(Akkad) several cities had grown opulent and practically independent. Dungi the second king of the Dynasty of Ur completed the subjugation of the northern country Akkad, although his father had already claimed control of the kingdom of Sumer and Akkad. Dungi was severe in his treatment of the city of Babylon, one of the more obscure cities at that time.

This Dynasty of the city of Ur consisted of five Sumerian kings, whose total reign lasted considerably over a century. The period of their control is chronicled in the year dates found on many thousand business documents of this period. The kings are:

> Ur-engur
> Dungi
> Bur Sin
> Gimil Sin
> Ibi Sin.

The first two kings made speedy conquest of the Sumerian and Semitic world on the Euphrates. They enriched many of the cities which they subdued, building and repairing temples and canals. The states in Elam were conquered. The problems in Elam were most troublesome in the time of Bur Sin, who maintained his father's position there with difficulty. The last of the five was overcome by the first king of the Dynasty of Nisin, to which city and its Sumerian kings the power passed. There were two distinct royal houses besides usurpers in the line of sixteen Nisin kings. The later dynasty was probably Semitic and became contemporaneous with the rulers of Larsa and Babylon.

The virility of Babylon was greatly augmented by a Semitic inflow from the western lands of Amurru, which led to the founding of the first great Babylonian dynasty. The accession to power of this last mentioned house marked the passing of Sumerian control. The only real competitor of Babylon was Larsa, which under its fourteenth and last king, Rim Sin, overthrew Damik-ilishu of Nisin. Rim Sin made an era of that event and for thirty-one succeeding years business men in Larsa dated their legal documents with reference to the overthrow of Nisin. Nisin had suffered previously at the hand of Babylon and Larsa's turn was near when it should be subdued by Babylon. But we are trenching on the next, or Babylonian Age, with which Nisin and Larsa were partly contemporaneous.

SUGGESTIONS FOR STUDY

1. Why would there be less encouragement to provincialism along the Euphrates than along the upper Nile?

2. Write on agriculture as a civilizing influence.

3. Reasons why republicanism did not develop in early Babylonian cities.

4. How late may tribal organizations persist in a civilization?

5. Suggestions of monotheism in the religion of Marduk.

6. Describe the artistic features of the Stele of Vultures.

7. Urukagina, a reformer or a demagogue?

BOOK LIST

Enc. Bib. I, 413 and 419 (i.e., Encyclopædia Biblica, 4 vols.).

H. D. B. I, 214.

J. H. BREASTED: Ancient Times.

W. ROBERTSON SMITH: Religion of the Semites.

W. ROBERTSON SMITH: Kinship and Marriage in Early Arabia.

GEORGE F. MOORE: History of Religions, Vol. I.

BREASTED: Development of Religion and Thought in Ancient Egypt.

CHAPTER VII

The Babylonian Age.—When the city of Babylon began to dominate and to give its name to the southern Euphratean lands, an impulse was given to scientific, artistic and literary endeavor which caught up and passed on to the larger world many of the accomplishments of the earlier Sumerian and Semitic culture. In thinking out the relation of Babylon's god to the other deities and of Babylon's position in the world, a new revision of myth and story took place. Prof. R. W. Rogers has given us a most useful collection of these sources in his Cuneiform Parallels to the Old Testament. Here one finds stories of origins, destructions, the strenuous effort of mythical heroes and legendary kings, accounts of creation, deluge, fragments of ritual, doctrinal and incantation lore, hymns, prayers, historical chronicles, all reflecting the world of thought in which the ancient peoples of Western Asia lived. These Babylonian models set fashions for education throughout that early world. Here were the summaries of such beginnings of science and philosophy as the Asiatic world possessed. The Hebrews drew upon the learning of the great nations. As in all ages, those who had inspirations conveyed them to their contemporaries in the styles of thought and language which could be used and understood.

Intellectual Achievements.—Any fair-minded person will be disposed, after an investigation, to give due credit for the mental ability which brought into

110

orderly systems the rough-hewn materials of Babylonian thought about the ways of gods and men.
Here were the text-books of the early world. The
Hebrew students among other pupils acquired knowledge of this wisdom and gave the world improved
versions of the stories of the foundation of the world
and the beginnings of human society. The Hebrew
seers impressed their superior monotheistic, spiritual ideas upon this common mass of learning and
gave us the lofty conceptions of Genesis. It is as if
the bullion of ancient lore had been coined for a
universal currency. A comparison of the Babylonian and Hebrew stories about the same subjects will
reveal not only the relationship of the two but the
genuine superiority of the latter.

The best-known Babylonian stories are those of
Creation and the Gilgamesh Epic. In the following paraphrase of part of the Creation Story it
will be seen that some observation and much reflec-
tion have combined to construct a pseudo-science of
the forces of nature.

When there was neither heaven nor earth as
such but an indiscriminate mingling of watery elements and before the gods came forth, the primeval
Apsu or ocean wastes as male principle and Tiamat,
the inchoate, as female principle, produced Mummu,
but little different from themselves. With the production of successive beings, the gods, better and
better order followed. First of the deities proper
came Lakhmu and Lakhamu, then Anshar and Kishar
or heaven and earth, and finally, the very ancient god
Anu. Order came very gradually out of age-long

struggle and terrific travail. Anu the sky-god and Ea the god of knowledge were able to overcome the blinding forces and the ragings that threatened all with chaos. Counsel and plan, agreement and rational endeavor succeeded against irrational force.

In the later expansions of the story of creation when Marduk of Babylon became the most exalted deity, the triumph of order over disorder and the slaying of the fearful dragon Tiamat was ascribed to him as chief among the gods. The story of his battle with Tiamat concludes with a scheme to split her into two parts like the halves of a flat fish. One-half became the firmament and apparently the other half was the earth and its visible waters. Next the seasons and their markers, stars, moon and sun, were set in their places. Of course these heavenly bodies were conceived as deities with their respective functions. Man was made and apparently the story, as we can read it now in a fragmentary state on the tablets owned by the British Museum, told of further features of creation.

Tablet number seven, the last one known in this series, refers to the creation of vegetation and to the religious ideas of the cultus.

It will be seen that such speculations are less scientific than theosophical. Instead of a long, patient accumulation and interrogation of actual data of experience on which safe conclusions could be based, these early orientals did as so many have done since. They leaped to certain grand conceptions of the divine and of a progressive series of beings, mixed these with certain acute observations and much skill and produced artistic systems of the origins of life. This was done again and again by the brilliant thinkers of early races and has produced some of our most beautiful poetic conceptions. These are stimulating but are frequently superseded by equally plausible plans of the universe, all of which exercise man's subtle powers without deeply informing him.

A very definite historical era began with Babylon's attainment of supremacy. It was not until about 2100 B.C. that this city became the head of the country north and south of it, which was after that to be known as Babylonia for two millennia. The power of Sumer had been weakened by Elamite incursions. As so often in the course of history the invaders could not dominate that which they helped to shake to its foundations. In the meantime a strong family of Amorite rulers in Babylon gradually succeeded to the chief place. The dates assigned to this the First Dynasty are usually 2225 to 1926 B.C. This strong house of princes of West-Semitic (Amorite) blood was for awhile subordinate to the late Sumerians and partly contemporaneous with the dynasties of Nisin and Larsa. As the Sumerians weakened the Elamites strengthened. The Elamites rendered thus an unwilling service to Babylon which helped that city to step into first place. Kish, Kasallu and Nisin contended with the growing Babylonian power. The long and able reign of the sixth king of Babylon saw the union of the country accomplished most completely. This was Hammurabi, "the Builder of the Country." (2123 to 2081 B.C.) He was one of the greatest, most versatile rulers of any age. The fame of long-lived

8

Babylon really began with him. In his thirtieth year he captured Ur and Larsa and drove Rim Sin, his leading competitor, from the country. In the next year he annexed the western border of Elam to Babylonia. He was by that time able to display the title "The Mighty King, King of Babylon, King of the Four Regions, King of Sumer and Akkad." The wars of Hammurabi were followed by a period of comparative peace, during which agriculture, trade and building and the general organization and development of the country's resources went on to a remarkable degree. Agriculture was the basis of Babylonian civilization and commerce its expression. Hammurabi patronized both of these. He ordered the digging of canals. He increased the security and ease of communication. He built fortifications, palaces, and temples. Every interest of the country seems to have been looked after during this brilliant reign. All the conquered territory was bound to the central authority by close imperial organization. The cities were reorganized and made to conform to the government of which they now became a part. Hammurabi's officers supervised the reformed organization.

An Early Empire.—The cities in the more distant provinces were kept in touch with the capital by systematic reporting. All the activities of the empire were greatly stimulated in favor of a firm government and a vigorous commerce. The calendar, police and post systems were improved. Laws were codified and published. Even as the countries and peoples were united under the administration of a strongly centralized government so the religion was centralized. Marduk the God of Babylon was supreme among the divinities of the land as the king of Babylon was supreme among the princes. It was probably believed that the god Marduk, being mightier than the other gods, had given victory to the king who served him over the servants of the other divinities and from the primacy of Marduk followed the political importance of Babylon and its king. The literature was colored and reshaped in accord with the new spirit and the new facts. Altogether the age of Hammurabi was an "Elizabethan" Age for Babylonia. It is interesting to compare the religious reforms of The First Dynasty of Babylon and The Eighteenth in Egypt by which Marduk and Aton were promoted to first place in their respective countries. (See page 58.)

Hammurabi had been preceded by five kings and he was followed by five kings. Unfortunately he was not equalled by any of his successors. His own reign of forty-three years was the longest in the period of his house which extended nearly three hundred years. Hammurabi's successors warred with the princes of the Country of the Sea. This enmity continued for nearly two centuries.

Ea-gamil, the last of the dynasty in the Country of the Sea, i.e., the Second Dynasty, invaded Elam unsuccessfully. He was not only driven back but was followed and conquered in his own country by the Kassite king Ulam-Buriash. The Kassite ruler Agum was also an invader of the Country of the Sea. He may have been the founder of the Kassite power

in the Sea-Land. At any rate the Kassites were
established in the southern part of Babylonia whence
they worked their way northwards until their kings
sat on the throne of Babylon. The First Dynasty
might not have succumbed to these attacks from the
south alone, but there is evidence that the Hittites
added to its troubles and prepared the way for the
Kassite triumph. Through all the vicissitudes of
political change, Babylon continued as the cultural
centre of the Asiatic world. Even when it was
destroyed by the Assyrian king Sennacherib, over a
thousand years later, its glory and prerogative were
too great for oblivion and his successor Esarhaddon
rebuilt the city. To Babylon, in the Assyrian period,
Assyrian kings went to strengthen their claim to
empire much as in later ages German kings went
to Rome.

The great law-code of Hammurabi is one of the most
remarkable monuments from ancient times. It was
engraved on a stone pillar over seven feet high and
was discovered by the French explorer, J. de Morgan,
December, 1901, at Susa. The block was in three
fragments and a part of the writing, the longest
extant Babylonian inscription, had been destroyed.
There were originally forty-nine columns running
horizontally about the monument and they contained
about eight thousand words. At the top was a picture
in relief exhibiting Shamash the sun-god in the act of
bestowing the code upon Hammurabi. The existence
of so complete a collection of laws is evidence of a
long period of legal development in Babylonia. There
has been a large amount of scholarly investigation

and discussion of the contents of the code. It has been compared exhaustively with other ancient codes, especially with those of the ancient Hebrews. Popular interest in old Babylonian culture has been stimulated. The other inscriptions of Hammurabi, his letters and the voluminous business records of the merchants of his day seem to bring his age with its customs very vividly before us. We have more complete information about the doings of this very early king and the culture of his day than about certain periods of European history.

Business Four Thousand Years Ago.—It is possible to speak with considerable precision of the business life that went on in the streets of such cities as Babylon, Larsa, Nippur, and several other places. For example, the private files of business documents and letters of men active in the life of these towns have been found. When one has handled dozens of documents belonging to one man, and has learned what kinds of business he did, what terms he made, the names of his neighbors by the score, the names of his relatives, one recognizes personalities as real, though four thousand years have passed since the transactions took place. Moreover, most of these documents are dated by year, month and day, occasionally in the forenoon of a given day. They mention commodities, measures and prices, terms of sale, lease, loan, partnership, quote from laws, customs, phrases of the street and the courts; mention the names of streets, temples, canals, districts, officials, priests, scribes, bakers, carpenters, smiths, and shop-keepers. Intricate details of social life were straightened out by the aid of the judges in court and the legal settlements of complicated business and religious affairs have been drawn up with seals, witnesses and oaths. For instance, here is a legal settlement dated the twenty-sixth of the month Elul in the fifth year of the reign of Samsuiluna the king of Babylonia, who was the son of Hammurabi. A man has borne the expense of rearing his daughter's child. When the father and mother of the child were able they paid a certain sum in grain to the grandfather to cover his expenditure so that neither he nor his sons might ever be able to lay claim legally to the child. One would suppose that such a matter would be adjusted privately, but evidently "business was business" in old Babylonia, so the matter was drawn up in legal form, sworn to by the names of the gods and the king, witnessed by seven persons. (A. J. S. L. xxxiv, 2 Jan. '18.)

Here is another document, this time a private contract which was probably never carried to court but carefully dated, sealed, and bearing the names of seven witnesses. It concerned a slave whose relatives, a brother and two nephews, bargained to release him for a time and to be surety, against his escape, to the owner. We have a good many similar documents showing that slaves were let out on a bail-bond. Very often it was the family of the slave who pledged securities for the slave's good conduct and safe return. (A. J. S. L. xxxiii, 3 April '17.)

One document in the Smith College Collection indicates that a father endowed his daughter in an office in the temple of the god Adad and also placed

her on an equality with her brothers as an heiress
to his estate. Still another contract from the same
reign would suggest the terms of a trial marriage.
(Cuneiform Documents in the Smith College Library, Elihu Grant, 1918.)

The fine specimen shown in these pages is a business contract from the sixth year of the rule of
Samsuiluna. It tells us that there is a piece of property, to wit:

Seven-eighteenths of a gan of clover field, of
which one side adjoins the property of Liblût and
another side the property of Inbi-Ilishu, while one
end bounds the estate of Amatum-Shamash and the
other Ili-matar. The clover field belongs to Ikunpi-
Shamash, the son of Ikunpi-Adad, who declares that
he has made no disposal of the same to Itti-mari-
Adad. At this time Asu-tabbu, the patesi, has
bought the property from Ikunpi-Shamash for its full
price, twelve shekels and eighteen she of silver
weighed out. In the future there shall never be contention over the clover field. Ikunpi-Shamash shall
be responsible that there shall be no return or com-
plaint. Ikunpi-Shamash has given oath by the divinities Nannar, Shamash, Marduk and King Samsuiluna. The witnesses are Liblût, a secretary; Tabum
and Awilili, merchants; Lunum, a priestess of Shamash; Shamash-asharid and Appâ, officials of the
Shamash temple. Dated in the month Addarum the
26th day of the sixth year of Samsuiluna the king.

Administrative Detail.—Mr. L. W. King of the
British Museum began to publish very important
political and social material from this period over

twenty years ago. In "The Letters and Inscriptions of Hammurabi" there are fifty-five letters from the great king to Sin-iddinam his governor in Larsa. There are over a score of letters from Hammurabi's successors in the dynasty. If all the matters within the scope of these letters came under the personal attention of the kings of Babylon, then royalty would be kept very busy, even though aided by a corps of scribes. Either able sovereigns had not yet learned how to delegate the details of administration to trained assistants or else they could not trust them, which amounts to the same thing. One is appalled at the burden which rests on the king who wrote or dictated about small as well as great matters. It would appear that Hammurabi investigated personally the details of litigation and business management of the government. His system took cognizance of everything that concerned internal development as well as outer politics. He built or repaired the canals and regulated the business done on them. We have evidence of his control through correspondence with but one of his vassal cities, Larsa, whose governor he addressed about daily business concerns. It is fair from this to suppose that the capital was united by vital lines of communication with the different parts of the empire. Delegates and couriers were employed. Hammurabi was an oriental Charlemagne. These Semitic rulers had inherited a civilization which taught its conquerors. Some of the devices employed had descended from Sargon of Agade. We may see in Hammurabi and his kind, though raised to be king of Babylon, the manners of

CLAY BUSINESS DOCUMENT FROM ANCIENT BABY-
LONIA IN THE POSSESSION OF MR. E. G. CLAPHAM
OF BOSTON. (SEE PAGE 119)

a patriarch. He possessed herds and flocks and was settled on the richest of the Asian lands. The unique greatness of Hammurabi was that he was not only able to hold his primacy as king over a large number of vassal kings of other cities, but that he was an accomplished organizer and that his governmental triumphs outlasted the personal power of his house.

Hammurabi paid careful attention to the interests of religion in the cultivation of the gods of his country. But he was broadly interested also in the divinities of other nations. This trait of catholicity in ancient rulers is remarkable and was shown later by such rulers as Cyrus and Alexander. Hammurabi was the patron of all the culture and science of his day as well as of the commerce and industry. His justice was notable. He sought to purify the practices of the courts, to encourage care in the selection of witnesses and to insure true testimony. He is one of the noble list of those who have published great and influential codes of law.

We should not be far wrong probably if we thought of the chief god in a Babylonian city as having to play an economic part as well as a religious. He was a legal person quite as real as a modern corporation. To carry out modern analogies we might think of his priests and other officers as comparable with a president, board of directors, corporation counsel, etc. One might be tempted to go further and think of Hammurabi as a trust magnate with his underlords as presidents of holding companies or industrial corporations under his control.

SUGGESTIONS FOR STUDY

1. In what ways were the Babylonians the school-teachers of the early world?

2. Compare the Babylonian cosmogony with the Greek.

3. Brief account of early British and French explorations in Mesopotamia.

4. Compare Hammurabi's age with that of Charlemagne.

5. Trace the steps of Babylon to headship.

6. Compare the Hammurabi law-code with the Mosaic.

7. Slavery in the early world.

BOOK LIST

JASTROW: Civilization of Babylonia and Assyria.

ROGERS: Cuneiform Parallels.

L. W. KING: Letters and Inscriptions of Hammurabi.

LAYARD: Babylon and Nineveh.

H. D. B. Extra vol. p. 584.

P. V. N. MYERS: History as Past Ethics.

KOLDEWEY: The Excavation of Babylon.

HARPER: Assyrian and Babylonian Literature. (Aldine ed.)

C. H. W. JOHNS: Babylonian and Assyrian Laws, Contracts, and Letters.

BUDGE-KING: Annals of the Kings of Assyria, I.

A. T. OLMSTEAD: Assyrian Historiography, University of Missouri Studies, 1916.

REVERSE OF THE TABLET SHOWN OPPOSITE
PAGE 120

CHAPTER VIII

Barbarians from the East.—The Kassite Age. The passage from one great age to another denotes a decline of those forces which made the former age great. Therefore we have usually what are to us dark, unintelligible years, or even centuries, in which readjustments were being prepared, between the ages of clearer history. This is the case in our study of the close of the age of the First Babylonian Dynasty. After lapses in our sources of information and scattered data we observe a new age for Babylon when the city was ruled by princes of alien blood, possibly akin to those Elamites who had suffered at the hands of Hammurabi. The people who came into power are known as Kassites. From the scanty data available we are able to gather the information that there were thirty-six kings in the dynasty of the Kassites, who ruled five hundred and seventy-six years and nine months. Names and inscriptions of nearly half this list have been recovered but the age is still a baffling one to the historian. Long ago Professor Goodspeed made a fourfold division of the Kassite Age which remains as useful as any suggested:

(1) The beginning of the Kassite rule.

(2) The appearance of Assyria as a rival of Kassite Babylonia.

(3) The culmination of the dynasty and the struggle with Assyria.

(4) The decline and disappearance of the Kassites.

The Kassites were an invading people from the eastern mountains, from the region of Elam-Media. They probably lived near the mountain routes by which Babylonian trade penetrated middle Asia. They became acquainted with the Babylonians very early. Kassite soldiers served in the armies of Babylon under kings of the First Dynasty. Kassite laborers found good pay, which meant better living, by helping in the harvest-fields and in other heavy work for the Babylonians. Their relation to the city and empire was not dissimilar to that of the warring tribes of central Europe and Rome. As the early Babylonian traders pressed into new and remote regions for profitable exchange they spread news of the land of comparative plenty from which they had come. Back over the trails of the traders came not only the returning Babylonians to replenish their stocks but many an ambitious native of the uncivilized tribes to serve the masters of the richer land. As the keener-minded among the new-comers saw a weakening dynasty losing its hold upon the prize of civilization their desire would be aroused to possess Babylonia. The Kassites must have been repulsed more than once in their gradual intrusion into the country. But, in the main, circumstances continued to aid them. As we have seen (page 116), a powerful people from the northwest, the Hittites, warred against Babylon and even sacked the city. Thus the collapse of the First Dynasty was not due to the Kassites alone, although they reaped the main benefit.

They have left us no assurance that they brought any notable contributions to Babylonian culture with them. They were barbarian pupils of their vassals and doubtless left an infusion of more virile blood in the population of the valley. The Kassites, as forerunners of the Persians, belong to the succession of Indo-European conquerors of western Asia. Very many Kassite names end in ash, said to be comparable with the Greek nominative ending in os. It will be seen that many Persian names end in a similar way, ush, ish, the vowel being changeable. The consonant s is the constant feature, whether followed by the aspirate h or not. Names with similar endings come from Urartu.

The Kassites established their power first in the very south of Babylonia, whence they spread over the whole country. Beginning as barbarians they were soon able to appreciate the advantages of civilization and by their greater force and enthusiasm to dispossess a worn-out dynasty.

We have an important inscription of the Kassite king Agum Kakrime, the seventh of his line in Babylonia. It consists of 338 lines. He styles himself King of the country of Kashshu and the Akkadians, of the wide country of Babylon and several other regions. An illustration of the way in which these Kassite barbarians gradually became Babylonized may be seen in the inscription. Already the dynasty had identified itself with the glory of the olden Babylon and delighted to honor the deities and priesthoods of the great city. In the assaults upon the capital by northwestern enemies, possibly the Hittites, the sacred images of the city gods had been captured. These Agum Kakrime succeeded in

regaining and installing in their proper temples
which he favored with his zealous bounty. Agum
Kakrime had, however, to be content with a smaller
empire than that of Hammurabi. Mesopotamia and
the West-Land were not under his jurisdiction. It
is commonly the case that when an empire breaks
up under the assaults of various neighboring races
the people who secure the prize of the capital and
the original land of the kingdom cannot possess the
provinces also. These become the booty of the nearest strong force which had its part in bringing about
the disintegration. When the contrary fact is the
case we have one of the great epochs of history.

The beginning of the Kassite rule was the age
of other restless Asiatic forces such as the Hyksos
and the Hittites. The synchronisms are not yet clear
for this period. The Hittite power was approaching
its meridian with great centres in Asia Minor
("Great Kheta," now Boghaz-Köi) and in Mitanni.
Furthermore, Assyria was rising into prominence and
the migrations of the Aramean peoples were soon to
take place, overrunning much that had been Babylonian possessions. The Phenician maritime city-
states were already active and a few centuries later
the Hebrew tribes would settle in Palestine.

But to return to the Kassites in Babylonia. Later
than Agum Kakrime was Kara-indash I, from whose
reign we have an inscription. An attempt was made
to regain Mesopotamia. Palestine became subject to
Egyptian rule. There is record of a boundary settlement between Kara-indash I and the Assyrian
King Ashurbelnisheshu. Messages passed between

Kara-indash and the Egyptian monarch of the day. Eleven letters from Babylon to Egypt are found in the Tell el-Amarna collection. Kadashman-Ellil corresponded with Amenhotep III and one Burnaburiash with Amenhotep IV. In these letters it is disclosed that the pharaohs had taken Babylonian princesses into their harems but had not sent Egyptian princesses in return to Babylon. Lapis-lazuli was one of the choice products sent from Babylon to Egypt and gold was sent in return. The Babylonian kings frankly made demands for presents in exchange for those sent to the Egyptian court. Political matters were not often treated in such letters as have been found. It is interesting to observe that in reality these kings were engaged in international trade and that they were exempted from the usual taxation upon such business.

Kara-indash II, the son of Burnaburiash II, married a daughter of the Assyrian king, and his son by the marriage succeeded as Kadashman-Kharbe II, who was murdered in a Kassite insurrection, and followed by one called Shuzigash, "the son of nobody." But the king of Assyria, Ashur-uballit, avenged the murder of his grandson and put his great-grandson Kurigalzu III on the throne.

Kassite Babylonia had to suffer the hostility of covetous neighbors just as Semitic Babylonia had done. Assyria gained control of Babylon and then lost it. Elamite invasions were suffered, precursors of a time when they would succeed in placing an Elamite in control of the city. As Winckler observes: "These wars prove that the conditions already exist which are always apparent in the future; Babylonia is the prize coveted by both Assyria and Elam. For the present she is able to cope with both, and if at times worsted, at others she proves superior. The contest is waged through the following centuries to the fall of Assyria. In later times Babylonia was a vassal state of the one or the other."

Following the Kassite dynasty came that of Isin or Pashe a little after 1200 B.C. Little is known of the line until we reach Nebuchadrezzar I who called himself the offspring of Babylon. This line of kings therefore may have been of native origin. There appear to have been eleven kings with reigns totalling 132 years. The same struggles with Elam and Assyria and in Mesopotamia as engaged the Kassites became the concern of this dynasty.

By the end of the Kassite dynasty Babylon was in a low state. The statue of Marduk had been carried off to Elam. This showed the loss of national independence and a decline into vassalage. Marduk would have to do obeisance in the temple of a foreign god and his client, the Babylonian king, would be subordinate to the Elamite sovereigns. Not until Nebuchadrezzar I had won such a decisive victory as enabled him to retake the statue of Marduk could he assume the title "King of Babylon." At that time the statue had been in captivity thirty years. Nebuchadrezzar I extended his boundaries as far as the Mediterranean and was successful against the Elamites as well.

From about 1000–960 B.C. affairs in Babylonia were in a deplorable condition. Foreign invaders made the country their prey and no less than three dynasties are recorded as ruling. Three names have been saved from the first, three from the second, and the third, so-called dynasty, is one lone king. The three groups are of different races. They are known as the Dynasty of the Sea-Land, the Dynasty of Bazu and the Elamite. The Sea-Land is the land about the mouth of the two rivers at the head of the Persian Gulf. Two of the names have been regarded as Kassite and may signify that the Kassites as they relinquished the country retreated southward. Bazu or Bazi is near or on the border of Elam. With the presence of an Elamite on the throne a similar condition of affairs obtained to those which were evident nearly a thousand years previous when Rim Sin was in authority at Larsa and was in contests with Semitic rulers. Similar fate met this Elamite for a dynasty (the so-called 8th) believed to be Semitic gained the ascendency. The presence in Elam of a king named Khumbanigash, in the latter part of the eighth century B.C., would seem to link the Elamite government of that age with a Kassite name.

Assyria was too weak during the time of these changes to interfere with Babylonian affairs.

The next great force in Babylonia was a race called the Kaldi or Chaldeans. Who were they? They seem to have come from the south where they must have been settling for some time before the development of sufficient strength to seize the valley. They bear Babylonian names. With them, we have a third factor introduced into Babylonian politics along with the Assyrians and the Elamites, all eager to dominate in

9

the ancient seats of culture and wealth. The Babylonians themselves were more and more ignored in the contest. The struggle thus became a three-cornered one between Assyria, Elam, and Chaldea. The Assyrian may have loftily assumed the rôle of protector of Babylon against the encroachments of the other two. Certainly Elam and Chaldea found it easier to make common cause, at times, with each other than with Assyria. In the long run Assyria was eliminated from the struggle by the fall of Nineveh, when Chaldea founded a Babylonian dynasty and rose to great power which lasted until the coming of Cyrus the Persian, who came from the ancient Elamite quarter.

In Palestine, the most interesting developments were taking place when Babylonian affairs were least stable. The division of the Hebrew kingdom was made while the Eighth Dynasty was ruling. For much of the succeeding period Assyrian emperors were dominant in Babylonia and were frequently recognized as kings of Babylon. Merodach Baladan (Marduk-aplu-iddina), of Biblical fame, was the contemporary of King Hezekiah and of Sargon of Assyria. This Merodach Baladan was a politician from the Sea-Land who had been active some years before and was to appear again in the days of Sennacherib and Hezekiah.

The Mighty Race on the Tigris.—The Assyrian Age. The imagination has been permanently impressed with the cultural claims of Babylonia and the warlike exploits of Assyria. This impression is in the main justified. But one must not forget altogether the campaigns of the southern country nor the agency of the northern in spreading the Euphratean civilization and disclosing many new regions to history.

As early as the days of Hammurabi there is mention of Asshur and Nineveh, the earliest and latest capitals of Assyria. Asshur or Assur stood on a rocky site by the Tigris. It was, so far as we know, the primitive Assyrian city, the seat of the national god. City, god and people bore this one name. Ilu-shuma of Asshur was a contemporary and combatant with Sumu-Abu of Babylon. Ilu-shuma's son Erishum is represented by inscribed material. A clumsy brick with carelessly ruled lines in a ladder-like column shows us that the language used was Semitic. There can be no doubt of racial and cultural connections between Babylonia and Assyria. The only question concerns the time and manner of the relationship. It is possible that the Assyrians of history were originally Semitic Babylonians who conquered the settlements on the Tigris River. Some as seen (page 91) prefer to think of them as a part of the same outward wave of conquering Semites which overran Babylonia. In either case we can only say that our earliest historical indication is of the subservience of the Assyrians to Babylon. The Assyrian type of Semite developed somewhat differently from the Semitic Babylonian. The result was a fiercer frontier stock more continuously and ruthlessly engaged in exploration and war. The early vassalage of Assyria to Babylon was changed by the fortunes which gave the city of Babylon to the Kassites. Assyrian kings contested with the Kassites and the advantages slowly accumulated in the balances on the side of the Assyrians.

Building the Assyrian Nation.—A goodly list of early Assyrian rulers may now be named. Ashur-uballit, Bel-nirari, Arik-den-ilu (formerly written Pu-di-ilu) and Adad-nirari I seem to have been occupied largely with the countries to the east and south. But Shalmaneser I made at least three great campaigns in the west where the Arameans were taking up the ancient seats of the decaying Mitannian and Hittite power. The chaotic elements of new and old nations were forced to yield to the strong-handed Assyrian. The Mesopotamian regions were quiet to a degree until the days of Shalmaneser's son Tukulti-Ninib I. Tukulti-Ninib's conquests of the regions around had their climax in his taking the throne of Babylon. The conqueror took back with him to Assyria the king of Babylon, the statue of Marduk and much treasure. With the treasure he set about building his triumphal city called "The Fortress of Tukulti-Ninib." His achievements should be credited in part to the preparations for them due to the notable energy of several strong ancestors who occupied the Assyrian throne before him, including his own father, Shalmaneser I, the builder of Assyria's second capital Kalah. In the beautiful new city which Tukulti-Ninib built out of the proceeds of his Babylonian triumphs he met his tragic death by the hands of a son. The conquest of Babylon was undone and had to be re-enacted in the next century. Frequently the ferocity of the Assyrian turned in upon himself in the awful palace intrigues and assassinations. The

Kassites were able to regain their lost control in Babylon because of the troubles in the north. It was the last flickering, however, of their power, which went out before the successes of Ashurdan I. This Assyrian king brought up the fortunes of his nation after their first serious decline. But it was long before the glories of the power of Tukulti-Ninib could be matched.

Meanwhile in Babylon where the Kassite Dynasty had gone out, a new house of rulers called the Dynasty of Isin or Pashe came into control. Although there were desperate encounters between Assyria and Babylonia during this age, both nations had more serious problems to face in the subjugation of hostile foreign races on their borders. The new king of Babylon, Nebuchadrezzar I, fought with the Elamites who had been for a long time annoying the people of the valley and struggled successfully as well to regain Babylonian power westward. He inscribed his record on the rocks of Nahr el-Kelb, the stream close by modern Beirut, showing the westward extent of his power to the Mediterranean.

Assyria's more natural enemies were to the north and northwest in Armenia and in the countries of the Nairi, Kummukhi, and on the frontiers of Khatti-land (Hittite). Assyria, too, had its campaigns with that doughty foe the Elamite. About the year 1120 Tiglath-Pileser I began to reign. During his rule the second period of Assyrian expansion reached its climax. This was the period of the last weak Ramses (the XIIth) of Egypt when the priests were about to form the Twenty-first Dynasty. It is easy to discern that it was not merely a lust for military conquest but the desire also to open up new possibilities of trade that helps to explain the restless activities of the great Assyrian kings in their many campaigns. Moreover, the very nature and fate of Assyria were such as to make necessary a vigorous, successful foreign policy in order to prevent dynastic troubles at home and to keep under the liberty-loving tribes whom the Assyrian controlled beyond its boundaries.

Within the half-century before the accession of Tiglath-Pileser I the peoples called the Mushki (Meshech) from Asia Minor had advanced along the upper courses of the Euphrates and successfully attacking Assyria's tributaries the Alzi and the Purukuzzi penetrated into the region of Kummukhi. Those Hittites who held control in Syria were disturbed if not displaced by this movement of the westerners whom some believe to have been of the same general race. The Syrian Hittites in turn being thrust against the Assyrian border provinces contributed to the embarrassment of Assyria. Tiglath-Pileser was to affect this whole situation very materially. His campaigns undertaken vigorously against very great odds cleared the mountainous countries northwest, northeast and then north. With the vigor of a Julius Cæsar he addressed himself to his heroic tasks. The Mushki and the disaffected Kummukhi were badly handled and the Assyrian authority assured in all those regions.

As we approach the year 1000 B.C. we are conscious of declining strength in Assyria and Babylonia. In Assyria the explanation seems to be exhaustion due to the excessive physical activity of the reign of Tiglath-Pileser, while in Babylonia civil strife accounts for the low fortune of the nation where three petty dynasties occupied about fifty years. Outside of those two countries the world of Asian peoples was moving significantly. In the southern part of Arabia there were flourishing small kingdoms which may date as early as this time. But the real interest for us now is in the peoples who had migrated from Arabia to the north and west. Chief of these in physical strength was the great Aramean folk already wedged between Assyria and Phenicia. The Hebrew tribes had pressed into Palestine from the south and east and the Hebrew state was forming under Kings Saul, David and Solomon. The Phenicians entered a new era of prosperity. It was a great day for the smaller nations.

The year 950 B.C. may be taken as the date of the turn in fortune for the three great nations Egypt, Babylonia and Assyria. In Assyria it was another Tiglath-Pileser (III) who began the recovery of Assyrian power which was to last two hundred years before another temporary decline, when still another Tiglath-Pileser (IV) was to restore Assyrian prestige and authority for another century, after which the end would come, lingeringly culminating in the final overthrow of Nineveh in 606 B.C.

Following Tiglath-Pileser III and his son Ashurdan II, Adad-nirari III (911–890) helped to further the rise of Assyrian power. He strengthened the defence of Asshur and is famous as a campaigner in wars of which details are lacking, except in the cam-

paign with Babylon over the boundary question. The
first of several encounters, all of which favored the
Assyrians, was fought near Mt. Yalman (Holwan),
in the eastern mountains. In the treaty that followed
the rival kings exchanged daughters in marriage and
the boundary lines were adjusted between the two
empires. Tukulti Ninib II followed his father with
a short reign (890–885). His fame as a conqueror
was long-lived. He inscribed the praise of one of
his campaigns on the rocks near the sources of
the Tigris.

Ashurnasirpal III (885–860) had a comparatively
long reign and was busied with many campaigns.
(See page 223.) He battled with the Nairi to the
southwest of Lake Van in what is now Armenia, also
with the Kirkhi and Aramean tribes. Like his father
he inscribed his exploits on the rocks at the head-
waters of the Tigris. He made a change of capital,
selecting an old one instead of a new site, and chose
Kalah or Kalkhi, at the junction of the upper Zab
and the Tigris. Here he colonized captives from his
conquered Euphratean provinces and from Hittite
land. He built the shrine and statue of his patron-
god Ninib. One of the regions which gave him especial trouble was Bit Adini in northwestern Mesopotamia. This was peopled with Arameans who aspired
to independence and had already stirred up rebellion
in neighboring principalities. It would look as if
these Arameans were hoping to set up a state that
would control the commercial advantages of Syria
much as Damascus did later. But Assyria was not
willing to relinquish any of its commercial power and

was ready to maintain it by costly campaigns. In a
series of wars the king conquered the allies of Bit
Adini, including the Babylonians under the command
of the brother of the Babylonian king. Bit Adini was
next attacked successfully. Then came the turn of
the Hittite stronghold Karkhemish, which fell easily.
After that Ashurnasirpal went to the Mediterranean
and received the submission of the coast cities, including Tyre, Sidon, Byblos and Arvad. The great prize
for which the Assyrians fought was an absolute sway
sustained by profitable commerce. This necessitated
among other things the control of the trade routes,
the commercial centres and the tribute of the merchants. With these the first fruits of the oriental
commercial enterprise Assyria had the wealth of the
ancient east in its power. The Assyrians learned
from the Babylonians the business methods that kept
the produce of the orient in profitable circulation,
thus stimulating agriculture, mining and manufactur-
ing. It seems certain that the civilized Arameans,
a race of traders, had combined with the Babylonians
to prevent Assyria from usurping the control of the
caravan roads, the lines of trade and communication
and the necessary emporia which were the way stations of exchange. The Aramean states were well
situated to perform the great service of middlemen.
This service must be performed whoever the masters
were. The Arameans were ambitious to reserve the
prizes for independent enjoyment. But the great
military power Assyria was not to be denied an
imperial control and share.

The well-known ferocity of the Assyrians finds its

most terrible illustration in the inscriptions of Ashurnazirpal.* It is fair to say that independent peoples when first conquered were not so harshly treated as the rebellious vassals of the king. However, the cruelty finds no possible excuse by either modern or ancient standards. Ethically crude and immature peoples exhibit unimaginative cruelty as the children of the race. Desert and mountain origins account for hardy tribes able to contend with the elements and with beasts. A mental fierceness and narrowness of imagination characterizes those who fight with men for the prizes that exist rather than invent new good. While the early orientals were highly civilized in material achievement and were gifted with many noble qualities, loyalty, daring, and religious fervor, yet at times it would seem as if they were ethically unborn. They derived from religious devotion the justification of many of their most atrocious deeds. They conceived of the minds of their gods as set upon just such horrible revenges. The Assyrian kings were most devout in ascribing to the great god Ashur the incitement to battle, leadership in it and peculiar satisfaction in the discomfiture of foes. Ancient oriental religion had fully as much emotional fervor and devotion to the will of divinity as now, but it was lacking in that other and equally important side the ethical and the humane.

Great wealth came to the conquerors. The booty of a dozen successful wars in all quarters must have been immense. Much of it is catalogued in the royal inscriptions. The royal treasuries were filled and

---

* See Olmstead in J. A. O. S. 38: 4 October, 1918.

great buildings were erected, magnificent palaces, temples and forts. Besides the rich and countless treasures accumulated by the Assyrians in these campaigns much was wasted, wheat fields were burned, cities and lands devastated. By adding the waste and the wealth together we may gather some notion of the opulence of the East. But what about this method of concentrating wealth? The property, camp equipage, and spoil of 50,000 slain citizens of the various hostile nations may well have been great. The markets, bazaars, treasuries, mines, forests, fields of scores of captured and pillaged cities, must have been enormously productive to the conqueror. The enforced tribute upon hundreds of thousands of subjugated people must have yielded magnificently, for these people were active in every known form of paying industry, agriculture, herding, mining, manufacture, transportation and barter. However, when all has been reckoned and one is awestruck at the splendor of the material wealth in fabulous quantity, we may confess that the method of its garnering would be like the burning of a forest in order that one may gather wood ashes or the drying up of the sea to secure the treasure of lost ships. When all has been said we have simply described robbery on a royal scale. The savings of a million people though each one be humble would make an imperial purse. So the great grain fields of Mesopotamia, the forests of the northern and western mountains, the caravans of the traders were made the possessions of the warlike Assyrians who slew the owners and appropriated the fruits of the toil of the multitude.

It was robbery sanctified by the name of the great god Ashur and made successful by numerous well-drilled troops. Nor was the warring harmful only to the conquered, for it eventually ruined Assyria. Exhausting campaigns cost a fair share of the treasure secured. Moreover, the citizens of Assyria were drawn upon so heavily that depletion of the strongest and best was inevitable. Ashurnasirpal stayed this decay by enlisting the troops of conquered races in his armies. But the cost in men from whatever race was never made up. Those unfit for war and heroic things were left at home and became the progenitors of the races that survived. Economically the East was sacrificed to the gods of war. Assyria is not to be unduly blamed. The races whom it fought were themselves incessantly engaged in petty wars. The only hope for the times was a well-ordered empire that should keep the kingdoms and principalities at peace. It would seem that Babylonian dominion was able to maintain comparative tranquillity with less devastating warring than Assyria. Why? The Babylonian state was predominantly commercial and cultural. It was not led by so fierce a race as Assyria. Its military class was probably not so highly specialized as Assyria's and did not overrule the peaceable population.

The empire of Ashurnasirpal III was left sufficiently stable to last a hundred years after him in the hands of his descendants. The energy of the dynasty seemed inexhaustible and its duties ever extending. Thus Shalmaneser III, the next king, reigned thirty-five years and records thirty-two expeditions in which he or his generals ranged far and wide, subduing and setting in order disturbed provinces or new lands. Surely the kings on the Tigris knew the strenuous life and were inured to hardship.

Shalmaneser introduced the custom of a definite yearly tribute payable by certain communities. This seems like a provincial tax. It was different for different countries and may have been apportioned to wealth or population. The organization of provinces was more regular and thorough than before and the limu list included governors of remote Assyrian provinces held by strongly centralized power. Assyria must have been succeeding better with the problem of provincial organization.

Shalmaneser III is credited with the building of a library at his capital Kalah. Here in charge of the royal librarian were Babylonian religious works, either the originals which were taken away from Babylonia in war or else copies which the scribes in the southland of culture had made of the originals.

Shalmaneser was called upon to interfere with Babylonian politics in 852 B.C. when the brother of the rightful king contested the throne successfully until an appeal to Assyria resulted in the death of the usurper. Shalmaneser was met in northern Syria by an organized opposition on the part of the Arameans, headed by King Akhuni, of Bit Adini. After defeating in detail the members of the league which fell to pieces soon after his approach, Shalmaneser proceeded in a direction never before traveled by an Assyrian conqueror. This was in the region occupied by three kingdoms, Hamath, Damascus, and Israel.

Hamath was eighty miles south of the Assyrian provincial outpost of Khalman and commanded the entrance to Cœle-Syria. Damascus was a hundred miles south of Hamath and the next territory was that of Israel, fifty miles southwest of Damascus.

Israel and Damascus had been at war with each other frequently, as had others of these South Syrian kingdoms. But at the advance of the common enemy, the Assyrian, they formed an alliance and evidently made Assyria's progress difficult for a while, for although Assyrian inscriptions claim the victory for Shalmaneser the facts that tribute was not exacted nor a further advance made for some time show that the Assyrian victory was not important, if indeed there was not a drawn battle. The land of Palestine was spared for a hundred years. Shalmaneser's son Shamsi-Adad had to come to the throne in the midst of a serious rebellion which clouded the last years of Shalmaneser and lasted six years into the new reign. The favor which designated Shamsi-Adad as the legitimate candidate for the throne before his father died had aroused another son to attempt to secure the succession for himself and to set aside both the king and the heir. Twenty-seven cities joined with the rebel but he was unable to secure the capital Kalah and the army. Thus Shamsi-Adad succeeded to the throne on the death of his father and after six years of contest was able to secure the empire for himself. Such internal disturbances must have been costly in the elements of imperial strength and security. The control over Babylonia had been lost in the meantime which illustrates how a rebellion disintegrated imperial influence. Shamsi-Adad was able, however, to reëstablish his authority over Babylonia.

The last king of the line we have been studying was displaced in a rebellion in 745 B.C. by a military leader who took the name Tiglath Pileser IV. He made good the name he assumed, revived Assyrian authority by campaigns in Babylonia against the Arameans, and the Kaldi, also in the eastern, northern and western confines of the empire, thus going to each of the points of the compass as was necessary when serious disturbances threatened the integrity of the realm. Northern Syria, Damascus, Israel and the Philistine country were attacked and despoiled.

Besides the exhaustion of life and treasure in great and frequent wars there were other insidious foes to political health. Sometimes regions which had been fruitful payers of tribute suffered from failure of crops and consequent famine. Shrinkage of supplies for the army made campaigns difficult. Pestilence threatened to annihilate populations. Palace intrigues, plots, treasonable and murderous, undermined legitimate authority and threatened law and prosperity by divisions of allegiance. Any sign of weakening or misfortune loosened the bands which held together restless provinces. Ambitious provincial governors might become disloyal, or subjugated kingdoms, ever chafing under bondage and tribute, might revolt. When one revolted other provinces joined in making trouble and the ruler had a series of campaigns to wage or else he must suffer in weakness the disruption of the empire. Rather than allow this a military leader would arise, seize upon the

authority of the weak king and go to reconquer the
dissolving empire. Tiglath-Pileser IV was succeeded
by Shalmaneser V who comes into prominence in
Biblical history. Palestine had become involved with
Assyria through Syria (Damascus). The two west
Palestinian states of chief Biblical importance were
Israel and Judah, the latter subject often to the
former. The king of Israel was deposed and the
pro-Assyrian Hoshea was seated on the throne of
Samaria. Soon he rebelled against Assyria. The
cause of disaffection seems to have been provided
or encouraged by Egypt which played a consistent
anti-Assyrian rôle through combinations of Palestinian states.

Samaria fell a victim to the Assyrian siege under
Kings Shalmaneser and Sargon. Sargon was the
name adopted by the great successor of Shalmaneser.
Who he was before that, history does not tell. He
headed a dynasty that ruled the Assyrian empire
during the last century of its existence. In certain
respects this was the most magnificent period of
Assyrian history. Sargon was assisted by the
priestly power in securing the throne. His chief foes
outside of Assyria were the Babylonians under Merodach Baladan, the Elamites who made common cause
with the Babylonians against Assyria, and the Urartu
(or Haldi). Sargon received the submission of
Samaria in Palestine which was still under siege when
his predecessor died. The chief peril of these little
Palestinian states was the diplomacy of Egypt whose
machinations kept making trouble for Assyria.

The combination of Babylonia and Assyria might

have been irresistible, but, just as in Egypt, in Palestine and other countries the old question of the north and the south with their fancied contrasts of interests and pride led to the destruction of both countries.

Sargon gradually overcame all his foes and was king in Babylon. When it was no longer possible for him to be present at the annual ceremony that validated his kingship of Babylon he was at least considered the governor of the city. The Babylonians were averse to permitting an absentee ruler to hold the royal title. Such incorrigible obstinacies or customs of the ancient city led Sargon's successor Sennacherib to destroy it as a seat of mischief. But sentiment and the powerful claims of its ancient prestige led Esarhaddon to rebuild it.

Other campaigns of Sargon were in North Syria and in Philistia. Notable were his contests with the Urartu of the far northern country now known as Armenia. Sargon undertook serious campaigns against Kings Rusash and Argishtish. The power of the Urartu was finally broken by the Cimmerian invasion. The aged Sargon lost his life while campaigning against these Cimmerians.

Sennacherib Became King in 705 B.C.—He met successfully the revolts incident to a change of rulers. He checked disturbances in Palestine where Hezekiah of Judah played a prominent part. It is recorded that Merodach Baladan of Babylon, the old enemy of Assyria, was the instigator of the revolt in Palestine. In Babylon Sennacherib placed his son on the throne while he himself sought to render impotent the forces and allies of Merodach Baladan. These

10

were Kaldeans, Arameans and Elamites. He fought in all the borders of the land, but was as persistently opposed. The enemy took Babylon in Sennacherib's absence and carried off the king. Moreover, the natives of the city joined with the Elamites against the Assyrians. Sennacherib's desperate response to this was the destruction of the city. The region about was administered as a province. This was the province over which Esarhaddon, son of Sennacherib, was made governor and from which post he succeeded to the Assyrian throne on the death of his father by assassination. Sennacherib came into contest with the Ionian Greeks of Asia Minor and carried off many captives of that race to his own country.

These recreant brothers of Esarhaddon, who were probably the conspirators in the murder of their father, had sought to supplant both father and brother in the political control of the empire. They were pursued by the heir and defeated. Esarhaddon then secured his title to absolute control in both Assyria and Babylonia.

In the East Esarhaddon was far more conciliatory than his father had been. He possessed a deal of sentiment about the old Babylonian seat of culture and set about rebuilding the city. After small encounters with the Kaldeans who were rendered negligible and with the Elamites who came to an understanding with Assyria, Esarhaddon turned his attentions to Phenicia. The cities there had made another bid for independence. Sidon was quite destroyed, although a new city named after Esarhaddon was immediately built on the site. Tyre was able to resist the Assyrian siege successfully, a notable case of Assyrian discomfiture.

The really unique enterprise of Esarhaddon was the conquest of Egypt. This country had lived on an ancient reputation for prowess through long ages. Its pretensions to first rank were now challenged by invasion and the fall of the ancient city of Memphis was a seal upon the passing of an ancient empire.

Symptomatic of the changing times were incursions into certain of the northerly and eastern provinces of Assyria by barbarian hordes of Cimmerians. They were related to the Medes and the Scythians, between whose migratory movements in Asia their own career is dated. Esarhaddon held them off with a minimum of peril, but they were able to throw new populations into those eastern countries who before the end of the century would help to overthrow Nineveh and in the following century Babylon.

When Esarhaddon started out on his last expedition westward to quell an uprising in Egypt he appointed one of his sons king of Assyria and another to rule in Babylonia. He himself did not survive the journey and his careful provisions for a peaceful succession went into effect.

Ashurbanipal was the appointee to the throne of Assyria and Shamash-shum-ukin became the king of Babylon. Ashurbanipal continued the Egyptian campaign and occupied not only Memphis but Thebes. He, too, met the serious problem of the Cimmerian hordes which were overflowing into new homes. Many peoples were endangered by these barbarians and some of the victims appealed to Ashurbanipal.

Perhaps the most notable of these suppliants was Gyges the king of Lydia.

The most tragic occurrence of Ashurbanipal's reign was the unfortunate but perhaps inevitable revolt of his brother and the Babylonians from their increasing dependence upon Assyria. Whatever solution of the political problems of the kindred kingdoms Esarhaddon may have had in mind when he constituted two thrones in his family was misconceived. For fifteen years the status was maintained. Then the effects of ambitious plotting and revenge began to appear. Without going into the sickening details of fraternal strife it is enough to say that Ashurbanipal survived. He was king of both countries for the next twenty-two years. He left a greatly depleted empire to two sons who between them reigned the last twenty years of Assyria's existence (626–606). Already Egypt had ceased to pay tribute. Gyges the Lydian ignored the alliance with Assyria and entered into one with Egypt. Scythians, Manda and Persians were moving in the old eastern provinces and regions neighboring to Assyria. It is not absolutely certain how these enemies of Assyria shared in the last wars upon her nor who at the last delivered the fatal blow at Nineveh which resulted in the fall of the most famous military capital of the ancient Orient (606). H. D. B. III, p. 310.

The Return of Babylon to Power.—The New Babylonian Age. The Chaldeans, those persistent claimants of the country of Babylonia and most consistent foes of Assyria, had the last word in the age-long contest. They were allies of those who overthrew

Nineveh and they provided the last ruling dynasty
of Babylon before the advent of the Persians. From
the fall of Nineveh to the conquest by Cyrus, there
were nearly seventy years in which much stirring
history was enacted. The spent powers of the Semitic nations were to be succeeded by the virile forces
of the new Indo-European peoples.

Nabopolassar headed the line of Chaldean kings
of New Babylonia. His great son Nebuchadrezzar,
second king of that name, is very well known to all
readers of the Old Testament. Nabopolassar's
twenty-one years' reign covered the entire time of
the last two Assyrian kings. Their weakness gave
wide opportunity for his great ability.

Nebuchadrezzar succeeded to the throne upon the
death of his father in 605 B.C. He is the king who
twice conquered Jerusalem in the days of Jeremiah
and Ezekiel the prophets and who, the second time,
utterly destroyed the Hebrew capital and shrine.
Each time he carried away Hebrew captives from
Judah. These captives and their children grew up
in Babylonia and became the founders of those eastern Jewish communities whose rabbinical schools
were established in the midst of the ancient Babylonian culture and partook so much of it.

Upon the fall of Nineveh what might be called the
normal boundaries of the two empires north and
south were observed. Cyaxares possessed the homeland of the Assyrians and the highlands as far as
Armenia and Asia Minor while Nabopolassar held
the Babylonian country, southern Mesopotamia and
thence westward to the Mediterranean as far south

as the border of Egypt. Necho the ambitious king
of Egypt who essayed to prevent this partition of
Asia was beaten in the battle of Karkhemish in the
same year that Nabopolassar died. The victory was
won by Nabopolassar's son Nebuchadrezzar, who was
vigorously clearing away the opposition to the new
status of Babylonia when he was summoned to the
vacant throne.

A brilliant renaissance of building, irrigating and internal improvements for the progress and the defence
of Babylonia resulted from the energy of the new
king. He had a long reign which was followed by
several brief reigns of small significance, after which
a revolution seated Nabunaid the last Babylonian
king on the throne.

The last king of Babylon might be termed a dynasty
by himself as he was probably alien to the blood of
his predecessors. He developed remarkable interests
and abilities more in the line of religious and antiquarian research than in that of politics. He did
thorough work in rebuilding the temples of his country and uncovered much valuable information concerning its early history. He will be remembered
especially for recovering thus the foundation bricks
of the early king Naram-Sin in the temple at Sippar,
although his high reading of the figures misled modern historians. Nabunaid was not equally well fitted
for the practical affairs of his kingdom and perhaps
no man of Babylon could have hindered the next
great figure in world conquest.

The contemporary king of the Manda was Asty-
ages, one of whose provinces in the northern part of

Elam was Anshan. This principality came to be ruled by Cyrus the Persian, who quickly overcame his Manda suzerain and succeeded to the empire of the north and northwest. Nabunaid was not displeased with this turn of affairs. He had no such relation of amity with the Manda as was maintained by his predecessors the Chaldean kings of Babylon. The city of Babylon was painfully factional and probably Nabunaid's own son Belshazzar represented the more warlike and patriotic party that resented the successes of Cyrus. Certain it is that after he had disposed of his enemies in the west under Croesus, king of Lydia, Cyrus began operations in Babylonia. Belshazzar was defeated. The people weakened and Cyrus' officer Gobryas came to the capital which was betrayed into his power. Cyrus followed in a few days, making a peaceful entry and pretending with consummate tact that he had been summoned by the god of Babylon, Marduk, to take charge of his city and to worship his divinity. This was very different from the old style of fighting which would have included Marduk as an enemy whose statue must be carried away so as to exhibit the inferiority of Babylon's deity to the gods of the conqueror. The new Persian way was similar to that followed by the wisest conquerors since. Conciliation is an aid to conquest.

SUGGESTIONS FOR STUDY

1. Describe the geographical features of Assyria.
2. Map the mountains and paths from which the Kassites came.
3. Possible connections between Kassites and Hittites.
4. Read descriptions of military scenes in Nahum.

5. The commercial rivalry of Assyria and Phenicia.
6. State of the world 1000 B.C.
7. Assyrian ethics.
8. Gog, Magog, Meshech (Mushki). H. D. B., II, 224.
9. Data about Merodach Baladan in the Bible.
10. Egyptian use of Palestine to hinder Assyria.

BOOK LIST

H. D. B., I, 176. Enc. Bib., I, 347.
WINCKLER: History of Babylonia and Assyria, trans. by Craig.
HOGARTH: Ionia and the East.
OLMSTEAD: J. A. O. S., 38, 209. (1918.)
H. G. MITCHELL: Isaiah.
C. H. W. JOHNS: Ancient Assyria.
OLMSTEAD: Western Asia in the Days of Sargon of Assyria.
JASTROW: Aspects of Religious Belief in Babylonia and Assyria.

CHAPTER IX

The Heirs of Assyria.—When Assyria, exhausted for the last time by the drain of incessant campaigning, fell, no more to be a factor in history, the domain of the Asiatic world was divided between New Babylonia, Media (of the Manda) and Lydia. (See page 148.)

New Babylonia had able kings for over half a century. Its ally Media, in the western Iranian tableland of central Asia, had been growing in importance and was among the destroyers of Assyria. The Medes traced their national existence to King Deiokes, who in the beginning of the seventh century B.C. made Ecbatana the Median capital. This city represented now by Hamadân, near Mt. Elvend, was in a fertile valley east of Assyria and the Zagros mountains. From a little kingdom extending itself by conquest over Iranian tribes, Manda-Media came to be an empire and the victor over Nineveh and proud Assyria. According to Herodotus, Deiokes was followed by Kings Phaortes and Cyaxares.

Lydia arose in Asia Minor and occupied part of the old Hittite regions. Gyges the Lydian established his kingdom as the successor of ancient Phrygia and put himself in control of the overland trade-route through Asia Minor. In 585 there was a treaty which made the Halys River the boundary between Lydian and Median possessions. Alyattes, king of Lydia, made firm his control over Asia Minor. He probably included Cilicia within his sphere of influence and as many rich Greek cities of the coast as he could persuade. Caria, a country whose mercenary soldiers had already proved useful to Lydia, was associated with Alyattes by marriage. His son Croesus, child of the Carian woman, was able to add Caria to the Lydian kingdom. Lydia had become a prosperous and powerful state. Its art and culture blended Babylonian and Greek elements. It became notable as a country of merchants and much merchandise passed through Lydian hands. The Lydian and neighboring Greek cities grew rich in consequence of the trade. Such places as Sardes, Ephesus, Miletus and Clazomenæ became great emporia wherein the arts of trade were refined.

Early Coinage.—Although the matter is disputed, some think that the Lydian business firms brought out the first coinage of money. In cutting up the bars of gold which were used by weight to serve the exchange of goods the ancients hit upon the expedient of stamping the smaller bits with an indication of their weight or value in some uniform manner which would facilitate business and yet preserve confidence. At least this function of coined money is discovered as early as the Lydians. Individual bankers were probably the first to devise the scheme which was later taken up by cities and states as a government right much as the use of postage stamps developed in America. Coins of King Croesus exist with the device of the forefront of a lion opposed by the head and shoulders of a bull.

Croesus had triumphed over many rivals on his

accession and brought under his authority the southern and western coast of Asia Minor. This made
him master of many Greek cities. By skilful treaties
with the Greek islands and with European Greece,
by reverent regard for their divinities and most lavish gifts to their famous shrines such as Delphi,
Dodona, Phocis and Thebes, Croesus secured the
friendly partisanship of the western world in preparation for the time when he might desire to pursue his
ambitions eastward. Moreover, he so amazed the
world by his resources as to bequeath to all time his
own name as a symbol of fabulous wealth though it
might better stand for lavish expenditure. Most of
the subjects of Lydia retained their own constitutions
and their native rulers. These paid tribute and
raised levies for the Lydian power at Sardes. The
climax came about the time of Cyrus' victory over
the Medes (see page 151). Croesus was secure in
power west of the Halys but crossed that river to
gain new territory.

The opposition of Cyrus was provided for by agree-
ments with Egypt and Chaldea. The Greek states
were sending aid and Lydian money secured mercenaries. News was taken to Cyrus by a faithless
agent of Croesus. Cyrus moved his Persian and
Median army across Asia so rapidly that he was upon
the Lydians before the allied nations had provided
their promised aid. Cyrus made his swift progress
by a short route through Babylonian territory instead of risking a detour through his own more northern and wintry regions. Such an act in itself showed
his contempt for Babylon with which he must soon

or later engage in war. The Lydians were taken by surprise but rallied and gained the advantage in the first contest. Later they were worsted and retreated upon Sardes, their capital. They counted upon the oncoming winter for a stay of operations. But Cyrus pressed on over the mountains and confronted Croesus whom he found almost without troops as the Lydian had disbanded part of his army. A desperate call for aid was of little avail and Sardes fell. Egypt, Chaldea, Tyre and Damascus could not hope to succeed where Lydia had failed. Cyrus had recognized his ablest foe and could after that win victories over the others in the order that suited his judgment. Cyrus left the pacification of Asia Minor to generals and governors while he returned to deal with problems in the farther east.

Persia was at first a small kingdom of allied tribes which inherited the seats of ancient Elam and was subject to the growing Median power. It rose to importance under Cyrus who was able to reverse the relative status of Media and Persia (549 B.C.). He became the master of all the Iranian peoples, including his former masters. The Persians belong to the Iranian branch of the Indo-European peoples. They were very hardy folk trained to feats of almost incredible endurance and valor. The ancient religion of the Iranians is usually known as Zoroastrianism after the name of the prophet Zarathushtra or Zoroaster. His date is uncertain. Possibly it should be set in the Seventh Century B.C. The religion taught the worship of the good principle in the universe, the Lord Wisdom or Ahura-Mazdā (Ormazd).

The writings of the faith came together, comparatively late, in the sacred collection called the Avesta. The Good Lord Ormazd with his patrons and attendants is forever opposed by the Evil One, the destructive Ahriman, who with attendant demons and powers wages continual war against all goodness. Eventually Ormazd will win in the protracted battle. Human beings are divided into corresponding parties according as they serve one principle or the other. Six attendant deities (Amesha-Spentas) and thousands of great spirits (Yazatas) are in the kingdom of the good. The future state of souls is quite as distinctive as the two kingdoms. The just will be blessed and the bad will be slaves of Ahriman. Except in the case of the king who was peculiarly related to the service of Ormazd, all the devotees were very dependent on the mediation of the great priestly class known as the Magi.

Cyrus the Great is represented in some of the legends as of humble origin, in others as a noble child who was brought up in the life of a shepherd in order to shield him from vindictive enemies. Other claims connect him with the royal Achaemenian line. When it was seen that Cyrus was of world-wide significance as a conqueror his romantic and unpreventable rise to power from so small a place was viewed with great alarm by the powers of the day. But by the oppressed he was hailed joyously as a deliverer. May he have sought to raise such hopes as an aid to his plans and ambitions?

The combination of the Medes and Persians was apparently a congenial one for those peoples. United under the Achaemenian kings of Persia they became the leaders of the world. Babylon, Egypt, Syria, Phenicia, Asia Minor, the Greek islands and cities as far as Marathon and Salamis became subject to the Great King. No empire before it had so widely extended a domain. The influence of the Persian thought upon Jewish and Christian doctrines was considerable. The Persians inherited the Babylonian civilization and wrote their language in its system of signs.

The Conquest of the East and of Babylon.—When Cyrus returned to the East from his war with Croesus it was to annex regions such as Bactria, Margia, Khoramnia, etc. The country of the Sakae, Cabul and Gedrosia was entered. These operations filled the time from 545 to 539 b.c. Then Cyrus was free to consider the case of Babylon which he had passed by twice with impunity to do more important campaigning. Nabonidus (Nabuna'id), king of Babylon, seems to have been interested chiefly in antiquarian research into the records of Babylonia. Whatever else may be said he kept his throne longer than some of his more daring contemporaries. To make up for his deplorable weakness as a sovereign his son Belshazzar (Bel-Sharuzur) appears to have been a creditable antagonist to the Persian. Babylonia was probably the prey of factional strife. The Jewish exiles hailed Cyrus as a messiah who should deliver the Lord's people from their captors (Isa. xlv, 1). Perhaps other parties within the state had similar hopes. Cyrus and his general Gobryas won several preliminary engagements before Babylon was reached.   On the sixteenth of the month Tammuz Gobryas entered the city without the necessity of an attack.   Cyrus followed the ancient Babylonian custom and "took the hands of Bel."   Thus he became a legitimate king of the ancient city and acceptable to the oldest civilization of Asia.   He associated his son Cambyses with himself as king of Babylon. Cyrus was more liberal and more successful in dealing with the Babylonian question than the Assyrian kings had been.   He posed as deliverer of the Babylonians and was so received.   He cultivated the religion of the god of the city, Bel-Merodach (Marduk), and all affairs continued in usual course.

Cyrus and the Jewish Captives.—According to the generally accepted tradition the Jews who were in Babylonia were permitted by a decree of Cyrus to return to Palestine.   Whether this was because they had favored the Persian side or because Cyrus wished to found vassal interests in western Asia is left untold, but probably the latter reason was the determining consideration as we know that Cyrus followed a similar policy with other victims of Assyria and Babylon.   In 536 a company of the more enthusiastic idealists formed a returning group.   They accomplished very little.   The people were poor and the attitude of those who had crowded into devastated Judah was hostile for political reasons to any rehabilitation of the Hebrew influence.   After fifteen years the prophets Haggai and Zechariah were successful in a vigorous summons to the people to build the temple of Jehovah at Jerusalem.

The Conquest of Egypt.—Egypt was the one great

oriental country yet independent of Persia. It had
been the ally and supporter of the enemies of Cyrus
and must soon or later receive the summons to surrender. Amasis was the pharaoh (569–525). Long
before this time the Greeks had become very influential colonists in parts of the Delta, although they were
looked upon with disfavor by the more reactionary
Egyptians. Amasis' predecessor, King Apries
(Hophra), had a successful reign until his soldiery
became mutinous. First it was the foreign mercenary troops that alarmed him by defection. Later his
native Egyptian troops were even more troublesome.
Apries sent Amasis who was a relative to treat with
the rebellious Egyptians. Amasis, however, was able
to win over the malcontents to himself if not to his
sovereign and was proclaimed king. Amasis, by this
coup, became a representative of the successful native
party. But, once seated in power, after his rival was
dead, Amasis was even more a friend of the Greeks
than Apries. He founded the purely Greek city of
Naukratis, which became a flourishing industrial and
trade centre. Amasis was deservedly very popular
among these foreigners. He was careful to nurture
the native support also, but was never able fully
to gratify the native ideal of a ruler. His navy
and other schemes of defence necessitated large revenues which he secured by encroaching upon the temple resources. He laid the foundations of a great
sea-power. Cyprus was conquered and organized as
a subject country. The rise of Cyrus, his speedy
conquest of Lydia and the fall of Babylon in 539
were all signs of the inevitable for Egypt, but both

Amasis and Cyrus died before Persians and Egyptians actually met in battle. Amasis' son Psamtik III was the pharaoh whom Cyrus' son Cambyses overcame in 525. Tradition has it that Cyrus lost his life in battle with the Massagetae about 529. He was buried at Pasargadae.

The two sons of Cyrus were Cambyses and Smerdis. While the former succeeded to the empire the latter was a provincial administrator under the authority of his brother the king. Plots, connected whether rightly or wrongly with the name of his brother Smerdis, led the hasty tempered Cambyses to compass his murder.

Legend has busied itself with the causes of animosity between Cambyses and Amasis. It is said that a demand by the former for a daughter of the pharaoh was met by subterfuge on the part of Amasis who, instead of sending his own daughter to the east, sent the daughter of his unfortunate predecessor Apries. The girl's name was Nitetis and she disclosed the trick to her royal husband. The Egyptians invented another story to the effect that Nitetis really married Cyrus and was thus the mother of Cambyses, who avenged her father upon the usurper Amasis. By this legendary device the Egyptians could claim that Cambyses was descended from the pharaohs. Ebers has written an interesting romance on the theme.

Cambyses in Egypt.—Cambyses had reached Gaza in pursuance of his mission against Egypt, when one of Amasis' mercenary leaders, Phanes of Halicarnassus, who had quarreled with his master, met

11

Cambyses and put him in friendly relations with Arabs who could manage for him the passage of his army over the desert. When Cambyses reached Pelusium he learned that the aged Amasis had died. At so great a disadvantage the new pharaoh Psamtik III undertook the defence of Egypt. Superstition and fear worked on the minds of the people and inferior numbers with which to oppose the Persian army was but one of the many hindrances to success. Fierce fighting was followed by a victory for the Persians, who proceeded to the reduction of Memphis, after which Egypt became a Persian dependency. Cambyses began his control of Egypt by measures tending to ingratiate him with the natives. But after meeting misfortunes in his attempts to conquer Carthage and Ethiopia he became subject to mental depression if not madness. He changed his policy of conciliation to a frenzy of outrageous treatment of every native susceptibility. He even showed himself insanely brutal against his own friends. He delayed leaving Egypt for a long time, which gave rise to restless conditions in home politics. As the Inscription of Behistun, col. 1, lines 32–35, says, ''untruth had spread all over the country, not only in Persia and Media, but in other provinces.'' A usurper, the Magus, Gaumata, pretended to be the king's brother whom Cambyses had ordered killed. Many were deceived and supposed that Cambyses' unfortunate brother, Smerdis, had really escaped and was now calling off the loyalty of the nation from the insane tyrant to his own claims. The rebellion headed by Gaumata came in

March, 521, and was successful in securing the allegiance of Persia, Media and the Iranian countries. Gaumata under the name of Smerdis was placed on the throne. The entire East followed his claims. Cambyses died just as he was setting out to punish the usurper. The inscription of Darius at Behistun says that Cambyses died by his own hand.

The Pretender.—The new king sought by every means to conceal his real identity and to curb the power of the grand dukes from whom he feared opposition. He sought to make himself secure in the provinces by exemptions from tax and military service. But the lords of the realm formed a conspiracy and succeeded in overcoming the impostor by assassination (521 B.C.). Darius was one of the conspirators and on him the choice fell for king. He became one of the greatest administrators of the Orient.

Darius the Great.—Darius' accession was the signal for revolts on every hand and only consummate ability and address saved him his provinces and throne. The trouble was that rapid changes in rulers suggested further usurpations and the constitution of the empire was such as to encourage rebellion. The provinces were ruled by powerful satraps who were in effect viceroys well furnished with military power and wealth quite at their own disposal and offering very tempting suggestions. In seven or eight separate regions of the empire insurrections broke out and ambitious claims were set up. Elam, Chaldea, Media, Parthia, Margiana, Asia Minor and Egypt revolted and set up local pretenders. The pretensions of Athrina who essayed to rule in Susa

were soon disposed of, but in Babylon, Nadinta-Bel,
who claimed that he was a son of Nabonidus, received
strong support. He took the name of Nebuchadrezzar III and was able to give serious trouble to
Darius, who defeated him in two engagements and
then besieged him in Babylon. This was a critical
hour for Darius. Media and Asia Minor were hostile at the same time, but Darius persisted in the
attempt to solve the Babylonian problem, sending
small detachments to secure loyalty in the other disaffected regions. An embassy to Sardes was successful in securing the adherence of Asia Minor.
The siege of Babylon dragged on while district after
district rose in arms. Even Persia heeded the claims
of a pretender who claimed to be Smerdis, the second
son of Cyrus, so slowly did the idea of that unhappy
youth's survival die out. Darius was able to take
Babylon in 519, when he turned his personal attention to the Medes, winning battles and putting to
death the annoying leaders of defection. Babylon
again revolted and was again reduced. By the end
of 518 the general strife was over and Darius was
proven to be a sovereign of unusual force and judgment. He had faced a most discouraging combination of trials and had successfully overcome them by
patient devotion to the tasks in the order of their
importance to his cause. He chose the pass of Bagis-
tana (Behistun) as the site for a great commemorative monument of his triumphs. His figure was
carved on the cliff, a foot resting upon one prostrate
foe while nine captives representing the pretenders
who had opposed him were ranged before him. A

three-fold inscription tells the story of the wars necessitated by the uprisings and his victory in each of them. It was the decipherment of this inscription by Henry Rawlinson that placed the reading of cuneiform writing upon a sure foundation. Darius next visited Egypt where he set about attaching the people to the Persian cause. The mad Cambyses had treated the Egyptians abominably. The priests were humiliated, their revenues forfeited and the people were scandalized. The Persian governor Aryandes fell under the suspicion of the king and was executed. Darius then sought to undo the mischief of his predecessor and by a reverent and sympathetic attitude towards the things which the people held dear was able to secure their loyalty.

Darius' Empire was a Conglomeration of Nations.— He encouraged local peculiarities, for they kept the provinces from agreeing upon any policy which would endanger his authority. He divided the whole empire into many satrapies, numbering between twenty and thirty. Instead of leaving the old-time power in the hands of an individual he appointed three officials to each province. One was a satrap or civil governor in whose hands was lodged the power of life and death over the subjects. The chancellor of the satrap was really an agent of the king to whom he reported the conditions of the administration. Besides these there was the commander of the military forces. Each of these three was in communication with the king and acted as a check upon the others. Post-roads with relays of riding animals were maintained between the capital and distant parts of the empire. The main route, for example, which ran between Sardes in Asia Minor and Susa in Elam, went through Lydia, Phrygia, Cappadocia, Cilicia, Armenia, Matiene and the country of the Cossæans to Elam. It comprised one hundred eleven stages or relays which could be accomplished in eighty-four days. Besides the regular couriers the king sent out annually special officers called the "eyes" or the "ears" of the king. They came unannounced and spied upon every detail of provincial management or mismanagement. All the parts of the empire except the home country of Persia were assessed. The total payment resulting has been estimated (Maspero) at over $130,000,000 annually. Babylon and Egypt were the richest of the provinces. The Persian coin, the daric, named after Darius, was struck to facilitate the business of tax-collection and of exchange, but the use of bullion was very common. Besides the imperial levies the provinces must bear other heavy exactions incident upon the administration. A satrap, for example, received no salary from the empire but was a charge with all his luxurious requirements upon the province which he governed.

Darius and the Greeks.—When Darius had secured the integrity of the empire of his predecessors he directed his energies to the reduction of the independent Greek powers who were his western neighbors. A large Greek population was subject to Persia in Asia Minor. It was made restless by the neighborhood of European Greeks across the Ægean. Many cases of intermeddling occurred and possibilities of disloyal ambitions were imminent. A conquest of Greece was a political desideratum. Sparta had rendered itself obnoxious to Persians on more than one occasion and Athens was a doughty foe to Persian expansion. The latter state came first in the plan of invasion. A direct passage from Asia Minor to the Attic country seemed more problematical than a roundabout campaign *via* the Hellespont. The latter route was adopted. A preliminary campaign against Thrace and the Scythian country beyond was undertaken to know what possible hindrances might be present in those regions and their peoples. Thrace alone was permanently occupied and garrisoned. Persia was now entrenched in Europe and a neighbor on the north of Greece. Revolutionary conditions threatened Athens. The citizens got rid of Hippias, their tyrant, in 511. Darius and his officers probably expected some of the Greek belligerents to call for Persian aid. Such a request would have afforded an excellent opportunity to divide and rule. The exiled Hippias asked to be avenged by Artaphernes the satrap of Sardes and later the Athenians sought help against Sparta. Hippias was held off until the Athenian negotiations fell through when his cause was undertaken. The second great stage of the Persian invasion of Europe therefore made the Athenian state its objective. Athens once conquered, it would be entirely feasible to throw Persian troops directly across the Ægean Sea by the short route without fear of Athenian naval hostility. Blunders and defections accompanied unsuccessful attempts to seize some of the Ægean islands.

These led by Aristagoras soon stirred up the Asiatic Greeks against Darius. Thus the second stage of the Persian war developed a Greek offensive against Persia, since several of the Greek independent states joined the Greek provincials. But with the fall of the city of Miletus the tide steadily turned towards a reconquest of the rebellious countries.

The third stage of the Great War opened with Darius determined to avenge the miscarrying of all his plans and the indignities suffered in his rightful realm upon the European Greeks. These had showed, more clearly than ever before, by their recent actions and sympathies the necessity of reducing their country. Athens in particular was recognized as the centre of Greek offenses. The new campaign conducted by Mardonius through Thrace brought Macedon under Persian control. A serious natural disaster befell this expedition. The fleet accompanying it was partially destroyed by a storm off Mt. Athos. The campaign was delayed until the passing of winter, when it was prosecuted by the generals, Datis and Artaphernes.

All through the year 491 preparation was made for a passage of troops directly across the Ægean against Athens. The Phenicians, natural commercial enemies of the Greeks, could be counted on to provide the naval vessels. A few of the Greek states allied themselves with Darius. When the great armament was once afloat the route was taken *via* Samos, Naxos, and Delos to Euboea. Eretria and Carystos were overcome. The army proceeded to the plain near Marathon and awaited news of an uprising in

Athens by the friends of Hippias, who were expected to turn Athens over to Darius. But the Athenian patriotic parties composed their differences and sent an army of about 20,000 men to watch the Persians, and, if possible, to embarrass their advance until more strenuous opposition could be provided. They hoped to win the aid of Sparta and others. An engagement ensued when certain of the Persian troops were being embarked for Athens by sea. This resulted in the discomfiture of the foreign army and was really the fourth stage of the Persian invasion.

The fifth stage was prepared for with great care through three years and was to be introduced with decisive activity in 487–6 when a diversion occurred in Egypt. That country revolted in 486 and Darius died before he had perfected his plans for its punishment. He had spent thirty-six years of great activity in the most difficult tasks that ever confronted a Persian king.

Darius is said to have built a canal for the Egyptians between the Nile and the Red Sea. He was antagonized more perhaps by the Hellenic Egyptians than by the native element.

The Deliverance of the Greeks.—Xerxes (485–465), who succeeded to the difficulties of the last years of Darius, possessed no personal qualifications for their solution. Whatever warlike activities might be engaged in by the Persians during his reign would be by sheer political impetus, not by any personal direction of their master's ambition. His hordes crushed the national movement in Egypt and stamped out a similar movement in Babylon. Thereafter the

dignity of the empire necessitated the prosecution
of the Greek war. In 481 the advance was made and
headquarters established at Sardes. We may easily
believe that the Greeks magnified the numbers in the
Persian army. But that is of little account, as, beyond
a certain efficient force well commanded, numbers
would prove a serious hindrance, especially such numbers of ill-disciplined levies and camp followers as
attended the Persian. This, the sixth distinct stage
in the Persian attempt to subdue the Greeks of
Europe, saw the Asiatics going *via* the Hellespont
in the spring of 480. The land forces were supported by a fleet of 1200 fighting ships and proceeded down the coast towards Athens. Many
of the Greek states had so far demeaned themselves as to forsake the cause of the homeland
and leave upon Athens and Sparta the responsibility of withstanding the aggressions of Persia. Perhaps they preferred to be satrapies
under the Great King rather than suffer the dominance of either Athens or Sparta. Perhaps they forgot Marathon in the remembrance of many a failure
of Greek armies in Asia Minor. It is possible that
Marathon had already been made to resound unpleas-
antly in the ears of lesser states than Athens. The
first conflict was in the famed pass of Thermopylæ
where Leonidas and his three hundred immortals
fell in a desperate chance against the Asiatics.
Athens lay at the mercy of Xerxes but its inhabitants
fled, many of them to the island of Salamis. Xerxes
expected overtures but in vain. The Athenians were
desperate. This they proved when the forces of the

Persian ships and troops crowded upon their retreats. The Greek navy, light and vindictive, assailed the Persians, inflicting heavy loss. It was then that the moral inferiority of the Persian leadership and motive was evidenced. Xerxes gave up the personal conduct of the campaign, entrusting it to Mardonius, and started for Asia.

The seventh stage of the war came the next season when Mardonius returned to Attica. The Athenians fled as before from their city. This time the Persians ruined the place and retired. They were followed by the Spartans and Athenians. Finally at Platæa, when Mardonius thought he saw an opportunity to wound his foe, battle was joined with resultant disaster to the Persians. Their leader was slain. Greece was saved. It was now the turn of the Greeks to invade the possessions of the enemy. And it was especially grateful work to wrest the cities of Asia Minor from the Persian wherever they were Greek. Soon the Greek coast was free and leagued with the homeland to preserve its independence of Persia.

In 465 Xerxes was assassinated by his officer Artabanus, who secured the accession of a younger child of Xerxes named Artaxerxes to the throne, designing thus to hold the real power in his own hands. But the conspirator's lease of life was short, he fell a victim to intrigue. Artaxerxes' position was strengthened still more by the failure of revolutions in Bactriana and in Egypt. In the latter country considerable success attended the native party at first, and Athens did itself much damage by an eager alliance with the Egyptians, all to no avail. Things

on the Nile settled back into oriental lethargy with
Persian satraps to administer it.

Persian Control in Palestine.—Whenever any Persian, movements against Egypt were conducted overland they would pass within a few miles of the foothills of Judah, which was part of one of the Persian
satrapies. It was in these days perhaps that the
book of Malachi was written giving us a picture of
the difficulties in the Jewish society of the times.
Nehemiah felt the call which drew him from elegant
service in the Persian court to the stony hill-top
where he built the walls of Jerusalem. His memoirs
are vivid with description of the racial and religious
problems of the neighborhood. The beginnings of
the separate community of the Samaritans may be
dated in the same century. Their holy mountain is
Gerizim and their community has lived to modern
times in Nablus, the city between Mounts Gerizim
and Ebal, about thirty-five miles north of Jerusalem.[1]

The Jewish ecclesiastical state was established in
the latter part of this century and the sacred law became the chief glory of the nation. It is customary to
refer to the people after that event, not merely as
Hebrews, but more particularly as Jews. The political control of the Persians was probably as liberal as
any under which the people ever served and much
scope was allowed for the development of the peculiar
institutions of the Jews who formed a state within
the state, a religious community within the empire.

Travel between the Jewish colonies in Babylonia
and the city of Jerusalem was not uncommon, and

---

[1] See a modern description of the Samaritans' Passover in
"The People of Palestine," pages 125–129, Philadelphia, J. B.
Lippincott Company.

on more than one occasion special groups of returning Jews came back to the Holy City. Such a delegation accompanied Nehemiah and probably an especially zealous party came with Ezra, perhaps about 397 B.C., during the reign of Artaxerxes II. Not until the third Artaxerxes do we hear of harsh treatment of the Jews by the Persians.

Peace Between the East and the West.—The long struggle between Greece and Persia was telling heavily upon Athens, for it was that city that had to bear the heaviest part and often to battle with jealous Greek states besides. A treaty between Persians and Athenians was consummated which was a great relief to both parties (449). Those Greeks of Asia who had been leagued with Athens in the Great War were recognized as free. The Persian navy it was agreed should not enter their seas, nor a Persian army go nearer than three days' travel to the Ægean shore of Asia Minor. The merchant ships of the two treaty nations were permitted to go anywhere. Thus a status was recognized which exhibited the shrinkage of Persian power since the days of Darius. The vocation of Persian Monarchs henceforth would be to amuse themselves. Their avocations were building, administration and the suppression of intrigues.

Artaxerxes (Longimanus) died in 425 and was succeeded by Xerxes II who reigned two months and Sogdianus his murderer who reigned seven months. Darius II (Nothus), who had been known as Ochus, reigned from 424 to 405. His wife and queen was the infamous Parysatis whose cruelties belong to the

catalog of queenly horrors. Revolts were frequent
in the west where the Greek question had not ceased
to be a factor but was kept alive by ambitious satraps.
After the disaster to Athenian armaments in Syra-
cuse, Sparta assisted Persia to regain the Greek
cities of Asia Minor and thus aid in the humiliation
of Athens.

There were two claimants among the sons of
Darius II for his crown which death took from him
in 405 (4). One was Arsaces, who actually succeeded to the throne as Artaxerxes II (Mnemon).
The unsuccessful one was a Cyrus who had as his
powerful aids the fact that he was born after his
father became king and that he was the favorite of
the queen Parysatis. Arsaces had not been born to
the purple, but while his father was a satrap. Cyrus'
ambition had been forwarded by great bestowal of
power in Asia Minor where his father appointed him
to the most influential post in the empire. This was
at Sardes. In the war between Sparta and Athens,
Cyrus was the ally of the victorious Spartans, and
thus managed to attach to himself the dominant party
among the Greeks. He was present at the coronation
of his successful brother and rival and was there
denounced by Tissaphernes, the powerful western
satrap. Delivered from that peril, Cyrus the prince
hurried back to his domains to plan revenge. He
led an army eastward as far as Cunaxa, near Babylon, to fight with his brother for the empire. His
soldiers were victorious until he himself fell in the
engagement when they dispersed. Ten thousand
Greeks, led by Xenophon, made their way back to

the shores of Asia Minor, having discovered the hollowness of the vaunted Persian power. The weakness of the administration of Artaxerxes Mnemon was taken advantage of by the satraps of Asia Minor, who were in almost constant revolution or plot during the last part of his reign. In Egypt his representatives were driven out and native pharaohs contested his authority with the aid of Greek mercenaries. Amyrtæus, of the Twenty-eighth Dynasty, Nephorites I, Hakoris, Psamuthis II, Mutis, Nephorites II, Nectanebo I, Tachos and Nectanebo II followed in quick succession in disturbed Egypt. But the Persian was unable to quell the native movements until the days of Ochus, who succeeded to the throne of Artaxerxes Mnemon under the title of Artaxerxes (III) Ochus. The new king was a stronger character than his predecessor and proceeded to deal vigorously with the numerous revolts in the west. He even planned an invasion of Greece, but on account of revolts in Judah, Phenicia, and Cyprus and the renewal of hostilities with Egypt, he had to forego more ambitious designs. He overran Egypt, where his bearing reminds one of the insanities of Cambyses in the same country. The holy bull Apis he caused to be drowned, and proposed the ass as the sacred animal of Egypt. The Jews fared ill at the hands of this king, who exiled some of them to Hyrcania, near the Caspian Sea.

During this reign a notable figure appeared in the politics of Europe, Philip, King of Macedon. The Athenians appealed to Persia for aid against the Macedonians, but were refused. Ochus fell a victim to the plot of the eunuch Bagoas, who set up a son of the king on the throne, Arses. He also was murdered (339 B.C.) by Bagoas, who then caused the accession of Darius III, a great-grandson of Darius II. This king was the avenger on Bagoas of that servant's crimes.

Darius III (Codomannus) acceded in 336. Bury says "a mild and virtuous prince beloved by his followers but too weak, both in brains and will, for the task to which fate had doomed him." He was the last of the Achæmenian dynasty, for he was confronted by Alexander of Macedon.

Alexander the Great.—Alexander's army is said to have numbered 30,000 infantry and 5000 cavalry. The large proportion of cavalry was one of the new military ideas of Philip his father. The chief divisions of the army service were heavy cavalry, phalanx, and the light infantry or hypaspists. Darius had immense armies and great treasures of wealth at Susa and Persepolis. His empire was more united than usual. Many of his satraps showed considerable persistence in their loyalty. His army included thousands of trained Greek mercenaries. But there was no leader for these resources and men. The organization of the army was old fashioned. Alexander's troops had the benefit of the most advanced military organization of the day, for Macedonians had constantly improved the service, thanks to the ideas of the great Philip. Alexander's captains were Parmenio and his two sons, Nicanor, who was in charge of the hypaspists, and Philotas, who was in charge of the heavy cavalry. Then there was Menander,

who commanded the mercenary Greek hoplites. Antigonus was over the confederate Greek hoplites.
Clitus had the royal squadron of heavy cavalry under
Philotas. Callas was in charge of the Thessalian
cavalry with a corps of other Greek horse attached.

Alexander had the tolerant Greek spirit and an
unusually generous and chivalrous nature. He
greatly endeared himself to his followers and was
able to secure the confidence of many peoples among
whom he sojourned. Unlike some of the bigoted fire-
honoring Persians of later days he placated and
soothed the religious and superstitious sensibilities
of various subject peoples. He seemed naturally
reverent and devout in spite of his rash and impetuous youth. Sacrificing to appropriate divinities at
the various shrines, he showed a knowledge of the
mythological and religious past and a sense of his
great vocation.

A preliminary opposition to Alexander was provided by an army of 40,000 raised by Persian satraps
to defend Asia Minor. The leading general for
Persia was a man of Rhodes, Memnon. This army
gave Alexander more trouble than the immense forces
which later were led against him by the Persian king
himself. Alexander spent two years in seizing all
the strong places on the shores of the eastern Mediterranean, thus reducing the importance of the
enemy's fleet,to which he could oppose nothing comparable in the way of a navy. This, as Bury says, was
a blockade of the sea from the land. After Miletus
came the reduction of Caria and the capture of Halicarnassus. For the next cold season Alexander made

12

a division of his forces, some to Lydia, himself and
a division to Lycia, while he sent home to Macedonia
for reinforcements to replace the drafts on his
numerical strength by the garrisons left behind.
The meeting place in the spring for these three was
to be Gordion, capital of the ancient kingdom of
Phrygia. The Cilician gates were passed and Tarsus
was taken easily, the surprised enemy fleeing in dismay at Alexander's rapidity of movement.

The Conquest of the East by the West.—The king
of Persia now appeared to try to check Alexander.
The immense host of the one under the leadership of
an enfeebled mind and the small army of the greatest
genius of the ancient military world were encamped
on the two sides of Mt. Amanus. The Persian army
was well situated for a proper display of its great
forces, but gave up its position and moved into the
narrow space between the mountain and the sea at
Issus. The issue of the battle turned on the flight
of the Persian king (333 B.C.). Alexander did not
follow the Persian army but besieged Tyre and
reduced Palestine and Egypt to submission. In the
latter country he placated the natives and built a
city called after himself. When he next turned his
attention in the direction of Persia it was to meet
Darius III on the battlefield of Arbela. After his
victory Alexander seized upon the cities and treasures of his foe and then overtook the runaway king
who fell a victim to one of his own servants.

SUGGESTIONS FOR STUDY

1. Relations of Manda, Medes, Persians to the European races.
2. Rise of Lydian commerce.
3. Early coinage.
4. Reasons for the enmity between the Phenicians and the Greeks.
5. How did the defeats of the Greeks turn to moral gain?
6. Read of the achievements at Jerusalem in the days of Darius the Great. (Haggai and Zachariah.)
7. Remnants of Zoroastrianism (Parsees, etc.).

BOOK LIST

H. D. B., III, 310.
HERODOTUS: (Stories about Croesus, Cyrus, etc.)
GEORGE EBERS: Novels.
KING and THOMPSON: The Inscription of Darius the Great at Behistun. 1907.
A. V. W. JACKSON: Persia Past and Present.
A. V. W. JACKSON: Zoroaster.
GRUNDY: Great Persian War.
BURY: A History of Greece.
HIRSCHY: Artaxerxes III. Ochus.

CHAPTER X

Mediterranean Influences Mingle with Arabian.—
Besides the Egyptian, Babylonian, Assyrian, Hittite
and Persian factors in shaping the ancient oriental
world there were two more elements specially influential in making Palestine. These were the Desert and
the Sea, Arabia and the Mediterranean. From the
West as well as the East came peoples, customs and
trade which modified the blended life on the Syrian
shores. Cretan or Ægean would best describe this
western influence. Crete is a large island about the
size of Palestine. It is situated in the eastern end
of the Mediterranean about equally distant from its
European and Asiatic neighbors. It is the most
southern of the Ægean lands and was the leader of
the island civilization. It was the outpost of Europe's
communication with Egypt which was in touch with
the Cretans in the pyramid age. In stone, clay,
bronze, gold and ivory, in structural work and in
arts of design and writing the Cretans were apt
pupils and became eager members of the world of
commerce. Crete was an early Britain, depending
on its maritime power for a wide influence. The
early kings may have been mere vikings at first who
gradually developed a commerce by sea. This Cretan
sea-power was a predecessor and in some degree an
ancestor of the Phenician. The eastern Mediterranean was the first sphere of this activity and on
its three coasts the islanders probably established

trading posts and used methods which were followed by the better known Phenicians. The Cretans were united to Europe by many ties and pushed eastward and southward to remote regions. Egypt was at times teacher and suzerain. Elaborate theories have been proposed which would link the trade, the art and the myths of the Ægean and the South Arabian civilizations. Claims have been made in both directions, Mr. Evans, for example, claiming that the Ægean was the stimulator of the South Arabian, while certain continental scholars undertook to show that at a later time South Arabia repaid the debt, at least, by its influence upon the Greek islands. But a matter of special interest to us at this moment is that Palestine is believed to have provided the way-stations in the intercourse.

Crete and its Successors.—From Crete the influences of civilization awoke the slumbering powers of populations throughout the islands of the eastern Mediterranean and on the adjoining mainland. Tiryns, Mycenæ and Troy formed the continental rim of the Ægean world, culturally. The race which was responsible for these achievements is called the Mediterranean, from the sea whose shores it inhabited. After a while the highly civilized Ægeans were gradually displaced by forerunners of the Greeks who migrated from the Danubian regions about the time that the Kassites were displacing the Semites of Babylon. The change in the Ægean took a long time. The later phases of the Ægean life bring us to the Homeric Age. It helps the imagination to realize that the Homeric Life and Times in the Ægean world

was synchronous with the days of the earliest
Hebrews in South Syria. In North Syria there were
little Aramean states. Assyria, Babylonia and Egypt
were decadent after their most glorious age. The
Amarna letters were already lost in the débris of
Ikhnaton's forsaken capital. The strong priests of
the Twenty-first Dynasty had succeeded the weakest
of the twelve Ramses and Libyans were forging to
the front in Egyptian politics. While the great Semitic powers and Egypt were falling into decay those
of western Asia Minor, Greece, and the islands were
suffering similar change. The heaps of treasure, the
graves and other welcome evidence of the Trojans
and Myceneans were being covered to remain
unknown until the days of Schliemann and his successors. The delicately beautiful art revealed by the
excavations throughout the Ægean world would
require a large volume, even to exhibit it in outline.
It helps us to realize from what schools and masters
in taste the earliest Greeks drew their lessons.

The Ægean Migrations.—When the tribal folk of
Ægean lands overflowed the bounds they reached
Palestine as well as more northern Syria. And in
later times, especially upon the break-up of the
Ægeans, probably under the pressure of the forerunners of the Greeks, large numbers of the islanders
called Sea-Peoples were thrown upon the Syro-
Palestinian shores. When, nearly a thousand years
later, the Great Alexander carried Hellenism eastward to India and Persia, he was in the succession
of those Europeans, bearers of western culture to the
Asian lands. Europe and Asia met in Palestine at

several distinct historical periods in our human past. It is no longer possible to assign the precise credit for all of the intricate blend of cultural values of which Palestine has been the residuary legatee. It is interesting in the field of religion to remember that the divine descent of man was figured in the myths which centre in Crete and which make Zeus the parent of the kings of the island through the legendary Minos.

The Phenicians were the most famous of the earlier Syrian peoples. This was partly because of their wide commercial interests which brought them into touch with every nation and partly because they were well known to the literary people who have influenced our civilization the most, the Greeks. The Phenicians were described by the classical historians who passed on the tradition of their great importance as a maritime power. Indeed, before modern exploration uncovered the monuments of the really great oriental nations of antiquity it was often thought that the Phenicians were the inventors as well as the purveyors of the arts and institutions which arose in the East. The Greeks had a very inadequate notion of the great peoples and achievements which had preceded themselves whether in the Orient or on their own coasts and islands.

The Phenician coast of Syria is in the northwestern corner of the great rectangular land-mass whose southern portion we call Arabia. The Mediterranean shore of this great peninsula has made a fertile homeland for many Syrian peoples. The Phenicians settled on that part of the coast which lies between Mt.

Carmel and the angle of shore which Syria makes
with Asia Minor. The best harbors were along that
part of the coast and there were a few tiny islands
which encouraged seafaring. Fishing and boating
have probably always been carried on by the population on those shores. Snefru, who belonged to the
Fourth Dynasty of Egypt, 2900 b.c., carried on commerce with this region, and that fact would point
to ports on the Phenician coast which had probably
dated from prehistoric times. The products of the
Lebanon and farther east were passed on to the
islands and coasts of the Mediterranean in exchange
for European and Egyptian goods.

The hills near this coast supplied ship-timber at
an early period. It would be interesting to know
whether the Syrian trees were first built into seafaring boats by the natives or by peoples from over-
seas who came thither to show the Syrians what use
could be made of such valuable wood. It is now clear
that the Cretan sea-power was much earlier than the
Phenician. In what sense was the Phenician a descendant of the earlier Ægeans? Some would go so
far as to say that a considerable part of the mixed
Phenician population was a colonial offshoot of the
race that once inhabited Crete and, later, the other
islands as well as the coast-land of Asia Minor.
Such a theory would explain the skill of the Phenicians in seafaring. Instead of puzzling over the
anomaly of a Semitic people taking to the very rim
of the continent and cultivating the sea so ardently
as to seek harbor from the land rather than from
the water, going on daring explorations throughout

the Mediterranean, we should have this more natural
state of affairs that an essentially island-folk
migrated, through centuries, to the Syrian coasts
searching for homes, and when they had prospered
returned over the waters to their former seats in pur-
suit of commerce. There may have been Cretan
trading stations on the Syrian shores before the coast
towns arose there. Is it not more likely that home-
seeking tribes from the islands wandered to the coasts
of Asia Minor and along the Syrian front, even
threatening Egypt as we know, and that the descendants of these Europeans found the water-routes westward easier because of racial reminiscence and connections than that desert tribes came to the shore's
edge from the East, and after being civilized explored
the European sea? Civilized, well-to-do nations are
not so apt to explore as hungry peoples of less substance. Those who reason in this way think of the
ancestors of the Phenicians as kindred with those
Philistines and others called Sea-Peoples by the
Egyptians. Such tribal names are known for them
as Peleset, Thekel, Denyen, Sherden, Shekelesh,
Weshesh. (See page 68.) These were unable to break
into Egypt and were dispersed through Palestine and
Syria where representatives of the same races had
been arriving for several centuries.

The most famous trade-route of the early eastern
world was the one which ran east and west through
Phenicia. Before its establishment there may have
been an overland route through Asia Minor, synchronous perhaps with the Cretan sea-power. As
the Cretan traders were succeeded by the Phenicians

so were these latter by the Greeks, whose merchants captured the business of the Levant. The dispossessed Phenicians sought compensation for the lost trade by sailing their ships farther west. Thus the Tyrians built up a trade in the remoter Mediterranean and sought their fortunes beyond the Gates of Hercules.

There was a time when the merchant cities of the Phenicians extended along the Palestinian coast south of Mt. Carmel, but it was the northern stretch of coast which came to be known as Phenicia. This was because of the good harbors in the north. The monotonous southern coast was almost harborless. Cities in southern Palestine were likely to be inland and they arose because of the great caravan road between Egypt and the East through the fertile fields of the coastal plain. Agriculture and the caravan trade enriched these cities, but they never became as powerful as the more easily defended cities on the northern harbors. The southern cities were not as readily observed by the Greeks and did not receive from them the name Phenician, but they are known to history as Philistine. The Philistine peoples were not as different in race from the Phenician as has been supposed, but differed in development certainly. Phenicia and Philistia are both included in the old geographical term Canaan. Each contained its quota of Semitic elements, in different degree, no doubt. It was left for historical times to determine whether in the racial blendings of Canaan the European or the Asiatic would dominate. There were strong influences from both sides,

THE MOLE AT SIDON

FISHERMAN NEAR MODERN TYRE

desert and sea, and these influences were often
repeated throughout history, but the Asiatic has
triumphed so completely that only of late has it
been realized how early and how important was the
European contribution.

Palestine the Meeting-place of East and West.—In
conclusion, then, Canaan of the older and Syria of
later history held a union of Asiatics and Europeans. On the one hand, there was a people which
hugged the coastal edge of the continent, even founding island ports, as if the land were more foreign
to them than the water, given to seafaring on the
Mediterranean. Such habits would hardly seem cred-
ible of a purely desert folk or of civilized Semites.
It is far easier to explain from the European side.
Those tours of the sea were not explorations by
land-peoples but they were the return over well-
known paths of an island and coastal folk. On the
other hand, the fact that the Phenician became so
thoroughly orientalized shows the power of the language and culture of semitized Canaan. Naturally,
the European immigrants in Syria would not be
abreast of the civilization of their more favored kindred at home. These rougher Ægean tribesmen were
educated by the Canaanites. They were to be found
in north and south Canaan. Wherever there were
seaports they kept the European outlook and sea-
going habits of life. Where they went inland as in
the south they became landlords rather than sealords
and came to be known chiefly by one of the old tribal
names, Philistine, from which is derived the name
of their country Palestine.

Sidon was the leading city of Phenicia in the earlier period, so that Sidonian and Phenician were almost synonymous terms. The Sidonians were known to Homer and to the oldest traditions of the Hebrews. Their supremacy lasted until about 1200 B.C. when Tyre succeeded to first place. The other prominent towns were Acco, Achzib, Beirut, Gebal and Arvad. The rivalry between Sidon and Tyre increased after they had outdistanced the others. Prominent among the adverse circumstances which drove Sidon from first place was the success of the Greeks, who secured the trade of the Ægean countries. Tyre was a more versatile combatant than Sidon and was able to bend to circumstances, to devise new schemes for securing business and to take the lead over Sidon. The Greeks kept their hold on trade in the Levant while Tyre opened up a new sea-trade in the west Mediterranean countries.

The wealth of Sidon and Tyre must have been very great. Consequently the best and the worst of the civilizations of the age would be found in Phenician social and religious life. They were able to pay their way among the great powers of the day and secure in comparative peace the world-trade. But when the overbearing Assyrian and its successor the New-Babylonian empire wished to control the trade as well as the tribute, they dealt heavy blows at Tyre, which was shut up more than ever to the far westward course.

The harbors of Phenicia would seem poor for modern requirements but they were the best on the Syrian coast and they lay in an excellent position to serve the business needs of the world's commerce. As the greater Phenician cities grew powerful they controlled more of the hinterland but their true empire was seaward. They felt at home on the water and feared attack from the land more than from the sea, where their navy was dominant. Tyre was built first on a tiny island and held a strategic position in Phenicia.

The Phenicians were colonizers for trade. Wherever a mine or other natural producer or an opportunity for barter existed, they established their outposts. Traders are the least offensive of invaders because they go with minimum numbers and offer a maximum of profit. Besides serving their own business ends, the Phenicians became the purveyors of the instruments and advantages of civilization.

Tyre held its place until the days of Alexander of Macedon. Its kings, as Abibaal and Hiram, were kings of the Sidonians. Cyprus, the island of copper mines, was acquired and the familiar Phenician name of Kart-Chadast or New-Town (Carthage) was given to its important city. The island city of Tyre became one of the best equipped and most splendidly adorned capitals of the old world. The vices of despotism, palace intrigue, death dealing, played their ugly part in the dynastic history. One of the successful usurpers of the throne was Ithobal, a priest of the leading divinity Ashtoret. He was a capable ruler for twenty-two years. His daughter Jezebel, Ahab's queen, was the torment of Elijah and the prophetic party in Israel. One of the later kings of Tyre, Pygmalion, gave his sister Dido in marriage to a priest

of Ashtoret. This priest tried his hand at usurpation
but lost both his cause and his life. Dido and a party
of sympathizers fled by sea to the north coast of
Africa where they began another and more famous
Carthage.

Palestine, the southern part of Syria, between the
Anti-Lebanon mountains and the Egyptian border,
is frequently called to this day The Land of the
Philistines, or Palestine. In Arabic this is Balâd
Filistin, or Filistin. The same country and its bordering regions has been known in other times by
such names as Kharu, Martu, Khatti, etc. Lesser
parts of it have been called by the names of inhabitants — Israel, Judah, Gilead, Ammon, Moab,
Edom, etc.

Early mention of Palestine is made in the biography
of Uni an Egyptian officer under Pepy I, Sixth
Dynasty, about 2600 B.C., wherein it appears that an
expedition was undertaken against Palestine by sea
as far north as the mountains and that land-forays
were encouraged against the sand-dwellers.

Prehistoric Palestine was once occupied by a
non-Semitic race with which the Arabian immigrants
blended. The mingled stock was firmly established
in the land and was able to assimilate a succession
of racial elements much as the native Egyptian and
Babylonian populations did in their countries. In
such lands there results a clearly distinguishable type
which is fairly well preserved though frequently
augmented. Philistines, Hebrews, Greeks and Crusaders have since joined with the stock of Palestine.
The presumption in any country is that the old-time

customs will assimilate the newcomer. Languages change, official religions shift, but folk-customs are more likely to persist. The difficulty with an innovating culture is that it may not be able to preserve its identity long enough to overcome the inertia of its predecessors. Should it, however, be strong enough to accomplish that result it would certainly supplant its forerunner. Usually a compromise results with the balance in favor of the older culture. Nothing seems alien to Palestine. Ancient civilizations met there in perplexing blend. The culture of the eastern Mediterranean met that of Babylonia and the Hittite crossed the Egyptian. Palestine was the great mixing-bowl of elements from the four quarters of the ancient world. Its seaward coast as well as the desert rim was important. It was as far as the sea-rovers could go without taking to land routes and as far as desert nomads could go without taking to the water. There must always be excellent reasons for believing that either change in an ancient habit has taken place.

The pre-Semitic peoples, who belonged to a neolithic culture and who disposed of their dead by burning, lived in Palestine five thousand years ago. Historical interest begins with the Semitic occupation of the country. This came in successive waves of different peoples who belonged to the Arabian stock.

The great Amorite conquest of Asian lands in the middle of the third millennium B.C. was the second at least of those major Semitic influences to reach the fertile borders of Arabia and was followed many centuries later by the Aramean migrations. We know that an earlier incursion than the Amorite had given Semitic rulers to ancient Akkad. Whenever such forces overran Babylonia we might expect to find clans of the same virile stock overflowing Palestine. When the pressure of these uneasy marauders met with weak resistance they made definite conquest of the country, after which they were likely to be assimilated to its life. The same invaders were frequently a menace to Egyptians, who referred to the intruders under names no more tell-tale of origin than our term barbarian would be. It would be of great value to the student of civilization to be able to resolve the mixed populations of early Palestine, to give to each element its proper credit for the items of culture. Many an archæological and historical problem may be traced up to the time of its entrance into Palestine-Syria, and what appear to be phases of the same problem are seen to issue later from the same country. The solution that would connect the two phases of the problem seems to belong to Palestine, but for us there is a blind spot which keeps us from seeing the actual development. Proofs are seldom available though the plausibilities are very seductive. An illustration of these problems is that of the origin of the alphabet. It is an interesting debate as to whether the Cretans or the Egyptians are chiefly responsible for origins of the alphabet, but it is pretty clear that somewhere in Palestine-Phenicia the actual alphabet was used and passed on to the Greeks.

We reach fairly solid ground to walk on in our search when we deal with the second Semitic con-

quest. This was the one by the Amorites to which
branch the great Hammurabi belonged. This king
of Babylon was also king of Martu, *i.e.*, the Syrian
coastal country, and it seems pretty clear that a people kindred with his stock lived in Syria. The early
Hebrew tradition of Palestine preserves names much
like those which we meet in the Babylonian and call
West-Semitic.

The Hyksos must have affected Palestine considerably. On being driven out of Egypt they retired
into Palestine where they retained power for a longer
period than their Egyptian sojourn. The Hittite
and Mitannian peoples traversed the country and left
racial remainders in its population. The Hittites
conquered Babylon during the Eighteenth Century
and probably overran Syria and Palestine near the
same time.

The earliest Egyptian raids upon the coasts to the
north of them were merely retaliatory or to secure
valuable products of the country. Pepy had undertaken to punish annoying Bedawin and probably
found it expedient to strike terror to their kin in
Syria and Palestine. The chief gain for us is the
knowledge that confirms the statements made above
that Semitic people were living in Palestine at that
early time. The Egyptians called the land Kharu
or possibly Rutenu. Among the place-names of
the land found on Egyptian monuments are Carmel,
Megiddo, Taanach, Joppa, Aphek, Gezer, Edrei,
Ashtoreth-Karnaim, Jacob-el, and Joseph-el. The
real intimacy between Egypt and Syria was a result
of the Hyksos wars. The Hyksos relinquished the

country to two great successors, the Hittites of the north and the Egyptians, who were thoroughly aroused in a great patriotic movement that expelled the Hyksos and developed Egypt's empire in Asia. From Ahmose I (1580) to Amenhotep III (1411) Palestine was a dependency of Egypt and parts of the country still looked to Amenhotep IV as lawful suzerain. In the Fourteenth Century, however, the Hittites were the dominant influence in northern Syria and were influential farther south, though affairs at that time in Palestine tended to chaos. (See page 57.)

Palestine's Position in the Early World was Central.—One need go no farther in history to realize what has continued to be true of Palestine that its masters were many and its outlook cosmopolitan. It is the littlest of continental lands. National experiments are seldom made on such tiny plots unless they are islands or peninsulas. Within this little country several nations have lived as neighbors. What it lacks in acreage the country makes up in strategic position between the great countries of the world. The land itself, containing from six to ten thousand square miles of residual limestone, is most diverse in quality and the population quite as varied. There is considerable desert, much wilderness, highland ranges,mellow plains and the deep cleft of the Jordan valley. In the earliest times from which we can secure pictures of its life we have an impression of a country divided, in the most fertile regions, into cultivated tracts. The agricultural lands were dominated by the guardian walls of villages and cities. Between the richer tracts were ranges of wilderness which were given over to flocks. Raids by wild tribesmen were the constant fear of the border-towns. If any power were strong enough to repress the raiders the cultivated regions increased in size and importance. The more progressive rulers looked hopefully to Egypt for its powerful aid in repressing the nomads within their Arabian bounds. When Egypt was strong these rulers paid tribute and hoped in exchange to use the name of the pharaoh to local advantage.

Life in Different Parts of Palestine.—In those days the cities in the coastal plain could boast of considerable advancement in the arts of civilization. The population drew upon the riches of the fertile lands and the commerce of the passing caravans. The opulent citizens became familiar with the best that the most progressive citizens of that day could teach. (See page 55.) More remote Palestine of the interior, on the other hand, was in a stage of comparative barbarism, sometimes of desert conditions feebly harnessed on the frontier to agricultural pursuits. The population in the walled towns was a mixed one. The market-place and tribunal was just inside the gate on an open piece of ground. Elders, or heads of leading families, would "sit in the gate" and watch over their respective interests. Their chief might be called a king. When these cities were well managed wealth tended to gravitate toward them. They were the natural toll-depots on the lines of the great caravans. The exchange of goods stimulated manufactures. Around the cities daughter

villages sometimes came into existence, while around
the villages were orchards of figs and olives, vineyards and the wheat and barley fields. The uniting
bond of these many similarly placed centres of civilization was not necessarily race. It was language
and the superimposed culture of those greater peoples
who from age to age dominated their foreign connections and took tribute of their wealth. No national
mood ever held all Palestine together for a long time.
The land was not placed advantageously for a great
national development. In the first place, it was middle ground in the ancient world, and secondly, the
country is most diversified in its physical characteristics. It was admirably adapted to a secondary
or dependent civilization but not sufficient for its
own complete nurture or defense. These are reasons
for the fact that there has been less of that national
consciousness which so often leaves its expression in
large enduring monuments and lengthy inscriptions.
The little states of Palestine played an important
but not a large part in Asiatic and African politics.
They arose in the lulls of the activity of such great
nations as Egypt, Babylonia and Assyria, in comparison with whom they left few inscribed records. That
is why we are so dependent on the incidental notices
provided by the Egyptian and Assyrian monuments
and derive so little aid from Palestine for the early
periods. Systematic excavations have been undertaken in Palestine in recent decades. The significance of the remains has not always been accurately
gauged, but some light has been shed on the life of
earliest Canaan.

The Egyptian Control in the Thirteenth Century.—Such a city as Gezer or Taanach furnishes a panorama of the civilizations that passed over the country of which these were typical towns. Most of the articles found are mute but they point, sometimes unmistakably, to the actual course of ideals, cultures and events, especially when aided by hints in the inscriptions and traditions of other countries. The humble fragments of clay pottery have been most useful in indicating the successive dates of layers of débris and therefore of the large objects and buildings caught in them. As every period of time made its own characteristic styles of dishes, jars, and other earthenware vessels and vast quantities of such were left behind, usually in fragments, pottery affords the surest criterion for judging the chronology of the mound-layers in a Palestinian heap of ruins.

In the time of Ramses II Palestine was better organized and more closely related to Egypt than in any previous age. This state of affairs continued during the reign of Merneptah, his son, who carried on an Asiatic campaign and left a song of victory in which he mentions several places in Palestine, Askalon, Gezer and the name Israel, evidently for a people in Palestine whom he punished severely. (See page 66.) There was great disorganization in Egypt after the reign of Merneptah. Pretenders and officials vied in their endeavors to seize the throne. A viceroy in Nubia Sety II reigned a short time. One of the pretenders was a Syrian officer who gained supreme control for awhile. It has been customary to date the main Exodus of the Hebrew clans from the Delta into southern Palestine during this last quarter of the Thirteenth Century B.C. (See page 67.)

There was a stronger government in Egypt beginning with the Twentieth Dynasty. Domestic troubles were settled and a firmer policy followed in Syrian affairs. This was just in time to head off another invasion of the Sea Peoples who were moving down again from the northern coasts of the Mediterranean, abetted perhaps by Egypt's Libyan enemies. They swarmed southward toward the Delta. Ramses III met them in the north by land and sea. The power of the invaders was broken and their scattered remnants were flung about the land. These defeated raiders were also home-seekers and where they were not exterminated they must have been assimilated to the native population of Syria and Palestine. They were racially akin to the forbears of the Philistines, the Thekel and Peleset tribes.

The Kindred of the Philistines.—Although the Sea Peoples were checked for the time by Ramses they continued to enter Syria, where they disturbed the Amorite and Hittite peoples. The Hebrew tribes encountered the remaining groups of them in Palestine. By 1115 the Thekel folk were established as an independent kingdom at Dor, but probably they merged in the Philistines whose cities extended from Beth Shean through the plain Esdraelon to the sea-plain, thence along the coast almost to Egypt. This confederation and line of Philistine cities separated the northern Israelites from the southern and effectually prevented any ordinary efforts of the two to join. The Philistine stock was replenished by new arrivals from over sea and their chances must have looked bright for preventing the Hebrew tribes from consolidating into a nation. The Europeans were probably fewer in number than their Hebrew competitors but they were able fighters and developed into a skilled ruling class. They were the most serious foes of Hebrew unity and their numbers were increased probably up to the days of David.

The Philistines.—By one of those curious twists or prejudices of history the word Philistine has sometimes meant uncivilized, whereas in their own day, in Canaan, they may have represented the best in culture, law and order. They distributed the products of art and industry. If they deserved any part of their ill-repute it would be for an excessive commercialism and conventionality. It is hard to form a true judgment of those matters now and difficult to see how in their position they could have escaped the development of such traits. It was an age of zestful barter. It was not a forward age ethically. The world was decadent but considerable traffic passed over the ancient caravan routes of Philistia. These vigorous newcomers settled on the lines of a rich business and were educated by their opportunities. It was perhaps five hundred years too early to expect a more spiritual conception of life in just those circumstances. But the inscriptions of their kindred are still unread, so that we are unable to appraise the resources on which they might draw. Our chief information concerning them is found in the religious literature and the popular stories of their foes. The rugged Semitic tribesmen doubtless absorbed ideas from the Philistines as well as from other dwellers in Canaan. Upon the Hebrews, at any rate, the Philistines left their indelible impression. The conflicts of the hero Samson with the Philistines are recounted in delightful stories, just such as the unlearned might tell gleefully concerning the failures of the educated.

Whoever the Philistines were, mixed or pure, they became, to all intents, a people of Canaan and were assimilated to the stock of the land. They yielded in time to the traditions of the people among whom they lived and succumbed to that fate from which the Israelite leaders sought to save their people. Perhaps this easier and speedier assimilation to Canaanite culture accounts for the earlier civilization of the Philistines as compared with the Hebrews. The fact of settlement in the more fertile lowlands would in itself be enough to mature the Philistines earlier. But we incline to think that the Philistines had the advantage of time as well, in spite of the common opinion that the two peoples settled in Palestine about the same period. The centuries generally allotted to the Philistine and Hebrew settlements, 1200 to 1000, was a time when the problems of the great nations prevented them from interfering with these two groups who were becoming more conscious of each other and hence of themselves. Philistines and Hebrews suffered fates similar to those of other elements in the ancient Canaanite blend, but with this chief difference, that they were destined by long

persistence to make more definite contribution to and
modification of what they found. They stand as the
most eminent protagonists of West and East. It
was the Philistine who lost the battle for Europe and
the Hebrew who won it for Asia. But there never
was a battle of ideas wholly lost or won. As to language, there was one common tongue with dialectical
variations for the Phenicians and other Canaanites,
including the Hebrews and the east-Jordan peoples of
Ammon, Moab and Edom. There is good reason to
believe that the Philistines came to use practically
the same language.

The Conflict of the Two Races.—The memory of the
Philistine struggle was a strong influence with the
writers of the historical records. Genesis xxvi, 1,
brings Isaac and the Philistines together. Judges
iii, 31, makes Shamgar one of their opponents,
although Judges v knows nothing of them. By com-
paring Judges i, 17 *ff.*; iii, 3, and Joshua xiii, 3, we
may gather that the Hebrew invasion did not in the
early period affect the coastal plain nor arouse the
retaliation of its population.

The stories of Samson, Samuel, and Saul tell us
of the preliminary struggles between the lords of the
land and the Hebrew tribes who were growingly
conscious of their power and common interests. The
tribes sought alliances with each other so as to win
a foothold in Ephraim and Benjamin. The tardy
inclusion of Judah in the united Hebrew folk brought
about a national status that gave the Philistines much
concern. According to the books of Samuel the
Philistines offered the most serious opposition to

the establishment of the Hebrew people as a nation
in Palestine.

The relations of Saul, David and the Philistines
are at first sight confusing. It would seem that the
Philistines were hostile to the Hebrews only as the
growing solidarity of the latter threatened to change
fairly manageable nomads into a dangerous, because
united, foe to civilization. Even then such Hebrew
bands as did not join readily under Saul's standard
were on the old easy terms with neighboring Philistines as we see in the stories of David and Achish
of Gath. We must not exaggerate the duplicity of
David. As the story was told later by partisans of
the national ideal, David, about to become ruler of
the Hebrews, was made to appear consistently loyal
to Saul and his house and treacherous in dealing
with any foes of the realm.

David and his followers were the irreconcilables,
the competitors whom Saul's house jealously exiled.
When David rose to mastery over the heritage of Saul
he came, logically, into the same hostile relations
with the Philistines as those sustained by his predecessors. Such personalities as Saul and David
opened the new era of nationality and the Philistines
were unable to hold in check the flowering of Hebrew
development already due. More and more the term
Philistine became hazy as a racial term and more
common as a territorial one until Philistia supplants
it in usage. Probably by the time of the great
prophets the race of the Philistines was in no way
distinguished from other Canaanites, and rulers in
the former Philistine cities might be of any race.

Thus Philistia was an example of what the prophets sought to save Israel from, not realizing perhaps how pointed an illustration of their spiritual wisdom there was in the lowlands.

SUGGESTIONS FOR STUDY

1. Principal islands of the Ægean.
2. The legends told of Crete by the Greeks.
3. Early trade of Crete with Egypt and Palestine.
4. The story of Wenamon.
5. Where were the foreign colonies of Phenicia?
6. What are the leading theories of the origin of the alphabet?
7. Type of life in desert Arabia.

BOOK LIST

H. R. HALL: Oldest Civilization of Greece.

MOSSO: Dawn of Mediterranean Civilization.

E. HALL: The Decorative Art of Crete in the Bronze Age. Philadelphia, 1907.

NICHOLSON: Literary History of the Arabs.

HOGARTH: The Penetration of Arabia.

DOUGHTY: Travels in Arabia Deserta.

BLISS: Tell el-Hesy.

MASPERO: Popular Stories of Egypt.

DAHL: History of Dor.

MACALISTER: History of Philistines.

MACALISTER: Civilization of Palestine.

MACALISTER: Excavations at Gezer. (Palestine Exploration Fund.)

EVANS: Scripta Minoa.

Columbia University Series of Monographs on the Cities of Syria and Palestine, Gaza, Sidon, etc.

CHAPTER XI

Hebrews or Israelites.—This people is said to have been composed of many tribes. One count makes the number twelve. There may have been many more. Some of their representatives were in the land in sufficient force to be recognized among the conquered of Merneptah. They had probably been there a considerable time. Others of them, the family of Jacob, were indelibly impressed with the memory of odious bondage in the Delta or its neighborhood. Narratives of partial applicability were made to do for the whole people, much as Plymouth Rock becomes an American tradition. Kindred families were edging in from the desert. Some had more success than others. Probably as desert tribes came into Canaan they repeated much history even as they anticipated much in their assimilation to a resident population. Wherever possible the covetous, roaming tribesmen seized the treasures of the wealthier villagers. This but repeated the process by which the villagers themselves had passed from the life of the desert to settled abodes. Where a tribe was not able to carry things with a high hand it nevertheless pressed in with as much insistence as conditions allowed. For nomadic peoples are fluid and can approach more insinuatingly than any other kind. About the same time came the crystallization of Philistine power in the cities of Western Palestine. There had been border warfare between Philistines and the rough tribesmen. Thoroughly successful in the lowlands, the Philistines gave their attention to the semi-nomads of the highlands. But by this very menace the northern tribes came more closely together. They needed a dictator and could endure to serve under one in times of such danger. But when they made premature attempts at kingship, as we read in the stories of Gideon and Abimelech, they failed. With Saul the issue was squarely joined with the Philistines and there was somewhat more of political development among the tribes. In the south those who followed David had more cordial relations with the Philistines. With the immense popularity and success of David the seemingly impossible was accomplished and a kingdom formed of the North and the South after the failure of Saul's family. David accomplished much when he conquered his own capital. The logic of his position compelled hostility to the Philistines, a new policy for him and a bad one for them but the open way to nationality. The full political and social results of the monarchy came with the reign of Solomon. After him the division of the kingdom into Israel and Judah revealed the normal duality. The north seemed supreme. The south, however, survived the Assyrian wars. With the renaissance of the north came Samaritanism. In the south a perfected ecclesiastical state became the matrix of Judaism, which as a religious system may have been a wellnigh simultaneous phenomenon in Palestine and in Babylonia.

The persistent tradition of the Hebrews was that their fathers had come into a heritage of cities which they did not build and of vineyards and orchards which they did not plant. And there are plenty of

indications that they likewise entered into a civilization with its methods ready prepared for them. They
were assimilated to much of the Canaanitish life that
was best and to some that was bad. That is to say,
they were civilized in Canaan. Nomads from the
desert would bring neither laws nor institutions suitable for settled agricultural and commercial life.
The conquerors must submit to be taught if they
would maintain the prize of civilization. Israel was
not submerged. It inspired a decadent civilization
which it inherited. A complete experience of civilized life, the result of Egyptian, Babylonian, Hittite
and Cretan influences, had been wrought out in Palestine which was one of the most brightly illuminated
spheres of ancient culture. Into this hard-earned
heritage feebly held by the other Canaanites and but
temporarily by the conquering Philistines more
favored Israel came. Those parts of the nation
closest to the centres of culture matured more rapidly. But there was always the reserve of a vigorous
country folk and their desert traditions upon which
to draw. Bethel and Samaria might be softened
with indulgence but Tekoa and its sheep-pastures
could furnish an Amos. The faith of Israel did more
for it than its armies, even as the faith of Isaiah was
the main defence of Jerusalem.

Let us attempt to sketch the history of the
Hebrews in their occupation of Palestine, in outline
at least, by the following sixteen points:

(1) **Familiarity with the Land of Palestine.**—Certain
families or tribes of Israelites or their kindred are
known to have been in or near the land since the mid-

dle of the Second Millennium. These tribes and the East Jordan peoples were in close relationship. Marches, raids and campings of certain of these folk into the West Jordan country, especially in lax times, would almost certainly take place.

(2) **Weakening and withdrawal of both Hittites and Egyptians** followed by the occupation of the best of the land by the Semitic Canaanites and the Ægean folk. The less well occupied and less civilized interior, especially the mountains, would be more easily ranged over by nomads.

(3) **Migration into the land of families of nomads** here and there along the border. These found hindrances at certain points but opportunity to enter at other places. Certain villages would be encircled or even partly occupied. Even the nomad may accept gradually the methods of agriculture and a settled life. A small part of the wanderers near cultivated land tend to do this at all times when the government is tolerant or weak. The frontier bedawin move to different parts of Palestine with the seasons and return to the same regions at the customary time each year.

(4) **Occasional spirited grouping of allied tribes** against a dreaded foe, as Sisera. Local leaders arose to meet local needs. Certain of these "judges" may have been contemporaneous with each other.

(5) **New arrivals from the desert of more virile** members of the same racial stock. Perhaps certain clans of Arameans from Aram-Naharaim came in at this stage. War with villagers and with semi-nomads.

(6) **Border Warfare with the Philistines. Samson.—**

The Philistines when thoroughly successful in the lowlands turned their attention to the highlands and the East. The presence of opposing armies of well-equipped Philistines helped to educate the Israelites, who saw the need of massing their numbers under permanent leaders.

(7) **Premature Attempts at Kingly Rule.**—Gideon and Abimelech led in such attempts.

(8) **Ideal combination of pre-kingly functions of leadership in Samuel;** military, priestly and prophetic. The literary picture afforded by the Samuel stories symbolizes the social development of Israel.

(9) **Saul the First True King.**—The issue was squarely joined with the Philistines and Israel learned new political lessons. This applied to the middle and north country especially.

(10) **The disaffected South and David,** during the lifetime of Saul and afterward. Hebron. The union of the tribes under David; the new capital at Jerusalem; the new shrine.

(11) **The Ripening of the Monarchy.**—Solomon's reign was the culmination of all the tendencies to unity and strength, while the temple and its worship bade fair to hallow the national bonds.

(12) **Division of the monarchy into the two kingdoms,** Israel (Ephraim) in the northern part of Palestine, Judah in the south.

(13) **The development of the stronger northern kingdom of Israel** until its disaster at the hands of the Assyrians.

(14) **The development of the southern kingdom of Judah** until the Babylonian conquest.

(15) The renaissance of the North: Samaritanism.

(16) The perfected ecclesiastical state in the South: Judaism.

After this rapid survey let us take up certain of these points in detail, indicating progress by the numerals assigned to the separate points.

(1) Primitive Times.—The Hebrew historians of the early monarchy attributed the rise of their racial family to one Abram or Abraham. This name might be met at any time wherever the western Semites lived from Babylonia to the Mediterranean coast. The great Abram of the Bible moved along the Euphrates northward from the seats of Semitic culture in Babylonia and Mesopotamia and trekked by the famous routes of Palestine to the south, where his fame was firmly joined to Hebron. We are uncertain as to his date and must remember that more than one famous man may have borne the name. Too much effort has been expended upon the attempt to harmonize the fourteenth chapter of Genesis with the chapters which tell of the ancestors of the Hebrews.

In the names Habiri, Hebrew, Abram and Hebron a relationship is suggested by the persistent consonants *br*.

Not far from 2000 B.C. is the usual dating of an entertaining story which comes from Egypt. It is entitled "The Tale of Sinuhe" and tells how at the death of the pharaoh and while the succession to the throne was not yet completed the courtier Sinuhe fled the country, going into the land of the Bedawîn. There on the borders he met friendly tribes whose chieftains passed him on until he came to a fertile

country, presumably Palestine, where he settled
under the favor of a native prince whose daughter
he married. He described the country as rich in
figs, grapes, wine, honey, olive-oil, barley, wheat and
cattle. The hero lived the life of a hospitable shaykh
and was a successful captain in the wars of his new
country. The only grave danger in the whole happy
sojourn was the challenge of a powerful champion in
that region to mortal combat. However, our hero
treated him much as David did Goliath and became
more prosperous than ever after the exploit. The
tale continues to say that Sinuhe was eventually summoned to the Egyptian court where he found favor
and was able to close his days in his native land.
The story is rich in subjective detail and would repay
the student of moods, emotions and motives, but it
is interesting to us for its vivid picture of Palestine,
physically and socially, in primitive centuries. The
story belongs to the literature of entertainment but
seems to reflect an actual knowledge of conditions
in Palestine.*

(2) **The Clearing of the Way.**—We have seen how
in the ancient days two great peoples, Hittites and
Egyptians, sought across the whole length of Syria
to war with each other (page 63 *ff*.), until after what
was probably a drawn battle they came to terms in
the famous treaty 1272 between Hattusil and Ramses
shortly before the days of the Exodus. The messengers who bore this may have gone by land or sea,
as may their master a dozen years after, when the

---

* G. Maspero. Popular Stories of Ancient Egypt, New York. 1915.
(Putnams.)

Hittite monarch visited the Delta and bestowed his daughter in marriage on Ramses. Presumably the journeys were by land as the Hittites were no sailors.

Somewhere in Syria these delegations and royal doings passed over the international boundary agreed upon, but we do not know where to draw the line. It was doubtless some natural boundary such as has been suggested many times since between North and South Syria. Groups of Hittites would be met throughout Syria and Palestine. The tradition of them and their influence is persistent throughout the strands of the Old Testament. The successors of these two great nations north and south were two lesser but important peoples who approached each other more nearly from east and west across the breadth of the land. These were the Semitic elements among the Canaanites and the Island or Sea-Peoples from the Mediterranean, representatives of the Semitic East and the European West. They differed in intention from the greater Hittites and Egyptians in that they meant to make Palestine their permanent home. This fact made the lesser peoples more important for the life of Palestine, though settlers from both of the larger countries dwelt in the land.

(3) The continuing pressure of Semitic nomads upon Palestine maintained the supply of Asiatics in the country, whereas the time came when the European contingents practically ceased coming to the coast. The balance was soon strongly in favor of the desert arrivals. The nomads have always been able to hover near the borders of the land even when they have been forbidden by strong governments to enter. The

ancient Canaanites did not welcome them, for they were of marauding habits. But on the coast of Syria-Palestine the highly organized Phenicians and Philistines would permit only such landings as would seem profitable.

(4) A Sense of Unity in Peril.—It came about therefore that peoples kindred with the Hebrew tribes lodged in the less desirable parts of Palestine, where their hold was as precarious as the mood and means of the Canaanites chose.

Our earliest contemporary passage of Biblical literature is the fifth chapter of Judges and is invaluable for the fresh data it gives us. In it we read of Ephraim, Benjamin, Machir, Zebulon, Issachar, and Naphtali as clans which felt their relationship and responsibility seriously enough to unite in war with the Canaanites under Sisera. We read, moreover, of peoples whom the singer of the ode felt to be liable to such service in a common cause but who for reasons of their own did not come to the war. Such were the clans Reuben, Gilead, Dan, Asher and Meroz. Either they did not feel the tie that bound the others or else they did not feel that the peril concerned them. At any rate they are found two centuries later as members of the same Israelite nation under David. Certain other well-known Hebrew folk are not even mentioned as in the neighborhood.

The book of Judges is our best source for this age of settlement of Canaan which came about by the amalgamation of these related tribes. The fifth chapter shows us the inner and difficult workings of the process which a later writer, viewing the result

MISTS OF EARLY MORNING HANGING IN THE HILLS OF MIDDLE
PALESTINE

MOUNT TABOR, NEAR THE SOUTHERN BOUNDARY OF GALILEE

as an ideal accomplishment, describes as a thoroughgoing and speedy conquest. The result in either case is somewhat the same except for the historical imagination. When the process of Hebrew occupation and settlement had subdued the Canaanite and eliminated the Philistine it had educated the Israelites. Other cousinly nations, Ammonites, Moabites and Edomites, were left in the wake of the desert flow and, stranded east of Jordan and south of the Dead Sea, were not admitted into the organized kingdom.

(5) **Reinforcements from the East and South.**—The nomadic pressure which we have likened to the fluid movement of waves though coming from a dry sea, the desert, has continued to be the persistent historic experience of thousands of years. The nomad is always there on the border. When the control of Palestine is firm and friendly he stays on the border or near it, but should the government of Palestine weaken the nomad intrudes. At the time of the Hebrew invasion, which may be viewed as a process of centuries, the internal government of Palestine was growing weaker. The Hittite shrank away northward and the Egyptian neglected the land more and more. The Phenician cared little for the interior. The tracts of land which meant least to either Philistine or Canaanite were occupied by frontiersmen who learned in a humble way the advantages of agriculture as a means of eking out a desert living.

(6) **Education Through Opposition.** — The first chapter of Judges summarizes the process of conquest with a frank acknowledgment of the many dis-

appointments and setbacks which the ardent tribesmen experienced. Then the primitive stories in the
remaining chapters of Judges aside from the later
moralizing of the Deuteronomic school of editors
give us the particulars of the all but interminable
contests during which the Hebrews suffered much
discomfiture but had their triumphs whenever gifted
leaders arose in their midst. While we cannot at this
late date suggest a more severely chronological order
for the lives of the champions called judges, we shall
do well to hold to Judges v our most primitive document as the sheet anchor of our enquiry, follow it
with Judges i as the fairest summary of the occupation, and read the vivid anecdotes of the exploits
of the judges as the hero tales of those days. The
last five chapters of Judges and the early chapters
of I Samuel give very valuable social data. The
book of Joshua may be read most profitably after
the readings in Judges and early Samuel as reflecting
later pictures of a completer conquest and mingled
with administrative plans for a later Palestine.

(7) The reason why the Hebrew tribes did not have
a monarchical constitution earlier is suggested by the
stories of Gideon and Abimelech. Neither the state
of the country nor the mind of the people permitted
of such an advanced institution as a true kingdom.
The people were not civilized enough to tolerate the
restrictions upon their wilder freedom, yet they
were hard pressed by even fiercer nomads from the
east. A vivid picture of the frontier is given in
Judges vi, 11: "Gideon was beating out wheat in the
wine-press to hide it from the Midianites." Such

precarious agriculture as is there reflected when
raids are conducted at harvest-time suggests practical anarchy so far as the general government of the
land goes.

Gideon's father had an altar for Baal and an
Asherah or sacred post standing by it. When Gideon
destroys these he is in danger of death at the hands
of the neighbors. Gideon's father uses the rough
argument that if Baal doesn't like the treatment
received and is a god of any importance he will
take his own part. Gideon following the God revealed
to him at the wine-press faces the Midianites with a
carefully selected band of warriors. He has as
signal a victory with divine aid as that of Barak,
and similarly calls on the hill tribes to unite against
the foe but not until the foe is already in flight. But
the tribes-folk are very uncertain allies of Gideon.
His faithful band of three hundred are his main
dependence. When Gideon is assuredly victorious
and dominant "Then the men of Israel said unto
Gideon, 'Rule thou over us, both thou and thy son
and thy son's son also; for thou hast saved us out of
the hand of Midian'" (viii, 22). However, Gideon is
little better than a pagan and toys with idolatry
(viii, 27). One of the meanest of his sons, Abimelech,
essays to make capital out of Gideon's fame and fails
miserably. Another son, said to be the only one
who escaped the murderous Abimelech, has a brighter
fame than that of a king in that to him (Jotham) is
ascribed the beautiful parable in Judges ix, at once the
choicest prose and the daintiest piece of philosophy
in the whole book. Good and useful people are too

busy about their affairs and worthless folk too ready to assume rule over their fellows.

The next major figure was Jephthah, whose appointment to headship was by popular acclaim in an emergency. He was not of straight Hebrew lineage but compelled respect by his prowess. (Judges xi, 8–11.)

Jephthah's vow and the agony with which he carries out its consequences reflect the savagery and the superstition of the age. He has the same trouble with the tribesmen of Mount Ephraim that Gideon met. They are eager to fight in a sure cause where loot is the reward but are fickle allies in real trouble. Civil war followed and the taunt hurled out at the Gileadites by the Ephraimites was smothered in slaughter.

(8) Constructive Forces.—Beginning with the last of the Judges, Samuel, a transition figure of much importance, we are able to catch up the thread of political development rather more in sequence. The major part of the history in the first nine or ten books of the Bible has been saved for us by the energy of the prophetic disciples. The sources which they used are lost except as they included large portions from them. The Book of Jashar, The Book of the Wars of Jehovah, The Chronicles of the Kings of Judah, The Chronicles of the Kings of Israel and The Book of the Acts of Solomon are known to us only by the favor of the Biblical writers who quoted from them at length in the course of their religious and moral instruction.

(9) Seeking to Realize the Kingly Ideal.—In the

earliest story which we have of the choice of Saul
for king the enthusiasm for the goodly young leader
makes itself felt over the centuries.   There was
a man named Kish, a man of considerable substance,
who had a strapping son named Saul.   They lived in
the country not far from Jerusalem.   Farther to the
north was the district of Samuel, a much revered
good man with fame as a seer.   Saul was sent out
by his father in company with a household servant
to hunt for animals that had strayed.   It seems that
the servant had heard of Samuel and of his skill in
helping people in emergencies.   Saul hesitates to
ask advice of the man of God since they have no
present to offer as was customary in such cases.   But
the servant, always resourceful, produces a bit of
silver and the two set out to find Samuel.   They go
to the city where the seer dwelt and learn from maid-
ens who are near the well outside that a feast is on
for that day.   Feast and sacrifice are much the same
with them, but they await Samuel "for the people
will not eat until he come, because he doth bless the
sacrifice" (I Sam. ix, 13).   Jehovah had promised
Samuel that he would send on this very day a man
who should serve as prince of Israel in their struggles with the Philistines.   Saul met Samuel in the
gate, makes his errand known and receives special
honor from the seer at which the modest Saul mar-
vels.   Samuel continued his special favors to Saul,
instructs him, and in the morning anoints him in the
usual symbolic way with the vial of oil and the kiss.
Samuel gives Saul a list of signs which will follow
the young man on his way home.   These will certify

to the mystic potency in Saul which follows upon
Jehovah's choice of him and the anointing. First,
Saul will meet men who will tell him that the lost
animals are found and that Kish is anxious for his
son, the very things that had passed through Saul's
mind. Second, country people on their way to the
shrine at Bethel with sacrificial offerings will offer
some of them to Saul. Third, and most amazing,
a band of those primitive prophets of the times, similar to the modern dervishes, will not only meet Saul
but lead him into their own strange exercises. This
last event, so different from anything that anybody
had ever connected with the temperament and character of Saul, caused a proverbial saying to arise, "Is
Saul also among the prophets?" (I Sam. x, 11). Saul
is altogether a new man and ready for any emergency,
but his strong good sense and simplicity lead him
meanwhile to resume his home duties. The mettle
of the man is revealed when an emergency offers
as in the case of Nahash, the Ammonite (I Sam. xi).
Saul is the champion of the people and under the
drive of the divine fury delivers them. The people
are exultant because of their new leader and he
is made their king, all opposition being overwhelmed.
One may read in the remaining chapters of First
Samuel the career of the hero and his house. A
great change had come over the people since the
days of Gideon and Jotham. It is the change in the
people more than any difference in the heroes that
makes the kingship more feasible in Saul's age.

(10) David the Beloved King.—Even during the
lifetime of Saul, David, with an increasing band of

HILLSIDE NEAR THE MICHMASH GORGE IN PALESTINE. DISTANT (LEFT) AND NEAR (RIGHT) VIEWS OF A SMALL ARAB FORT DEFENDING THE EASTERN SIDE OF THE RAVINE

devoted followers, made himself a name in the
extreme south of Palestine and appears to have had
close relations with the Philistines. Gradually he
increased in power until the day of Saul's death,
after which he extended his authority northward until
he became king of all Israel. His prowess in war,
his qualities as a ruler and his versatility made him
the hero of all times. He was one of those heroes
whose magnetism stimulates the imagination and
quickens the affection of generations beyond his own.
By capturing as his own capital a city not previously
possessed by the tribes, David effected a fine stroke
of policy. His successes in the expansion and unification of the realm were not maintained, however,
beyond the time of his son Solomon. Our book of
Second Samuel in the Bible is devoted to David's
career.

(11) **The Age of Solomon** represented the climax
of the early monarchy. The king is a type of his
age and homeland. Indeed, the four figures Samuel,
Saul, David and Solomon are among the clearest
characters in literature. They reveal the unfolding
Hebrew folk. Solomon filled in the outline and expanded the plans of his great predecessors. Such a
ruler when furnished with ample means gives the
appearance of boundless versatility and elegance.
He was brilliant and friendly. He administered his
great estate in true oriental style. The state expressed the sovereign, a self-centred lover of the
material advantages of peace. Solomon's personality has been wreathed in a varying but perennial
legendary adornment. Wisdom, wealth, piety, volup-

tuousness, magic and might have all been credited to
him in supreme measure. The modern orientals
make him the hero of uncanny powers and gigantic
structures. The many tales tell of Solomon's perfect
mastery of occult forces, and any enormous ruin from
those of Romans at Baalbec to the vast reservoirs
south of Bethlehem are instinctively referred to
Solomon. The larger the structure the more surely
will his name be associated with it by the Syrian
peasants of to-day.

The friendship of Solomon with Hiram, king of
Tyre, made actual the natural fellowship of the two
leading Palestinian nations. The one controlled the
desert marches, the agricultural provinces and had
access to Elath on the Gulf of Akaba, an arm of the
Red Sea, and to Joppa on the Mediterranean. The
Phenicians were the greatest maritime nation of
Asia, controlled a rich supply of raw materials and
had some of the best artificers of the day.

The bargains between them enabled Hiram to
provision his people and Solomon to build the temple
at Jerusalem. The arrangement is one of the clearest
instances of political good sense from the ancient
world. Perhaps at no other time were Phenicia and
Palestine so well organized with reference to the
prosperity of each and the business interests of the
surrounding nations. A widespread culture would
result and as happy an age as the country was ever
to know until the age of the Maccabees.

(12) Tribal politics were at work to threaten the
unity of Solomon's realm even before his death. One
of the men who troubled the administration was

Jeroboam, the son of Nebat. He was compelled to flee and found asylum in Egypt. After the death of Solomon the opportunity came for the exile to return and head a revolt of the northern part of the Hebrew kingdom against the rule of the House of David. The impolitic scorn of Rehoboam, king at Jerusalem, was ill-advised and most unfortunate (I Kings xii). The larger and richer section of the kingdom set up for itself with Jeroboam as the new king. This secession of the North from the ruling dynasty was a revelation of the dual character of the Hebrew monarchy. The southern kingdom which remained loyal to the family of David had the advantage of a continuous ruling line while the northern kingdom suffered from usurpations. The southern kingdom had also the temple which Solomon built, but that shrine did not then have the prestige which came to it later. The religious leaders of Judah often reflected upon the defection of the northerners. It was considered by many as a great crime and the first king was referred to as "Jeroboam the son of Nebat who made Israel to sin."

When Jeroboam fled to Egypt and was given asylum, in Solomon's time, it was plain that the Egyptian government was not averse to his plans. Soon after Jeroboam's successful return to Israel, the Egyptians actually invaded Judah. In early times Palestine had been a dependency of Egypt, and probably the pharaoh was glad to prevent the growth of a strong united nation on his border. Egyptian politics offered a menace frequently which the prophets of Judah sought to remove. There was

often a pro-Egyptian group of citizens in Jerusalem
and it is difficult at times to distinguish such from a
strictly native or neutral party.

Judah waged war with Israel in the hope of
reuniting the kingdom under the Davidic House, but
to no avail, except to show all the more plainly how
inferior Judah was in military strength. Only when
Judah persuaded the king of Syria to attack Israel
could the latter power be overcome (I Kings xiv, 30;
xv, 6; xv, 16–22).

(13) **Israel the Northern Kingdom.**—For the while
Damascus succeeded Egypt as the dominating for-
eign influence upon Palestine. The friendship with
Phenicia was revived at times and even strengthened
by royal marriage. The strong dynasty of Omri in
Israel to which Ahab belonged was one of the ablest
and most widely known. The Assyrian referred to
Palestine as Omri-Land for over a century and
Mesha's inscription on the Moabite Stone (page 363,
Barton, Archæology and the Bible) tells of the prowess of Ahab's father. The prophetic party of Jehovah worshippers resented Ahab's foreign interests.
They feared corruption of the worship of Jehovah
and the old liberties, hence their relentless hostility
to the administration of Ahab and Jezebel.

As Israel was founded on military success its
kings were likely to suffer from violence at home if
they failed to win victories over the foes of the
country. Over and over again energetic military
leaders seized the opportunity afforded by a king's
unpopularity to supplant him. Omri himself was one
of those usurpers.

But the times were awaiting mightier movements than the little kingdoms of Syria and Palestine could set on foot. After one of those periods of exhaustion that came to Assyria occasionally and allowed the smaller peoples to play at politics, there ascended the Assyrian throne one of its greatest rulers, Ashurnazirpal. He advanced the boundaries of his country into new regions west and south until he reached the neighborhood of modern Beirut. He was indeed a "grande monarch" if also an atrocious despot. (See page 138.) The short reign of his vigorous father left Ashurnazirpal as a young man with large incentive to a policy of expansion. He carried through one of the most ruthless and successful series of cruel campaigns known to even Assyrian history. The historian Olmstead speaks of his "calculated frightfulness." One must remember the example of the fashion set for the world rulers by Ashurnazirpal in any attempt to estimate or appraise Omri and Ahab. They were thoroughly cognizant of the doings of the other nations. Omri felt within himself the stirrings of ability which has given to history such men as Hammurabi, David and Cyrus. With a small but compact material equipment at the start they join dauntless spirit and a despot's interpretation of rulership and opportunity.

The reigns of Omri and Ahab, father and son, were almost coterminous with the twenty-five-year rule of Ashurnazirpal III of Assyria. It was a period of large endeavors. It was Omri who made Samaria the new capital of Israel and he and his son adorned it with buildings. Remains of these buildings have

been cleared by the Harvard Expedition. Omri was
not so happy in his wars with Damascus and had to
come to terms with its king (I Kings xx, 34). Ahab
continued the era of prosperity and was even more
successful with Damascus though less so with Moab.
(Page 222.) The religious interpreters of Israel's
history found much fault with him on account of his
alliance with the Baal worship of Tyre which was
the religion of his Phenician wife Jezebel. A daughter of Ahab and Jezebel, Athaliah, married Jehoram,
king of Judah, and carried the foreign influence
into that kingdom. Circumstances had changed
since the friendship between Solomon and Hiram.
(Page 220.)

The alliance with the Phenician power at Tyre
must have aroused the enthusiasm of the progressive
court party even as it brought dismay into the hearts
of the old Israel group. But the patriots of the
Jehovah worshipping type had one of the greatest
prophets of the line as leader. Elijah's utter fear-
lessness was joined with a known probity, and when
in the name of his own God he stood across the king's
path to autocratic selfishness the conscience of the
people approved. The murder of Naboth in the
interest of expropriation of ancestral land was reve-
latory of the sinister side of the new politics. The
social injustice was joined in the popular mind with
the influence of Baal, the favored divinity of Jezebel.
The prophet of Jehovah stood for the old religion and
the old social freedom. In open conflict and in secret
conspiracy the contest between the partisans of the
two religions, which was really a social struggle,
continued. The dynasty of Omri was upset by a vio-

lence which reacted upon its opponent, the dynasty of Jehu.

Politicians of that day played a dangerous if thrilling game. No mercy was shown to the losers. The deeds in Israel may be compared to the treatment of the Aramean states and others who dared stand in the way of Ashurnazirpal. From the reek of Carmel to the holocaust in the house of Baal, even with the Deuteronomic retouching of the stories, we have a blood-lust in the service of reform. Above the mere historic value we have in these chapters of second Kings, closing with chapter 10, a social picture of an age in which prophetism has not risen to the ethical implications of Monotheism. These ethical implications were clearly seen by Amos and Hosea a century later.

SUGGESTIONS FOR STUDY

1. Why did not Israel make a success of kingship earlier?
2. Make a different outline of the settlement of Canaan.
3. Compare the story in Joshua with the account in Judges I.
4. Find parallels to Judges 5 in European poetry.
5. Chief reasons for the hostility between Israel and Judah.
6. Read a translation of the Moabite Stone. Barton, Archæology and the Bible, 363.

BOOK LIST

I and II SAMUEL.
MOORE: Commentary on Judges (Internat. Series).
PATON: The Early History of Syria and Palestine.
GEORGE ADAM SMITH: The Historical Geography of the Holy Land.
GEORGE ADAM SMITH: The History of Jerusalem.
PERITZ: Old Testament History.
MARTI: Religion of the Old Testament. (Crown Theological Series.)
CURTISS: Primitive Semitic Religion Today.
TRUMBULL: Kadesh Barnea.
FINN: Stirring Times.

15

CHAPTER XII

The ethical stirrings were present in the religious passion of the age but had not yet imbued the whole religious ideal. The obvious comment is that "They didn't know better." Perhaps this is true. The imagination of the world was dominated by imperial Assyria. Assyria conceived it necessary to strike terror into the hearts of foes and there is reason to believe that many were terrified into submission. A surprising number of princes and states were not thus overawed and usually paid the severest penalties. The states of Palestine were quite under the world-view of Assyria and in their lesser way are shown by the Scriptures to have followed similar methods. The Assyrian records name Ahab as one of the allies of Benhadad in the battle of Karkar, where the Israelites supplied 2000 chariots and 10,000 soldiers. This was a strong chariotry force. The westerners were able to hold off the Assyrians though the latter claim a victory. It may have been the year following that Ahab died fighting his one-time ally the Syrian. With his death the power of Israel was weakened. Moab was independent. Even Judah essayed to stand alone though without much success.

In 854 Shalmaneser III of Assyria began a series of campaigns in western Asia. He failed of his purpose at the battle of Karkar where Ahab's troops were present among the allies and had little better success in several other attempts against the Syrian states. The cost to the smaller western peoples was heavy. The misfortunes of the period are reflected in II Kings viii. Judah lost its vassal Edom and probably came somewhat under the domination of Israel. The house of Ahab had strengthened an already powerful influence over Judah by the marriage of Ahab's daughter Athaliah to Jehoram (Joram), king of Judah. If the states of Syria and Palestine could have made common cause consistently they might have continued to ward off Assyrian conquest. But internal wars and reprisals weakened the western coalition so that a century later Assyria was able to crown its western campaigns with success. Hazael was perhaps one of the most harmful politicians of the age. He had succeeded Benhadad, king of Damascus, after assassinating him and had then avenged himself on his southern allies because they had weakened in their resistance to Assyria. Moab secured its independence definitely and its king Mesha has left us a priceless record of his own review of the history of the time. The Mesha inscription on a stone slab was discovered in 1868 by a German missionary named Klein. After various perils and misfortunes this much coveted slab was mostly deciphered.*

Jehu, a military commander, put an end to the power of the house of Ahab in Israel by a successful revolt. In the same disturbance the nearly related and subject king of Judah was killed. But the strong-minded and imperious Athaliah preserved her hold in Judah. It was about 800 B.C. that Adad Nirari subdued Mari' of Damascus, thus relieving Israel of

---

* See Barton. Archæology and the Bible, p. 363 f.

its northern oppressor, Syria. Judah again came under the domination of Israel.

Home and Foreign Politics in the Eighth Century.— Thus as the Eighth Century opened the Palestinian states were securing more immunity from Syrian armies and were able to gain certain small successes of their own. During all this period the ancient Armenians (Urartu or Khaldia) were making matters increasingly difficult for Assyria. While the general condition of Judah was that of subserviency to Israel, the two long reigns of Uzziah of Judah (790 to 740 B.C.) and Jeroboam II of Israel (784 to 744) made for internal growth in both kingdoms. In Israel especially an era of prosperity was at hand. Temporary political eclipse came upon Assyria during the middle third of the century. Jeroboam was able to make the most of his opportunity and to bring his country to the very acme of outward splendor. But the reign though outwardly glorious was not based upon social justice and such mutual consideration as would beget a patriotism of all classes. This is clearly discernible in the prophecies of Amos.

The fortunes of war and peace involved both the northern and southern kingdoms during the Eighth Century until the fall of Samaria, after which Judah continued expanding for a century of growth, most of the time under Assyrian suzerainty. Doubtless one of the contributing reasons for the great interest felt in the history of the Biblical land of Palestine is that it is varied enough to illustrate in epitome the history of humanity. Leaving to one side in the consideration the great movements around, into and across Palestine before the days of the Exodus and omitting the mighty movements that have affected it since the days of Hadrian, we find in the twelve centuries of the Biblical History alone inner developments and outer contacts that go far toward explaining the experiences of the race. Among the more dramatic and crucial political events seven major conquests are recorded. These were launched by Syria, Assyria, Egypt, Babylonia, Persia, Macedonian Greece and Rome. Syria was the only one of these against which Palestine had any measure of military success. Judah ranks permanently with several of them as a contributor to the world's wealth of ideas. This was because Judah functioned according to her own genius. Several of her mightiest foes are known to history chiefly because they used their strength against the authors of the Biblical ideals. The detailed history of Judah herself is of wide interest because it reveals so frankly the development of those ideals through a course in typical humanity.

The rise of Hebrew prophecy was of greater significance to history than Assyrian-Palestinian politics. Doubtless the ancient Jews felt that the Sacred Law was their peculiar treasure but the world has appraised Prophecy even more highly. We discern the operation of the prophetic forces in the obscurity of the Hebrew religious development from the tenth to the eighth centuries. This gave us the beginnings of the prophetic literature of the Jahwistic and Elohistic types. While most of the workers in the field are anonymous to us, yet a few personal names rise to mention. Such are Samuel, Nathan, Gad, Ahijah,

Micaiah ben Imlah, and notably Elijah followed by the lesser personality of Elisha. There is an increasing amount of space devoted to these greater personalities in the Old Testament until we reach the Elijah-Elisha stories which form the equivalent of a book of the size of certain of the prophetic monographs. Those prophets of whom we have separate memoirs are often referred to as the literary prophets and have been particularly influential in the course of religious thought.

The Services of Amos.—Amos, the first of this distinguished line of literary prophets, was one of the greatest moral heroes of olden times. He appeared about 760–750 B.C. at the famous city and shrine of Bethel in the northern Hebrew kingdom of Israel. His own home was in the southern kingdom at Tekoa a little south from Bethlehem. There he was a sheepherder. The scanty biographical material is in the very first verse and in chapter 7, verses 14 and 15. Amos scorned the implication of any connection with the professional prophets. His call was a special one in a grave moral emergency. His message was startling in its directness, force, and lofty moral tone. It combined a practical grasp of history, politics and social conditions with a deep appreciation of the essence of true religion. At that early date he saw clearly the necessity of a close identification of practical morality with religion.

Amos' lofty monotheism led him to think of Jehovah as sovereign of the world. The same belief gave an oracular tone to his speeches which were brief and powerfully impressive. While we may not have a record of all his public utterances we can readily believe that we have a good portion of them and somewhat in the order in which he spoke. His words and manner would be preserved more accurately than the messages of a less forceful genius. His book therefore gives a satisfactory impression of the spirit of his teaching and is one of the clearest in the Bible. Its strikingly modern quality impresses us because of his keen sense of justice and the forceful logic of his argument. His great service was a moral one, his field was the social relations of men. He spared no sinner no matter how rich or how high his station. Men and women who sought luxury and not human weal he scored terribly. His word like an electric flash revealed the corruption in society and the false attitude towards the world and its God. The great wickedness that Amos charged against all the surrounding peoples, and against Israel most of all, was inhumanity. Israel was guilty of cruelty and oppression in trade relations and in the treatment of the victims of war, corruption in the courts and in the practices at the religious shrines. In a word, the privileged classes were wicked in their attitude toward their less fortunate fellow-citizens.

The language in which these arraignments were made was pure and vigorous. The sentence structure is concisely crisp and often epigrammatic. The paragraphs are clear and logical. The first great speech is a masterly arrangement of paragraphs in climactic order. The orator caught his hearers as in a rhetorical net.

The audience would be aware of the events to

which Amos referred and would enjoy the words of denunciation which the prophet poured upon foreigners. Syria with its capital at Damascus was particularly hateful because of the recent wars. In Jehoahaz's reign "the king of Syria oppressed them" (II Kings xiii, 4), "for the king of Syria destroyed them and made them like the dust in threshing" (vs. 7). With that sure point of contact with his hearers Amos wove his denunciations fairly around the land of Israel. The second people mentioned was the Philistine with their leading city Gaza at the remotest corner of Palestine from Damascus. Next Amos assailed Tyre on the northwest, then Edom at the far southeast and the remaining neighbors Ammon, Moab, Judah.

The audience would follow the denunciations of these foreign nations with keen interest which would be heightened when the prophet included his own country. The impressive repetition of the formula, "For three transgressions of ...... yea for four I will not turn away the punishment thereof; because they ....
But I will ...."
would arouse a fascinated curiosity as to the specifications of each new victim, its crimes and punishment. When at last the name of Israel was uttered the tenseness of the situation would be terrible. The magnetic effect of the skilful and powerful approach with the awesome dread induced would account for the fact that Amos was permitted to continue and expand his inditement. It would be difficult to imagine a more forceful presentation of the subject of the first two chapters.

The Social and Religious Condition of Israel in the Time of Amos.—In the Israel that Amos knew, social lines were drawn sharply. A class of rich was set off against a class of the very poor. The advantages of production fell to the rich. In criminal connivance with the rich were those who were the judges and the religious leaders. The religious leaders should have brought inspirational power into the social life. The judges should have been impartial arbiters of disputed rights but instead of that they were partisans of the wealthy oppressors and it was useless to appeal to them. These conditions arose more easily since Israel was an agricultural people. The natural tendency was for the richer people to acquire larger and larger holdings, to press the peasant farmers down in the social scale until there were but two classes, land-owners and serfs. Such a condition of things was fruitful of the most aggravated kind of selfishness. These wealthy nobles seem to have taken long steps into profligacy and to have withdrawn their abilities from any productive work in the country. The nobles had become drunken with the enjoyment of unfettered power. They were wanton and reckless in their sinning. Their fat valleys were at the same time their stay and their snare. The national development of wealth hastened like precocious fruit to untimely maturity. The mischief had its beginning in the division of the kingdom. One section of the country was preëminently agricultural. Judah was a rougher country and demanded more effort from its people. Israel, despite its hills, was chiefly a garden of softness and food. The two sections were as body and soul and ought never to have been separated.

The greatest peril of Israel lay in the fact that her nobles were not statesmen. They were not even patriots but mere voluptuaries. The peasantry ought to have been the well-handled feeders of the national prosperity but instead they were the victims of it. Thus the two classes of capitalists and laborers drifted apart in unpatriotic estrangement. Professor Mitchell thus summarizes the characteristic sins of the wealthy nobles: "unprincipled avarice, unfeeling oppression, unblushing immorality, unbridled voluptuousness." * The avarice was so unprincipled as to defeat real prosperity: the oppression so unfeeling as to dehumanize both sides: the immorality so unblushing as to be a trait. Old and young, man and son, yea even the women turned vile and as soulless as cattle. The voluptuousness was so unbridled as to become disease and madness.

The oriental is accustomed to despotism. It is eastern philosophy. But those familiar with despotic conditions have a lively sense of the quality of mercy. To be without mercy seems to be in defiance of heaven, itself the highest despotism, for in a despotism the chief despot is jealous of the exercise which inferiors make of their more limited power. To defy the great Sultan, God himself, was practical atheism, and, whatever else the Semite is, he is not naturally an atheist. Retributive justice seems very real and imminent to Semitic minds. There is among the common people in all the world a popular repulsion to wanton cruelty.

---

* Amos. An Essay in Exegesis, Boston, 1900, p. 85.

With such conditions as prevailed in Israel a people loses the knowledge of right and wrong. Justice and faith were mockeries to the poor, as they were but rhetorical figures to the rich, to whom material things were the realest facts of life. A blighting censorship was in effect by which the nazirites were forced to break vows and prophets were forbidden to prophesy. Thus the spiritual needs of the nation were not declared and Israel failed to interpret its own mission.

All this leads to another significant fact. There was no religious ideal to stimulate the people. They had sold their birthright to materialism. In effect they believed in a maudlin god who in his brute strength could be kept on their side by regular ritualistic feeding. At the altars was a subservient priesthood involved in the same mischievous dulness of spirit. The most serious place from which to drive out faith and the sense of religious appeal is the heart of the common people. The common people began to lose sight of any meaning in life. In his revolt from this condition of affairs Amos was in line with the belief among orientals already mentioned that the helpless have a champion in God, and they look for something terrible to happen to those who persecute relentlessly or sin against this popular conscience.

The Great Questions Growing Out of These Conditions.—The conditions in Israel made a national problem. In the minds of priests and princes there seemed to be no questions. That was the most fatal aspect of the national peril. There was no seership among them. Such was the dearth of spiritual initiative in Israel that Jehovah in sheer pity must take a

layman from the peasantry of the neighboring kingdom and use him in the emergency to prophesy to
the fatuous crowd. One might ask the question:
Would Assyria have been held back or defeated if
Israel had been good? Amos seems to assume that
something of the kind would be true. It is interesting
to compare in this connection Isaiah's faith that
Assyria could not cope successfully with Jerusalem
when it trusted in Jehovah and the Biblical account
of the confusion of the Assyrian host under the very
gaze of the beleaguered city.

Amos seems not to have been so much a restorer
or a healer as an announcer of certain woe. Sometimes it would seem as if others may profit but not
his hearers. His offers of repentance seem to have
been rhetorical echoes of a lost opportunity. And
yet it is possible that his severity was designed to
awaken a people for whom there was the possibility
of better things. Otherwise the office of prophet
would be simply declarative of God's judgments.

Amos came to declare God's attitude toward all
those who sinned against their fellowmen. God's
vengeance is aroused against sinners anywhere. No
people, therefore not the Hebrews, can truly claim
that they are favorites of the divine when they sin
and that they will be immune when God punishes.
Thus Amos opposed certain religious notions of that
day or tried to do so. Chief among these was the
popular idea that because the Hebrews had been so
greatly favored of God they would be specially
shielded when God dealt with the world. They looked
forward hopefully to God's judgment of the world

thinking that when the nations were punished Israel would profit by the event. But Amos told them that their elaborate worship, as at Bethel, was odious to God while they were immoral in their lives. Had they been peculiarly near to Jehovah? Then they would be held peculiarly responsible for their sins. Amos in common with the thinkers of his time held that physical evil was a punishment from God upon sinners. He couldn't point as certain later prophets did to present misfortunes as his proof but declared that God was their enemy and would certainly ruin their nation. He was interrupted in his course of denunciation and was bidden by the authorities to leave Bethel. The high priest, doubtless voicing the princely attitude, told Amos to go and speak his words in his own country.

Israel's Own Prophet.—Hosea who preached in Israel soon after the appearance of Amos is a very different personality from the southern prophet. He belonged in the North and he betrayed no such consciousness of the rich and privileged people as a class. Perhaps he belonged to one of the more favored families. He may have been a hearer and disciple of Amos. Hosea's early message seems much like the teaching of Amos in its stern ethical quality. But in contrast with the oracular aloofness of Amos and the grim logic of his analysis of Israel's failures and doom, Hosea's prophecies seem to relate him more sympathetically to the people whom he denounced. Two motives play their part in the prophet's message, the afflictive and the affectional. The doom of wicked Israel is clear in Hosea's words. Equally with Amos he heard God's demand for righteousness. Perfunctory fulfilment of outward requirements will not suffice. "I desire goodness and not sacrifice" (vi, 6). But Hosea went beyond Amos and made a distinctly Hosean addition to the growing religious ideas of the prophets. He taught the fatherliness of God and his persistent love.

Hosea introduced a dilemma into religious thinking which might be stated in such a problem as the following. If God surely punishes sin and if He is the persistently loving father of the people, what will be the result if the people persist in wrong doing? That God would destroy sinners, was Hosea's belief, but he held also to the hope that it was possible for the love of God to redeem and perhaps convert a disloyal and treacherous people to a repentant and faithful one. It is possible that Hosea, like many others, did not harmonize his positions at different times, his instincts on the one side and his logic on the other. But if Hosea believed that Jehovah's love would win did he fall into the easy popular error about God's chosen people which Amos refuted? In chapter six Hosea's attitude toward that error may be surmised. In the first three verses he impersonates, mockingly, the spineless religiosity of the folk and in the next few verses he speaks God's mind about the matter. There may be greater prophetic genius in Amos. There is more pastoral and persuasive power in Hosea. Hosea not only saw clearly what is right but felt truly the spiritual values in human life.

It is difficult to appraise Hosea's literary style. His book does not afford much opportunity for judg-

ing of his continuous discourse. The bulk of it depends no doubt on the precarious memories of those
who heard his teaching.

**Conditions at Home and Abroad in the Times of
Isaiah.**—A new era of Assyrian prosperity began in
745 B.C. with the enthroning of Tiglath Pileser IV.
In that year he warred against the Aramean tribes
along the Euphrates River and in the south in Babylonia. In the next year he invaded Armenia on the
north and Media on the east. This was the year in
which Jeroboam II of Israel died. Then followed the
two very short reigns of Zechariah and Shallum.
These kings lasted, the one only six months and the
other a single month (II Kings xv, 8 and 13). Menahem, who followed, reigned a little less than ten years.
Thus in less than a year Samaria saw four kings.
During those chaotic times Judah improved the
opportunity to slip the leash which bound it to Israel
(II Chronicles, xxvi, 2–15). Judah was still under the
reign of the long-lived Uzziah, who died a leper in
740 or 739. He was followed on the throne of Jerusalem by Jotham, who must have ruled about five years
as Ahaz was probably king by 735 B.C. The period
just reviewed may have covered the time of Hosea's
ministry in Israel.

By 740 Tiglath Pileser had concluded successfully
his campaigns against Armenia and Arpad. In 738
he defeated a Syrian coalition headed by Azriyau of
Ja'udi.* He records that as a result he received tribute, with submission, from a number of kings of western Asia, among whom his inscription names Mena-

---

* See Hall, A. H. N. E., p. 463 *f.* and Note 4.

hem of Israel. About 735 Menahem of Israel died
and Pekahiah followed him with a short reign of
little over a year. He was assassinated by one of
his officers, Pekah, who joined with the new king of
Damascus in a policy of resistance to Assyria. They
attacked Judah, doubtless because it would not join
them in resisting Assyria. This was near the close
of Jotham's short rule in Judah and the troublesome
situation was inherited by the next king of Judah,
Ahaz. Ahaz was in a quandary. It may have been
his distress of mind that led him to the horrible act
mentioned in II Kings xvi, 3. Such a deed had been
the turning point a century before in the misfortunes
of Moab (II Kings iii, 27). But Ahaz appealed to
Assyria instead of joining his tormentors, Israel and
Syria, against that country (II Kings xvi, 7 *ff*.).

This is a situation synchronous with the seventh
chapter of Isaiah and will explain that interview
between the prophet and the king. The response of
Tiglath Pileser of Assyria to Ahaz's appeal was a
war against Israel and Syria in which Israel suffered
severely. Its northern and eastern provinces were
captured and many prisoners sent into captivity.
The woes of those times for Israel are referred to
in the eighth and ninth chapters of Isaiah. All these
things took place in 734 or 733. Damascus was next
besieged and Israel was too weak to be of much help.
Pekah the king of Israel was killed by Hoshea, son
of Elah, who was willing at first to be a vassal of
Assyria. In 732 Damascus, the capital of Syria, fell.
Assyria was thus dominant throughout Syria and
Palestine. Ahaz made a visit to his overlord the king

HOUSETOPS OF JERUSALEM, WESTERN SIDE OF THE CITY

THE VALLEYS SOUTHEAST OF JERUSALEM.   CORNER OF CITY-WALL
(LEFT); MOUNT OF OLIVES AND VILLAGE OF SILOAM (RIGHT);
KING'S GARDENS (RIGHT FOREGROUND)

of Assyria at Damascus after that city had been taken. He was so apt a pupil of Assyria that he refashioned some of the temple furnishings according to patterns which he saw in Damascus (II Kings xvi, 10).

The acts of Ahaz's administration were very obnoxious to Isaiah, who with his followers must have been gratified when Hezekiah became king of Jerusalem since the prophetic party was much in favor with that king's administration. One of the most difficult reigns to date in this period is that of Hezekiah. It is generally conceded that Samaria was captured in 722–1 B.C., and II Kings xviii, 9 f., says that this was about Hezekiah's sixth year. But II Kings xviii, 13 f., says that Sennacherib's raid upon Hezekiah's domain (in 701) was in Hezekiah's fourteenth year. So we are in doubt as to what year between 727 and 715 saw the death of Ahaz and the accession of Hezekiah.

At any rate, the years of the known public service of Isaiah fall between 740–700 B.C. Tiglath Pileser died in 727 and was followed by Shalmaneser V. Hoshea, king of Israel, broke fealty to Assyria and joined a plot against her. Some say it was an Egyptian plan. This sealed the doom of Israel. Damascus no longer, as for a century, served as a bulwark of defence. The Assyrian border regions which included former Israelite territory now impinged upon Israel. No movement of the latter could escape Assyrian notice. Nothing could save Hoshea when once he opposed the greater force, except a rapid disintegration of Assyrian power such as did occasionally befall the nation. But just now there was a succession of strong rulers in Assyria. What could have led Hoshea to so fatal an attitude cannot be clearly discerned. Perhaps it was the imminent danger of dethronement by ungovernable elements. Assyria probably made egregious blunders in her violent treatment of subjugated peoples. All the fault cannot have been with her restless subjects. Her tributes were laid on heavily and she crushed relentlessly. So long as there was any spark of national life in a people Assyria's treatment fanned it until the life of the nation burned out in hopeless rebellion or else favoring circumstances gave the coveted opportunity to escape so hateful an oppressor. A suspension of payment was considered by Assyria as rebellion. Thus no overt act was really necessary to precipitate a revolution. The impoverished ruler, unable to command the resources which would gratify the rapacious creditor, was driven to ally himself with anybody who promised help, as the last desperate chance for existence. Assyria was an utter failure as a constructive administrator of provinces or vassals.

In 724 B.C. an Assyrian army came into Israel to annex the country and secure booty. Samaria provided a most satisfactory resistance for nearly three years. This showed fully as much resource as the resistance of Damascus, a decade before. Perhaps, if such resistance to Assyria were possible, it seemed well worth while to try for independence, for much might happen in two or three years to change the politics of western Asia. As the siege proceeded the desperation of the people of Samaria must have become great. They knew very well what

happened to cities taken by Assyrian armies after
such difficulties. For the sake of Assyrian prestige,
it was important that no uncertainty should mark
the outcome of the contest. Shalmaneser V died during the progress of the siege and Sargon, one of the
greatest of Assyrian rulers, succeeded. He soon
brought about the downfall of the beleaguered city
(721-2; *cf*. Olmstead's Sargon.)

King Hoshea of Samaria with 27,290 of his people
are recorded as having been carried away captive to
Harran, the river Chabur, and the highlands of
Media. It is not impossible that the descendants of
those colonized in Media may have had their revenge
in the subsequent overthrow of Nineveh near the end
of the following century.* McCurdy (H. P. & M. i,
400 *f*.) considers that Sargon dealt mildly with Israel
in taking so small a number captive and that he may
have sought to found a goodly sized province with
Samaria as its capital which should be in strategic
command of that important region; for Megiddo was
near, that battleground of western Asia, and trouble
was possible from the south and west. But if a docile
province was anticipated, Samaria did not immediately prove to be such. In two years it was joined
with the next northern provinces, Simirra and Damascus, in a conspiracy which included Hamath.
Ja'ubidi of Hamath was leader of the attempt which
was futile. Possibly the total number of Israelite captives includes those taken on this as well as on the
earlier occasion.

---

* The tragic fall of Samaria must have produced conflicting
emotions among the inhabitants of Judah.

(14–16) The Spirit and Achievements of Isaiah.—
With Isaiah we come to a great mountain peak in
the religious life of old Palestine. Rooted in a sensitive appreciation of the common life and its needs he
towered to sublime heights of thought and expression.
There is reason to believe that his speeches were preserved in a number of little collections or booklets
and that these were freely annotated by their owners
or students. A number of these little booklets must
have been brought together comparatively late with
two other collections of prophetic writings which
were composed a century and a half or even two centuries later than Isaiah's lifetime. Thus the whole
book as we now have it consists of three main sections: chapters 1 to 39; chapters 40 to 55; and chapters 56 to 66. The first section, only, belongs to the
age of Isaiah the prophet of the eighth century b.c.
As suggested above, there is reason to believe that
this first section, which is usually referred to as
I Isaiah, is a growth from smaller books. Perhaps
the endings of those books may be seen in chapters
12, 27, and 35. Chapters 36–39 are supplementary
and are taken from II Kings. Even within these
smaller sections of I Isaiah the order of the chapters
and passages is in a very disturbed state. The book
has always been valued more for the sublimity of its
ideas and the beauty of its poetical passages than for
the course of history which it might help us to trace.
It will be noticed in reading it how little connection
there is between certain chapters. Attention has
been called by Professor Gray to the probability that
no prophecy took Isaiah more than four or five min-

utes to utter. As these prophecies were in noble
poetic form the effect of their utterance upon an
audience must have been profound.

The best possible Biblical preparation for the
study of Isaiah the Prophet is a thorough acquaint-
ance with the work of Amos and Hosea, for Isaiah
is. their logical successor and the completer of their
thought. He owed much to the two preceding
prophets and with his superior genius produced the
prophetic classic of the age. Not least noteworthy
of his gifts was a remarkable versatility, for he was
possessed of unusual ability in politics, religion, letters, and oratory. With all of Amos' intellectual
power and stern logic he combined the Hosean emotional gift. He was a powerful preacher, a finished
rhetorician, a saint and a consummate statesman.
A man of the city, leader of a devoted party of disciples, he was well educated and influential. His
personal character was of the loftiest and his genius
sublime. Because the prophet dealt on terms of such
ease and equality with the king himself and with all
dignitaries it has been commonly thought that he was
of royal lineage. But an Isaiah would not need such
an aid to composure in the presence of kings. Even if
it were a fact royal relationship would not explain
his attitude sufficiently. His superiority was personal and moral. In all probability he had a considerable party of followers. One notable difference
between the work of Isaiah and that of Amos and
Hosea was that those earlier prophets were called to
short services in emergencies, Isaiah to much service
during a long career.

A faith that produced a marvellous equanimity in the presence of grave peril was the fruit of Isaiah's religious experience.   When the city of Jerusalem was invested with the all but irresistible Assyrian army, Isaiah calmly declared that the enemy would not enter the city.   Thus Amos' doctrine of the universal sovereignty of Jehovah in the affairs of the nations was put to the severest test by Isaiah's firm reliance upon it.   He consistently urged the leaders of state when in peril to trust in Jehovah and not to make matters worse by calling in the help of other nations.   Had his advice been heeded in this particular it is entirely possible that Jerusalem and its temple would have lived on a century or two longer or perhaps have never been so utterly ruined.   His policy was well expressed in the following sentences: "Take heed and be quiet," vii, 4, *cf.* vii, 9; "In returning and rest shall ye be saved, in quietness and in confidence shall be your strength," xxx, 15.

His spokesmanship for God was extra-national as a great prophet among the Hebrews always conceived it.   Jehovah is the majestic one terrifying the whole earth (ii, 20 *f.*).   Idols are nothing.   Assyria may think that it is doing wonders in war and conquest, but its strength is used by Jehovah's permission.   He will punish Assyria if need be after he has used her as an instrument against other recalcitrants.

There were times when Isaiah though heard was not heeded by the governors of the people, as in the times of Ahaz.   There were times, as particularly in the reign of Hezekiah, when his ideas guided the administration.   At all times his influence must have been great.

Chapter 6 of Isaiah illustrates a number of things: the sublime thought and imagination of the prophet, his poetic diction, the life-nature of his call to the service, the disheartening features of it, the divine compulsion which he felt, and the later reflective mood in which the chapter was composed, interpreting life's experiences in their afterglow by the aid of results.

Micah the prophet is remembered by the aid of one of the smallest of the books and, in parts, one of the clearest. The figure of the stalwart peasant who was as sure of the divine spirit within him as that he lived is very distinct. He was especially conscious of the gross iniquity of the privileged class. Against people who held high position he charged falsehood and oppression. He said that God cannot tolerate such doings nor can he, the prophet of that God, forbear to publish the facts. Such men as Micah must have made the rulers uneasy, for the people were not incapable of overturning a dynasty or revolting successfully against those in power. To dispose at once of such a fiery public speaker was not easy or politic, because the dread of the voice of Jehovah speaking through chosen men was upon all and sometimes such spokesmen were popular. One cannot but wonder what the personal relations of these strange men were and especially what was their bearing towards each other. Probably such men as we have studied, especially Amos and Micah, were not often led to speak and it may have appeared to them and their contemporaries that their speaking was so dependent on a special visitation of the divine suggestion

that they were somewhat different men in those
moments than in their usual daily course of life.

We may be sure that these men represented the
finest religious consciences of their day and were
esteemed for their high plane of moral living. We
may also understand that they, more clearly than
others, held and taught that God is one and that true
worshippers must worship him in truth.

Micah the prophet, in his origin, reminds us of his
fellow-countryman Amos. He was reared in the
country westward from Tekoa, among the foothills of
southwestern Judah. Like Amos, too, in his message,
his voice was raised against immorality, unbrotherli-
ness, and social wrongs. He was the peasant prophet
who had to contend with fierce opposition and whose
denunciation was fiery. His time falls about the middle period of Isaiah's ministry. Jer. xxvi, 18, preserves a tradition that Micah's prophecy was in the
reign of Hezekiah. It is interesting to find in this
passage a hundred years later than Micah a reference
to the latter and a direct quotation from him. These
four great leaders of thought and conscience, Amos,
Hosea, Isaiah and Micah, give the Eighth Century
a permanent place in human interest.

Turning now to political events in Judah one comes
to the time of King Hezekiah. His small kingdom
had been made tributary to Assyria by Ahaz's policy.
No buffer state stood between Judah's northern boundary and Assyrian territory. Isaiah's policy might,
perhaps, have left one there. In the beginning of
Hezekiah's reign Merodach Baladan, a Kaldean
prince of Bit Jakin on the Persian Gulf, sent agents

to propose a league with the Palestinian states against Assyria. Ekron, a Philistine city, refused to join and the king, Padi, was seized and sent to Jerusalem as a prisoner. However, Sennacherib appeared before the allies were ready and the league dissolved. Tyre was the only Phenician city to resist the Assyrian, with the result that Sidon was granted preferential treatment designed to give it the advantage over its rival. Askalon in the south was taken and battle joined at Altaku, where Sennacherib overcame Arabs and Egyptians. Ekron was taken and the Assyrian overran Hezekiah's territories. A large clay cylinder with an inscription which describes Sennacherib's campaigns says that he took forty-six of Judah's walled cities, captured many people and much booty in cattle and other property. Hezekiah was besieged in Jerusalem. Padi was given up and restored to his old place in Ekron. Ashdod and Gaza also shared in the conqueror's favor. (II Kings xviii and xix; Isa. xxxvi and xxxvii, and the Taylor Cylinder.)

Relations of Prophets and Kings.—There was harmony and good understanding between the prophetic and the royal parties in the days of Isaiah and Hezekiah, but in the reigns of Manasseh and Amon following there was a severe reaction. The prophetic religion with its more spiritual interpretation and worship of Jehovah was dishonored and a rigorous persecution stifled any protests. During the latter part of the period Egypt was weak and Assyria began to decline. As one consequence Judah's political opportunities increased and this must have seemed to some

like a justification of the course of religious affairs.
(See Jeremiah xliv, 15 *ff.*)

Manasseh may have followed Hezekiah about the
beginning of the new century. He was a contemporary of Esarhaddon and Ashurbanipal and may have
ruled but little territory outside the city of Jerusalem until the latter part of his reign when Assyria,
having wrecked Egypt, began to show the weakness
of exhaustion. Amon, the son of Manasseh, ruled a
short time and was murdered. The next king was a
boy, Josiah. With his accession the prophetic party
came back into favor. Probably the young king's
tutors were of the prophetic persuasion (II Chron.
xxxiv, 3). The principles of men like Zephaniah and
Jeremiah gained ground until a reform spirit gave
the entire country over to the prophetic side. The
public policy was entirely changed. There may have
been a movement to reclaim the old domain of Judah,
as Assyrian control weakened, and even to annex
some of the former Israelite lands. The great powers
of that day were menaced by the Scythian raids.
Somehow Jerusalem escaped any serious consequences, perhaps because of its isolation in the hills.
Indeed the sweep of these destructive forces through
Assyria's Palestinian provinces may have favored
Judah's expansion. A bright day of national prosperity seemed about to dawn. Prophets were encouraged by the government, a new order was to be enforced throughout the country.

The Revival of Prophecy.—Zephaniah's is the first
recognizable voice after the anti-prophetic age of
Manasseh. In view of the paganism of the people

(i, 1–12) he says that the Day of the Lord (i, 14) will come with distress for the sinners (i, 17) and possible hiding for the meek who do righteousness (ii, 3). Treacherous prophets and profane priests are contrasted with the God of unfailing judgment and righteousness. Zephaniah is very much indebted for his teaching and his expression of it to the preceding prophets. It is hard to find distinctive matter in his discourse. His distinction is that he is so thoroughly representative of the older prophetic doctrine. His date is about 630 B.C., shortly before the call of Jeremiah to prophecy. It looks as if there had been a quiet gathering of the old prophetic teachings of the Eighth Century by the persecuted disciples who kept their faith through a half-century of discouragement. They had passed on the essentials of the true message of religion until the days of the youthful Josiah when the prophetic folk was again free to preach and teach openly. Zephaniah is the best possible proof that such a religious people had not altogether died out. His word is just such a message as would come from one who had been taught the old prophetic lore. He kept the line of their teaching unbroken and prepared the way for the next advance in prophetic revelation, that given us in the teachings of Jeremiah.

Nahum was, perhaps, the most brilliant poet of the middle period of prophecy. He used his gifts in exultant glee over the discomfiture of Nineveh. That proud capital was nearing its doom. Assyria, the terrible nation, the dreaded scourge of the ancient oriental world, was exhausted and tottering. The fact was fairly obvious to all the peoples. The question that most interested the politicians in the nations roundabout was "Who will inherit Assyria's provinces and the headship when she falls?" What interested Nahum was that the bloody and ruthless city (iii, 1 *ff.*) was to be the victim of Jehovah's wrath, that Isa. x, 12 *ff.*, was to be fulfilled. The haughty destroyer who, as an instrument of the divine, had presumed to go beyond its commission or to ignore its master was to be horribly destroyed. The den of lions (ii, 11 *ff.*) that had ranged everywhere is itself to be ravaged.

Chapter 2, verse 3, through to the end of the third chapter is most assuredly of the times just described and is for so brief a passage a wonderful example, with its picturesque invective, of the fiercely taunting reproach of the oriental. It is savage eloquence even though Nineveh and the Assyrian may have richly deserved their fate. We are led to ask whether Nahum was really a prophet at all in the larger sense. May he not more properly be described as a poetic seer yielding his genius to the frenzy of revenge?

Jerusalem the Place Where Men are to Worship.— During Josiah's rule the Deuteronomic code of laws was established as the law of the land (621). He sought to enlarge his boundaries. The approaching collapse of Assyria was plainly visible in those times. Egypt loomed ambitiously on the horizon of world politics. Assyrian control in Samaria was so weak that Josiah was able to dispatch an expedition to that country in order to destroy the shrine at Shiloh. The Great Reform of Josiah sought to abolish the worship at the many high-places, shrines and sacred spots throughout Palestine in order to prevent corruption of the true religion of Jehovah. Jerusalem, its priesthood and its methods of worship, were officially declared to be the orthodox standards for the whole land.

The Fatal Mistake.—The nations expected benefits to fall to them when Assyria collapsed. Pharaoh-Necho of Egypt was one of these ambitious watchers for the fall of Nineveh. He moved his army northward so as to increase his influence when the hour struck. Josiah mustered his patriotic troops and went to meet the Egyptians. Why he did so has not been fully understood. It was as ill-advised as the policy of Ahaz a century earlier. It contradicted the famous advice of Isaiah (page 246) and as events proved was totally unnecessary even from the anti-Egyptian point of view. Josiah was killed in the battle of Megiddo; Judah came temporarily under Egyptian control, and Necho's army moved on only to be defeated by the Babylonian army of Nebuchadrezzar at Karkhemish. Thus the chain of events dragged Judah under the control of the conqueror. Jehoiakim, Jehoiakin, and Zedekiah were the last kings of Judah. The first siege of Jerusalem by Nebuchadrezzar's Kaldeans was in 597 and the second in 586 B.C.

The Times of the Prophet Jeremiah.—We are especially fortunate to possess the book of Jeremiah, for it is an important source of information on the period which saw the break-up of Assyria, the downfall of Judah and the rise of the new empire of Babylon.

Jeremiah's life fell in the most discouraging times which a Hebrew could know, the days of the decay and fall of Jerusalem. He was a patriot doomed to see the wreck of his country approaching and accomplished. It was one of the most critical times of ancient oriental history. No man could tell just how things were to turn, as turn they did in rapid succession. Asshurbanipal had made the dreaded Assyrian power particularly odious to an unhappy world. His reign was brilliant but ruthless. A path of devastation showed the line of his conquering marches. After his day there was no strong sword-hand to maintain the unnatural federation of provinces. As early as 624 Cyaxares, leader of the Medes, invaded Assyria, but was called off by the Scythian peril.

We have seen how in view of the imminent collapse of Assyria both Egypt and Babylon had hopes of profiting by the partition of the Assyrian domain, how an Egyptian army under the ambitious pharaoh, Necho, started northward across Palestine to seize upon any advantages that might be obtained and that for some unknown reason Josiah sought to block his path with an army from Judah. It was in the resulting battle of Megiddo (609) that Josiah, king of Judah, fell and that Palestine became a province of Egypt for four years.

But Nineveh did not fall until 606 and Nebuchadrezzar, the Kaldean king of Babylon, had ambitions identical in content with those of Necho of Egypt. He met the Egyptian advance at Karkhemish and won. Thus in 605 all Palestine came under the Kal-

deans of Babylon. But Egypt tried by indirection to
stir up trouble for the Kaldeans and thus to keep
them too busy to attack Egypt itself. Against the
consistent advice of Jeremiah Judah inclined to heed
the Egyptian plots and was drawn into a dangerous
conflict with its Kaldean overlord which resulted in
the conquest of Jerusalem in 597. But this did not
cure the Jerusalemites of treasonable negotiations
with Egypt, on which account the Kaldeans captured
the city a second time and destroyed it (586). At both
victories over Jerusalem many captive Hebrews were
carried off to colonize other parts of the empire.
Some of these captives were settled in Babylonia and
in the first party to go eastward was the priestly
prophet Ezekiel.

Life and Teachings of Jeremiah.—Probably Jeremiah was born during the long reign of Manasseh,
the king who so harshly repressed the prophets, but
his youth fell in the more favorable times of King
Josiah. Jeremiah was from Anathoth, a place three
miles northeast of Jerusalem, where the modern village of Anata retains the site and the name. He was
of a priestly family but he was thoroughly convinced
that Jehovah had summoned and inspired him for a
special life-work (i, 4–10). The consciousness of
this distinctive call made Jeremiah a fearless denun-
ciator of evil and a single-minded proclaimer of the
religion of the heart and spirit. The nearest he ever
came to favor at the hands of his own people was
during the life of King Josiah. After that king's
death his life was tragically painful. Yet through
persecution and defamation he kept on his consistent

way, a messenger of true things to a people who did not wish the truth. His sagacity discovered the weakness of kings and their policies in Jerusalem and saw that Babylon and not Egypt was to be the agent of God in organizing the world out of the chaotic elements left by the disruption of the Assyrian empire.

Because Jeremiah saw clearly the right thing for Judah to do he counselled his nation not to provoke Babylon and not to heed the plots of Egypt. This gained for him the hatred of all the friends of Egypt among the Hebrews at Jerusalem who accused him of favoring the Babylonians against the Hebrews. Of such a charge of treason Jeremiah was innocent. But when during the siege of Jerusalem by the Babylonians, he counselled surrender because he saw the futility of resistance, it was not hard for his many enemies to make a plausible charge of traitorous dealings with the enemy. The Kaldeans themselves regarded him favorably, perhaps on account of current opinion about him, but Jeremiah accepted no material advantages from them. He remained in his own country with the wretched survivors of the second siege of the city. He was a patriot to the last, seeking to build the spiritual fortunes of his people and land but not blind to the facts of the situation. Against his will he was dragged to Egypt by the refugees who feared Babylonian revenge though Jeremiah tried to dissuade them. Tradition says that he died a martyr to his life-long habit of rebuking evil and pointing to the true worship of Jehovah.

The most salient characteristic of Jeremiah was

his persistent loyalty to God, and to the ideal of a
pure people who should serve Him. He is one of the
saddest figures in all history. He was a man of fine
sensibilities, of affectionate nature, sociable, sensitive, and incorruptible. He was a man on whom individuals and nations could depend for the truth. He
did not thrust himself as a busybody into the affairs
of others but was under the pressure of moral compulsion to utter the truth in the face of bitter hostility.
He was unwilling to compromise the message of
Jehovah and consistently called for obedience to
God's will. But the times were out of joint and a
healthy soul was an abnormality.

The Message of Jeremiah.—Jeremiah stood for the
spiritual religion of the heart and of the individual.
He believed in a redemption for his people which
was to be wrought out in his native country. He saw
in Babylon God's chosen instrument. He rebuked
selfishness and immorality in people, priests,
prophets, and kings. The intimacy of the spirit of
the human with the spirit of the divine in Jeremiah's
teaching and practice is the most remarkable thing
about him. "But this is the covenant that I will make
with the house of Israel after those days, saith Jehovah: I will put my law in their inward parts, and in
their heart will I write it; and I will be their God,
and they shall be my people. And they shall teach no
more every man his neighbor and every man his
brother, saying, Know Jehovah; for they shall all
know me, from the least of them unto the greatest of them, saith Jehovah; for I will forgive their
iniquity, and their sin will I remember no more."
(Jer. xxxi, 33*f*).

17

This message was a consistent development of the prophetic thought of the Hebrews. That thought had grown in volume from early times. It declared that God is a righteous God and that he seeks the moral conformity of the worshippers' life and thought to the principles of divine truth and mercy. Thus Jeremiah taught and prepared the way for the full doctrine of personal responsibility before a righteous God. His message was probably much like characteristic parts of Deuteronomy, hortatory in manner, fervently spiritual, declaring that God looked with immediate favor or disfavor upon the good or bad man. Of course Jeremiah was a monotheist. He saw that the spirit of man can easily evade the requirements of any written law and so he sought that spirit of obedience to the divine law which would be an integral part of the people who obeyed it.

Jeremiah and the Great Reform.—In his early prophetic ministry Jeremiah may have aided the practical reforms of Josiah's eighteenth year (621), which sought to abolish the many local shrines throughout the country in favor of the one shrine at Jerusalem, the temple which Solomon built. This reform which was in the interests of uniformity of worship may have taken years to complete. It was first attempted when Hezekiah was king. There were manifest financial and political advantages in a move which would centre the attention of the country at Jerusalem. By appointing the sacred feasts, the sittings of courts of judgment, and the business interests of the country in the capital the dynasty would make Jerusalem dominant in the life of the people. But the unsuccessful effort of Hezekiah was well-nigh forgotten until the prophetic party revived the plan in Josiah's time. It is entirely possible that there was more priestism than prophetism in the later movement.

The ideas of the reform party are expressed in Deuteronomy. It was hoped to improve religion and morals by the suppression of the many centres of sacrificial worship. These old-fashioned shrines, each with its local associations, where priests and worshippers mingled the remnants of paganism with the variant methods of Jehovah-worship, gave too many opportunities for corrupt practices. Whatever worldly motives may have mingled with the spirit of the reform it was probably a step in the right direction. Great enthusiasm must have attended the harmonious working of a prophetic party and a kingly administration, except where old vested rights of priesthoods and cults were invaded. Many priests in the country districts were impoverished and some inconvenience took the place of the old enjoyable freedom of the country worshippers at their traditional altars. The reform at its best could hardly be profound enough for Jeremiah. But he may have helped it for what it was worth.

The Effect of Politics on Prophecy.—The lifetime of Josiah was the most favorable opportunity for prophetic influence in a century. The unfortunate loss of Josiah was far-reaching in its effects. Prophetic religion seems to have lost with him any hope that it had of saving the state. Succeeding kings Jehoahaz, Jehoiakim, Jehoiakin and Zedekiah gave it no opportunity. Jehoahaz, who might have been friendly, fell a victim to the Egyptian policy. The Egyptian party and the prophetic groups were always diametrically opposed. Jehoiakim, the candidate of the Egyptians, was utterly impatient with the prophetic teaching in general and with Jeremiah in particular.

Jeremiah was the least successful of the prophets during life. But his influence was most persistently useful. So lofty was the estimate of him in later times that he came to be known by the simple designation "The Prophet." His personal experiences of suffering, humiliation and steadfastness became folk ideals and he seemed a type of afflicted Judaism. His character is better and better understood and he has become one of the most beloved and revered of the prophets. His influence on Ezekiel was so great that many have thought that the latter was a pupil of Jeremiah. Teachings which began with Jeremiah are taken up and developed in Ezekiel. Many psalms seem to reflect his life and the book of Job is his logical descendant. Much of the chivalric attitude toward the Hebrew and Christian ministry on the part of prophets, apostles and ministers may be traced to Jeremiah.

In the Eighth Century one is attracted to the question of the effect of prophecy upon politics, but in the Seventh Century one thinks more of the effect of politics upon prophecy. As in the former century there are four great prophets named, so in this one there are four notable prophetic figures, Zephaniah, Jeremiah, Nahum and Habakkuk.

STEPPED STREET OF JERUSALEM, REMINDER OF THE HILLS ON WHICH THE CITY IS BUILT

JERUSALEM AND ITS SUBURBS FROM THE NORTHEAST; SIMILAR PERHAPS TO TITUS'S FIRST VIEW OF THE CITY IN 70 A.D.

Habakkuk.—Whatever question there may be as to the moral purpose to be subserved by the exultation of Nahum there can be none with reference to the main course of the thought in Habakkuk. He was frankly puzzled about the distressful problems of his times but he emerged clearly with a sure word of prophecy. The Assyrians had ceased as a nation. Their capital had been destroyed (in 606) and was no more to be known until the European explorers of the Nineteenth Century of our era discovered its ruined palaces and fortifications. The Kaldeans, conquerors of old Babylonia, were among the instruments of the divine punishment upon other guilty folk (i, 6 *ff.*). But these Kaldeans were idolatrous and had no notion of Jehovah (i, 11, 15 *f.*) and sometimes the less wicked was swallowed up by the more wicked (i, 13). It caused anguish in the soul of the prophet to see the course which events were taking and he asked if there was not a law from the everlasting and holy God that would regulate the wild doings of this new scourge of providence (i, 12 *f.* 17). The answer is found in chapter two, in the third and fourth verses. The patient faith of the loyal believer will be rewarded, indeed it is its own reward. Habakkuk really shows a resumption of prophecy in its pristine power and dignity. He may be dated sometime between the battle of Karkhemish in 605, when it seemed clear that Kaldea and not Egypt would step into the place vacated by Assyria in oriental politics, and the first capture of Jerusalem by the Kaldeans in 597; 600 B.C. is a convenient date to assume.

In the Years of Exile.—When the army of Nebuchadrezzar captured Jerusalem the first time in 597 and carried off the flower of the population into exile there was in the company of prisoners a priest by the name of Ezekiel, who was destined to perform a ministry for the Hebrews in captivity corresponding to that attempted by Jeremiah on behalf of those left behind in Judah. Ezekiel was a younger man than Jeremiah and was perhaps his pupil. This is often assumed to be the case because the teachings of Jeremiah are so sympathetically upheld by Ezekiel.

Ezekiel was born to the station of priest but added to that the service of prophet, by which he was best known. His call to prophetic work came in 592, or five years after his exile to a foreign land. He was living among the Hebrews in their colony at Tel Abib by the river Chebar. The site is unknown now and was probably on one of the great irrigation arms of the Euphrates or Tigris. The people among whom Ezekiel lived in captivity were considered both by him and by the prophet Jeremiah as the more hopeful portion of the Hebrew race. Jeremiah had designated the captives by the symbol of a basket of choice figs in comparison with whom the remainder at Jerusalem were seen as a basket of worthless figs (Jer. xxiv). In Ezekiel's estimation the remnant in Palestine (Ezek. xxxiii, 23 *ff*.) were idolators whose foul corruptions of the true faith and of the temple would lead to the destruction of city and temple. It was customary for the exiles to assemble at Ezekiel's house and listen to the prophetic warnings and advice, but these did not greatly affect them because they were filled with the notion that they were to go back to their city and temple, to worship God there. News passed back and forth between Babylonia and Palestine and it served to confirm Ezekiel in his declaration that things at Jerusalem were beyond remedy and that the city was doomed. When the news came that the Hebrew capital was besieged, the prophet, in his sorrow, ceased speaking, and when it was known that Jerusalem and the temple had been burned by the Babylonians consternation seized every Hebrew heart. Their nation and their hopes were crushed. (See Ezek. xxxiii, 10, and xxxvii, 11.)

Building the Morale of a People.—In this terrible hour the magnanimity and the value of Ezekiel the prophet were seen. He strove earnestly to persuade the people that they need not give up hope, but that God still lived and that they might worship him acceptably and fruitfully as a group of his people and also as individuals. It is probable that his voice was more heeded at that time than formerly, since he was seen in his true character as a declarer of the counsels of Jehovah. Paradoxical as it must have seemed to them he now assured the Hebrews that they might look forward to a return to their country as the bearers of a holier, more spiritual faith and with a law written upon their very hearts.

So long as the city and the temple stood the people seemed to let that material fact be their dependence. They failed to look through the material symbols to the moral demands of the invisible deity. And yet the prophets were continually trying to show the people the real nature of religion which consisted not in the things used in worship but in righteousness. No wonder that the prophets came to feel that the outward things must be destroyed so that the people might understand God. The prophets, therefore, believed that they saw in the great political changes and warlike events of the ancient world the agencies of God, who was thus making the Hebrew people understand him better. The prophets came to believe also that the other nations would understand the message of God better because of the events of history.

During the early years of the exile the Hebrew captives were saved from their despondency by the rallying summons of Ezekiel, who was a true pastor as well as a prophet. Their character had been purged by the fiery ordeal and there was more likelihood that they would accept the spiritual teachings of the prophets. Henceforward they would be a more religious nation, cured of heathenish customs and idolatry. Thus true faith would be revived in the ashes of their old hopes. The significance of Ezekiel is not likely to be overestimated for that critical point in the history of religion. Viewed more broadly he was a great transitional character who served in the double capacity of pre-exilic and exilic prophet. Hebrew prophecy was always very sensitive to actual conditions and needs. In the age before the exile the prophets were consistent denunciators. That was because they found a conceited people prosperous in material things and complacent about their obligations to God and humanity. They slipped ignorantly into serious perils which involved their destruction. The prophetic interpretation of national history had been fulfilled by the exile. That calamity called for a new kind of ministry, to the broken-hearted survivors. And just because true prophecy is always timely in the sense that it is spiritually alert to the real needs of the people, so now there was a message of comfort and edification forthcoming. As suggested above, this turn in the prophetic thought occurred within the ministry of Ezekiel. From Amos to Jeremiah the course was straight and its great consistent trend was maintained in the first part of Ezekiel's work until the year 586 B.C. (Chapters 1 to 24.) In that year the lowest mark of Hebrew fortune was reached. Thereafter prophecy was more often consolatory and constructive. It was less sublime and terrible, less poetic and fervent.

The Individual in the Nation.—Ezekiel taught the people of the exile how they might have faith and how Jehovah might have a people even though there was no city and no temple. The doctrine of the individual in religion was clearly brought out, and that in two aspects; the individual's responsibility for himself and the sacred responsibility of the watchman which in no way conflicts with the former. (See Chapters 33 and 18.)

Because of Ezekiel's priestly training and temperament the ecclesiastical element holds a large place in his plans. During the latter part of Ezekiel's life he busied himself with plans for an orderly and painstaking arrangement of public worship in a new temple that was to be built in the homeland whither he hoped the people would return. The conception of an ecclesiastical state began with Ezekiel.

Ezekiel's prophetic activity was between the years 592 and 570 in his mature manhood. He was more immediately successful in his own lifetime than most prophets. Perhaps that was because he was satisfied with lesser achievements. A genius of the first rank, an Isaiah or a Jeremiah, placed the goal too high for practical success. However, their value is more persistent in the world of ideals than Ezekiel's. Was it the obduracy of the people or the diminishing genius of prophecy that gradually reduced the altitude of the prophetic idealism? At any rate, the time came when the people adopted advices of the prophets as moderate steps in actual social progress.

Perhaps the most important teaching in Ezekiel for the general history of thought was one which grew out of the teaching of Jeremiah and was elaborated by Ezekiel, viz., that the individual has rights, privileges and duties. The destruction of the Hebrew state threw the individual Hebrew more upon his own resources than ever before and broke his dependence upon the outward and material institutions of religion. The spiritual doctrine of the prophets led, logically, to the same thing, but the awful overthrow of the city and temple and the breakup of society with the seeming withdrawal of Jehovah from the people emphasized it most powerfully. The Hebrew captive in Babylon felt his individuality as never before. Therefore the religion that Ezekiel offered was for the individual, though the prophet began at once to bind his parish of captives together and to plan for its social reconstruction.

Dreams of Restoration.—In his careful provision for every detail, Ezekiel furnished a solution for a practical economic difficulty which resulted from the great reform of 621. The Levites who had been attached to the outlawed shrines of the country were to be provided with duties at the temple in Jerusalem. (See Deut. xviii.) But it was impossible to give all the country priests good places at the temple. This problem appeared before the captivity so that Ezekiel was well aware of it, and in chapters xliii, 18, to xlv, 8, we may read his provision for the Levitical families in his constitution for restored Palestine.

The period of the Exile in Babylonia was a rare opportunity for the most earnest and devoted among the captives to enforce the lesson of true religion upon the minds of their fellow-Hebrews. Many of the worldly interests that had competed with the prophets' messages in Palestine had been taken away by the conquest. In Babylonia the fact that they were poor and despised drew the captives closer together in their deeper human interests. They saw, as they and their ancestors were not willing to see before it happened, that the doom of their country had been sealed, as the prophets so often declared, and they agreed with the prophets that it was because of the nation's sins. This led them, under such teachers as Ezekiel, to honor more humbly the dignity of their offended God.

It is not likely that the Kaldeans interfered very much with the religious exercises of their captives, and there must have been much freedom for the religious leaders to work as much as they wished in their labor of love. In Babylonia there would be no Jeroboam, no Manasseh, no Jehoiakim, no powerful court party, no corrupt Hebrew politicians with power to hinder the truth, no strongly situated priesthood jealous of its rights and its income, no false prophets who could make a comfortable living by catering to the powerful. If any one worked for religion in Babylonian captivity it must have been because his heart was in it. As the Hebrews found new homes in the cities and on the fields of the rich eastern countries, many of them developed profitable business connections and probably gave less attention to thoughts of homeland and faith. But priests and prophets and others with a conscience for the welfare of their fellow-countrymen would seek to keep alive the customs of the Hebrews and the faith in Jehovah. In time, a considerable religious nation of Jews was built up in Babylonia. The community had its institutions, officers and teachers and looked upon Babylonia as its home.

But before such a measure of prosperity came to the Jewish people abroad they were naturally thinking much of their ruined country and their losses. They could think of no favor that God could do for them equal to that of sending them back to Palestine. Many of the most devout continued for ages to feel that way about returning to Jerusalem, though many more gave up the expectation after a few years. The majority may have preferred their new homes and prosperity.

The Lessons of the Exile.—One of the inevitable results of living in Babylonia would be to educate the

Hebrews in the largeness of the civilized world and to bring them into close relationship with one of the oldest civilizations and all its rich lore and art. Any day they might behold the elaborate worship of the great gods of the foreigners and hear the numerous stories, hymns, prayers and incantations that concerned the Babylonian divinities. An alien is likely to become possessed of two cultures, that of his homeland and that of the country of his residence. If he is an apt pupil his education may be richer than that of his native neighbors. A comparison of the religion of the Hebrew prophets with that of the Babylonian priests would surely occur to the better Hebrews. Any keen Hebrew would conceive a deeper reverence for his sublime deity, Jehovah, as he saw the motley deities of the east, essentially gross and selfish, worshipped under all the opulent circumstances of a materialistic civilization. A really spiritually minded Hebrew would be quick to surmise that the gods of the Babylonians were really symbols of human passions, power, profit, and war. He would still believe in his heart in that august deity who hides his splendors from the eyes of flesh and writes his laws in human consciences.

The exile was more than a national calamity. It was to those who would receive it a thorough-going discipline. Those who specialized in ideas and who worked at the great moral and religious problems of their day would be more likely than those who grew rich in Babylonian business to look fondly towards the Holy City and to remember any word of promise that God would bring about their return.

There was, probably, much earnest writing as well as thinking and talking done by the idealists among the exiles. In the clearer light of experience these saw their country's history as a whole and reasoned upon the significances of its events and personalities. They studied the prophets diligently as the accredited geniuses of their race and revered their words. Those words they sought to interpret more minutely and saved many a fragment of the old-time teaching of teachers whose names we no longer possess. They compiled from all available sources, documents and memory, a great interpretive history of their race. They saw new meanings in the old tales of their ancestors concerning the movements of nations and the march of events. They looked into the past and philosophized on the providence of Jehovah. With the unconquerable optimism of the human heart they could not help but hope that the future would show why God had so signally punished them as compared with other sinning nations. The exile was a large influence in the gathering together of a national religious literature which we might call the Bible of the early Jews. It was a great prophetic literature which saw God in everything and created a theology and a program to interpret history religiously.

The influence of such orderly minds as Ezekiel's was especially in favor of having a constitution ready for the day when the Hebrews might be permitted to live in their own land again. He, indeed, planned things far in excess of any possible fact, but the basis of his scheme is clearly discernible in the laws of the later Jewish priests.

The Comforting Prophet.—It is, perhaps, strange that we know of no other name of a prophet in the period of Ezekiel. But we have the writings of unnamed prophets scattered through our Scriptures and a large body of words from that time and later are appended to our book Isaiah. Everything after the thirty-ninth chapter of Isaiah may be so regarded as well as many passages in the first part of the book. Similar additional passages from the time of the exile and after are found in most of the prophets.

The rather unattractive designation "Second Isaiah" has been given most frequently to the chapters 40 to 66 of the present Book of Isaiah. By that name is meant simply the second part of the volume.

To those exiled Hebrews who were most eager to return to Palestine any political disturbance in the great world might appear as the moving of the divine power to better their lot. They were ready to believe that Cyrus the Persian conqueror might be one of God's messiahs coming to deliver His people from Babylonian bondage (Isa. xlv, 1). Profounder souls saw in the afflictions of the Hebrew people a preparation for a great vicarious service. The Hebrews were being developed into missionary people. What Jeremiah had suffered and stood for on an individual scale, the nation had undergone. Thus they answered their problem of evil. Through despite, yea even martyrdom, Jehovah's Servant would go his sorrowful way to the glory of God, the salvation of the peoples, and the justification of the heroic soul himself. (Isa. xlii, 1–9; xlix, 1–13; l, 4–11; lii, 13, to liii, 12.)

SUGGESTIONS FOR STUDY

1. Why did social ethics advance in Palestine beyond that of Babylonia?

2. Write paraphrases of selected passages from the first four chapters of Amos.

3. Discuss the merits of Isaiah's policy of neutrality for Judah.

4. Compare Isaiah's experiences as an anti-administration man in the days of Ahaz with his pro-administration career under Hezekiah.

5. Compare the prophetic party in the reign of Manasseh with modern persecuted sects.

6. How does Jeremiah's religion show advance upon that of the eighth century prophets.

7. Who were the foreign masters of Jerusalem from 610 to 600 B.C.?

8. Any reasons for the greater immediate success of Ezekiel as contrasted with preceding prophets?

9. What were the chief details of Ezekiel's hopes for Palestine? Ezek. 33 to 48.

BOOK LIST

AMOS, HOSEA, MICAH, ISAIAH, ZEPHANIAH, JEREMIAH, NAHUM, HABAKKUK and EZEKIEL in the Bible.

SOARES: The Social Institutions and Ideals of the Bible.

DRIVER: The Book of the Prophet Jeremiah.

Commentaries on the various prophetic books in the International Critical Commentary and in the Cambridge Bible: see the introductions to the volumes.

HERODOTUS.

CHAPTER XIII

The Difficulties of Reconstruction.—In the terrible Sixth Century B.C. with its calamities and agonies there were two crises of peculiar danger. One was the day which Ezekiel saved when, after the news in 586 of the destruction of city and temple, the prophet turned the people from infidelity to renewed faith. The other was the gray day of disillusionment when the returned band of Hebrews faced the facts of a hostile neighborhood in an inhospitable country and on making an attempt to rebuild their temple were brutally and peremptorily checked (Ezra iii and iv). There followed sixteen dull years of an attempt to overcome material difficulties, a struggle which was scarcely ameliorated by any comforting enthusiasm of religion. Then arose Haggai and Zechariah to show the people the true source of inspiration, solidarity, and triumph, in their sublime faith. Stirring appeals to the people which linked their evils with their faint-heartedness and little love for God's concerns resulted in a noble enthusiasm to build the house which should symbolize their newly aroused social conscience. The prince in charge was Zerubbabel, a scion of David's house, and the high priest was Joshua. International politics of the day seemed to be offering one more of those frequently anticipated but disappointing turns in affairs which might at any time give back to Jerusalem its former independence and glory. The early chapters of Ezra tell about the events which form the background of these related prophecies. Ezra v, 1, and vi, 14, tells us that these two prophets, Haggai and Zechariah, exhorted the people to rebuild their temple.

Haggai and Zechariah and the Second Temple.—It is natural to treat of these yokefellows together, though they illustrate, as in the case of Jeremiah and Ezekiel, a sympathy, in the common cause, of two very different men. Haggai was more nearly a man of a single idea than was Zechariah. He was incisive, and, with his narrow weapon of persuasion, saw but one explanation for the misfortunes that were plaguing the people and one remedy for the distress, the temple which they ought to build. But sometimes a simple consideration does not give easily daunted humanity enough scope, and so in this case the interest of the people was flagging when Zechariah, a more versatile and resourceful man, because a broader and more imaginative one, stirred up the enthusiasm again and, together, these prophets buoyed the peoples' endeavor until the temple was built. With their idealism, thus expressed in a common enterprise, the people were in a way to prosper in all respects.

The dating of the words of Haggai and Zechariah will show how they worked together on their great religious drive:

Hag.	1: 1	Darius' reign	2nd yr.	6th mo.	1st day
"	1: 15	" "	"	" mo.	24th day
"	2: 1	" "	"	7th mo.	21st day
Zech.	1: 1	" "	"	8th mo.	
Hag.	2: 10 and 20	Darius' reign	"	9th mo.	24th day
					(2 utterances)
Zech.	1: 7	" "	"	11th mo.	24th day
"	7: 1	" "	4th yr.	9th mo.	4th day

Haggai appears to have sounded the first appeal in Darius' second year on the first of the sixth month and on the 24th the people responded with the beginning of the work. Seven weeks after the first sermon Haggai urged on the work with a glowing forecast of the importance of the new house of Jehovah. A week later Zechariah spoke and urged the people to heed the lesson of their ancestors' failure to listen to God's message by the prophets. In the ninth month and the twenty-fourth day Haggai resumed with an encouragement of the zeal of the people. He reminded them that their former laxity was really profanity and that God had reduced them in material circumstances because of it. Another utterance was directed to Prince Zerubbabel (Hag. ii, 20 *ff.*) assuring him that he would be God's special care in an approaching day of calamity to other rulers and their people. In two months (11mo., 24) (Zech. i, 7) it was Zechariah's turn to speak for Jehovah, and while the earth was declared to be still and at rest a reassurance of God's special grace towards Jerusalem was given. Zechariah vii, 1 *f.* appear to be nearly two years later than the former chapters, *viz.*, Darius' 4th yr., 9th mo. and 4th day.

Obadiah's Message.—The Edomites were the most hated kindred of the Hebrews. The feeling was rooted in a history of grievances which culminated in 586 B.C. when the Kaldeans sacked Jerusalem and carried numbers of its people into captivity. At that time it was charged that the Edomites aided the enemy. The little Book of Obadiah, shortest in the Old Testament, specifies the offences.

"In the day that thou stoodest on the other side, in the day that strangers carried away his substance, and foreigners entered into his gates, and cast lots upon Jerusalem, even thou wast as one of them." Obadiah, vs. 11, see also vs. 12–14.

Ammonites and Arabs were hostile to the distressed Hebrews in those same awful times, as we may read in Jeremiah xl and xli.

These foes and others continued through centuries to arouse the enmity of the Jews. Nehemiah mentions certain of them among his opponents. Not until the Second Century B.C. were they wholly restrained. We read in 1st Maccabees v, 3–8, how Judas fought with the Edomites and avenged Israel upon them with great slaughter, humbling their pride and impoverishing them.

We wish that we had data from the viewpoint of the Edomites. What an irony of fate was that which brought Idumean (Edomite) kings to the throne of Jerusalem in the persons of the Herods!

Hebrew society in Palestine during the Persian period was undergoing a change that was destined to make a religious congregation of the people, comparable with the ecclesiastical citizenry in certain New England towns during one period of our colonial life. With the disappearance of Zerubbabel, representative perhaps of political aspiration, as of the Davidic line, the energies of Hebrew leaders turned more and more to perfecting a religious organization which should centre in the temple. All the prophets of the period show the ecclesiastical influence. The day of

classical prophecy was drawing to a close, **the priest**
and the apocalyptist were growing in favor.

But there were many obstacles and discouragements, chiefly those in human nature. Our book
Malachi reveals the fact that after the enthusiasm
aroused by Haggai and Zechariah had declined the
people provided certain very troublesome problems
for the guardians of morals. There was the evil of
divorce (Mal. ii, 16) which cut two ways. It resulted
in the breaking up of Hebrew homes and was often
followed by marriage with foreign women who
brought disturbing religious influences into Hebrew
life. There· was a sordid contempt for religious
obligations which led to the attempt to palm off
blemished creatures for the sacrificial offerings.
There was a growing cynicism which led some to say
that goodness doesn't count and that wrongdoing
pays. The moral and religious problems of the day
were so discouraging that prophecy felt the need of
a forerunner who should rough-hew and refine
society before the appearance of any messiah could
usher in a day of salvation. Probably it was the
priests and the many Levites of the lesser grades who
gave this conscientious messenger his deepest trouble
and concern because their example among the people
was so bad. A precious memoir remains of those who
were righteous and obedient (Mal. iii, 16–18). One
should read the entire book Malachi in order to
enter into sympathy with the sadly perplexed author
who sees nothing for it but a day of fiery cleansing
which will separate the good from the bad. Malachi
i, 11, is one of the most catholic notes in Old Testa-

ment prophecy, "from the rising of the sun even unto the going down of the same my name is great among the Gentiles, and in every place incense is offered unto my name," etc. Which amounts to saying that from east to west, wherever any one offers sincere worship, it is acceptable to God.

A New Statement of the Law.—The Hebrew leaders were convinced that Judah needed a new constitution. The laws in Deuteronomy required restatement, expansion and revision. Ezekiel's proposed constitution was the basis for the new document and the last hundred years had revealed many needs that Ezekiel had not provided for. The entire machinery of worship, sacrifices, feasts, and ministerial service was overhauled. There was a clearer and sharper line of division between priests and other servants of religion. The sense of sin was symbolized in an elaborate ritual of devotion, purification and atonement. It was hoped that ceremony might be made the language of human need and divine relationship. Society in all its variant moods was being organized into something comparable to a church. The authorities hoped to develop the conscience of the people and to perfect a moral folk. The Persian government demanded certain political virtues and tribute but provided little help for the development of that individual and social character which make good subjects of a people. The priestly guides organized a nation with an unusually strong inner life within which politics first found its affiliation with law and patriotism its expression in conscience. This legal development was a continuous one, but looking back one can see certain epochs. The main course of development from Ezekiel to Ezra culminated before the opening of the Fourth Century. The traditional date has long been given as 444 B.C. when the complete priestly revision of the law was published. Whether it was just then or a few decades later the custom has arisen of using the terms Jew and Judaism instead of Hebrew and Hebraism thereafter. We refer to the Hebrew as a Jew ever since the day that he founded a state within a state, an ecclesiastical state within the Persian empire.

The Persian period through which we are reading may be outlined more clearly by a list of The Early Persian Kings:

Cyrus	c. 550–529 B.C.
Cambyses	529–521 (conquest of Egypt)
Darius I Hystaspis	521–485 (Greek war)
Xerxes	485–465 "
Artaxerxes I Longimanus	465–425
Xerxes II	(two months)
Sogdianus	(seven months)
Darius II Nothus	424–405–4 (Egypt revolted)
Artaxerxes II Mnemon	404–359 (Xenophon)
Artaxerxes III Ochus	359–339 (Egypt reconquered)
Arses	339–336
Darius III Codomannus	336–333 (Alexander)

It helps the imagination to realize that vigorous strength marked the life of the classical people of Europe during the period of Persian decline. Socrates died in 399 B.C. and the great schools of Grecian thought were forming. Although the Gauls wrecked Rome about 390, the city was soon rebuilt and the Romans developed greater strength.

The Information in Ezra-Nehemiah.—These books belong together and are, in fact, a part only of a larger literary work which included our I and II Chronicles. This continuous work sought to rewrite history from the beginning of the world, for what purpose will be pretty plain to the reader. The sources which it used are for the most part in our Bible and consisted of the Books of Samuel and Kings. It was satisfied to cover the earliest periods of time by lists of names in genealogical succession. Its chief interest lay in the history from David's time onward and especially in the story of Judah and the Jewish church.

When the Chronicler, as he is commonly called now, reached the end of the history given in the Book of Kings and came to the Persian period, he proceeded to write the history of the Hebrews and of Jerusalem for that time. This gives us the Books Ezra and Nehemiah. Disturbances have disarranged the books. Anyone trying to read a consistent story is forced to make certain explanations and to attempt certain rearrangements if not reconstructions.

The story in Ezra begins with the proclamation of Cyrus King of Persia that a house be built for Jehovah at Jerusalem. Hebrews are encouraged to go to Jerusalem for the purpose and their neighbors are urged to contribute gifts. Cyrus himself made contribution, bringing forth the sacred vessels which Nebuchadrezzar had taken from the first temple and delivering them to Sheshbazzar, the prince of Judah

(i). A list of those who returned in 538–6 B.C. is
given. It is a great caravan of over fifty thousand
persons.

The first act concerned the temple and the altar
(ii, 68 *f.*; iii, 2 *f.*). They set up an altar and began
to reconstruct the temple. But many adversaries
arose who discouraged the builders (iv, 1–5). That
brought the history down to the reign of Darius
(521). Chapter iv, 6, refers to the reign of Ahasuerus
(? Xerxes, 485) and iv, 7–23, refers to the reign of
Artaxerxes (I? 465) while iv, 24, refers to the reign of
Darius again. There is a letter to Artaxerxes and
his reply, the subject being the walls of Jerusalem,
the finishing of which the enemies desire to prevent,
although in one place it is said that the walls are
finished (iv, 12) while in another it appears desirable
that they be not finished (iv, 16); iv, 24, with its
strange return to Darius' time concerns the building
of the temple, which is the subject taken up in chapter 5 with the story of Haggai and Zechariah and
much extra material not hinted at in the books of
these prophets.

Chapter 7 brings us to the time of Ezra himself
and dates his journey to Jerusalem in the reign of
Artaxerxes, but can this be the same king who
appears so hostile in iv, 7–23, or, the second king of
the name, *i.e.*, between 404 and 359 B.C.? At any rate,
Ezra is said to have gone to Jerusalem with a caravan
but without a guard of soldiers (viii, 22). At Jerusalem Ezra found much to make him grieve over the corruption of life. Especially was he distressed that
so many of the Hebrews had married foreign wives.

He secured promises that these marriages would be dissolved (viii, 32 to 10).

Nehemiah's account begins with the time of King Artaxerxes, which one is not stated, but it has always been supposed to refer to the First (Longimanus) and to the year 445. Nehemiah was the royal cupbearer but became a patriotic governor of Judah. He arrived at Jerusalem and rebuilt the walls of the city in 444 B.C. in spite of persistent opposition of those outsiders who did not wish to see the city fortified. He put through needed reforms and greatly improved the standing of the province. All these things are told in the first six chapters of Nehemiah, which are generally accredited as the most original in the book.

Chapters 8 to 10 tell how Ezra the scribe brought the book of the law of Moses and how, after reading and teaching it to the people, all subscribed loyally to its demands.

Professor Torrey claims that Nehemiah vii, 70, to viii, 18, originally followed Ezra 8. (E. S., p. 18, note 5.)

Chapter 11 opens with a scheme to secure sufficient population for the city. Chapter 13 indicates that Nehemiah's term as governor had come to a close and that he was back at his duties in the Persian Court. But he went to Jerusalem a second time in 432 B.C.

During recent decades there has been some critical dissent from the general position of scholars with reference to the Exile, the Return, the work of the scribe Ezra, the publication of the law in 444 B.C., the relations between him and Nehemiah, and the

credibility of the books Ezra and Nehemiah as they
stand. Howorth, Kosters, and Torrey have led in
the discussion, notably the last named. In 1896, in
his monograph on the ''Composition and Historical
Value of Ezra-Nehemiah,'' and in 1910 in ''Ezra
Studies,'' Professor Charles C. Torrey of Yale University has made a thoroughgoing reconstruction of
the history and significance of the Persian period.

Torrey's contention is that the Chronicler was
''the sole author of the Ezra story, of all the Book of
Nehemiah after chapter 6 and of the Artaxerxes
letter in Ezra 7 '' (E. S. ix). Of the Chronicler's
work in general he says that it was ''a great under-
taking with a single very definite aim well executed,
an elaborate and timely championing of the Jewish
sacred institutions, especially in opposition to the
Samaritans.'' (E. S. ix.)

The Chronicler's history was originally in somewhat different form from that now presented in either
the Hebrew Bible where Chronicles follows Ezra-
Nehemiah or in the English Bible where Chronicles
has been restored to its original position before
Ezra-Nehemiah, but not to its original form, as witness the duplication of the last two verses of the
present II Chronicles in the first three verses of
Ezra. Other disarrangements and confusions have
been noticed by readers of Ezra-Nehemiah for a long
time. Without halting for such, we notice that one
of Professor Torrey's principal points is that the
first Book of Esdras in the Apocrypha is really a
large remnant of the old Greek translation of the
Chronicler's history, not as it originally appeared,

but as it was generally held in the last century B.C. (E. S., p. 18) and when the whole work which we call Chronicles, Ezra, and Nehemiah was one continuous history. That history was in Hebrew-Aramaic and contained the Story of the Three Youths which was not in the original history nor does it appear now in our Ezra. (See I Esdras.)

In I Esdras v, 6, appears a date at a point in the text where Torrey discerns the evidence of a juncture of the close of an interpolation with the old narrative. He reads by correction, "in the second year of the reign of Cyrus, the king of Persia, in the month Nisan, on the first ·day of the month" (E. S. 27). This he concludes was the original dating by the Chronicler of the return from the captivity. Moreover, he claims to recover to the original Ezra and to believe to refer really to Cyrus, the passage I Esdras iv, 48–57. With such corrections and rearrangements of the texts Torrey restored the original order of the Chronicler's narrative thus: I and II Chron.; Ezra i; I Esdras iv, 48–57; iv 62 to v, 6; Ezra ii, 1, to viii, 36; Neh. vii, 70, to viii, 18; Ezra ix, 1, to x, 44; Neh. ix, 1, to x, 40 (Eng. 39); Neh. i, 1, to vii, 69; Neh. xi, 1, to xiii, 31. The story of Ezra (see E. S. 259 *f.*) falls in the reign of Artaxerxes II Mnemon (404–359 B.C.), or, more particularly, April 1, 398 B.C. It is thus that Torrey removes the puzzle of the anti-climax according to the traditional account which has it that Ezra went to Jerusalem in 458 B.C., published very drastic rules about divorcing foreign wives, appears to have gone into obscurity from which he did not emerge until 444, when

Nehemiah came and essayed milder reforms, where-upon Ezra read forth the entire law which he had brought with him nearly fourteen years before. But although Torrey thus rearranges the records in order to secure literary consistency he does not hold that Ezra was more than the Chronicler's invention in order to idealize the antiquity of the law and custom of the Jews. In support of this it is to be confessed that outside these books Ezra does not figure in the Biblical literature but that Nehemiah is the one always referred to. (See Kent, "Students O. T. Histor. and Biog. Narratives," and Ecclus. xlix, 11–13; II Macc. i, 18–23. Join with this the way in which Ezra is ignored in much of Nehemiah.)

One of the main results of Professor Torrey's thesis is the removal of the Exile and the Return from the experiences of the main body of Hebrews and the doing away with the conception of great liter-ary productivity on the part of mourning exiles who provided a complete system of law and ritual to be laid upon the renewed community at Jerusalem. Holding to the statement in Jeremiah lii, 28–30, that the total deportations by Nebuchadrezzar on all occa-sions amounted to 4600 persons, Torrey remarks that such removals would not seriously deplete Judah. He believes that these captives never returned and that the Babylonian communities of Hebrews became engrossed in their own pursuits and never had much influence on Palestinian Hebrews. The story that Cyrus sent back a delegation with orders to build the temple but that after a feeble attempt they did little for sixteen years and that they carried with them to

Jerusalem the sacred vessels which had been preserved by the Babylonians and captured by the Persians to be restored to the Hebrews, all this our author treats as a picture of fond idealization made three centuries later by the Chronicler (c. 250), because of his theory that every good thing in Judaism had grown within a ceremonially pure Jewish stock which returned from Babylonian exile and refused to be contaminated with the mixed elements that remained in Palestine after the Kaldean wars.

What really occurred, according to this thesis, after the overthrow of the city of Jerusalem in 586 B.C., was that most of the inhabitants, who were not killed, escaped into the regions about and that, after the army of Nebuchadrezzar had withdrawn, they crept back to reoccupy their dismantled city. They gained the upper-hand of their poverty and other difficulties slowly, worshipped at the site of the ruined temple which they may have partly restored in an unsatisfactory manner. In 520 B.C. these people, who are referred to not as exiles but as a "remnant" (see Hag. i, 12 and 14; Hag. ii, 2; Zech. viii, 11; see also Neh. i, 3), were exhorted by the prophets Haggai and Zechariah to arise and build. They did so, completing the temple in a few years. In the next century the patriotic governor Nehemiah rebuilt the wall of Jerusalem (444 B.C.) and to that time belong Chapters i, ii, iv to vi. Thus slowly but surely there grew up in Palestine a Judaism that steadily advanced, producing a native restoration, stimulated by prophets, psalmists and wisdom writers, a religious people not chiefly bound by legalism but by freer ideals. Palestine suffered before Nebuchadrezzar's time and ever afterwards from the continual dispersion of its inhabitants over the civilized world. Hebrews were found in all the more prosperous large cities and although, sentimentally, they looked back to the traditional home-land yet they knew that they were more prosperous where they were. (See E. S. 308.)

A result of these positions for literary history is the claim that all the books of the Old Testament were composed in Palestine. The Pentateuch was necessarily in its present form before the Samaritan secession which Torrey dates about 336, since the Samaritan and Hebrew Pentateuch are substantially the same. The Samaritans under the expelled Manasseh, excluded from the Jerusalem temple, built a temple of their own on Mt. Gerizim, and the anti-Samaritan motive in Hebrew literature had its beginning at that time.

Whatever else may be said of any or all of these theories in "Ezra Studies" the resultant picture is a much more attractive one than the picture that is displaced. This result so common in criticism is of course not the guiding motive, but rather an earnest search for the truth, which may have been undertaken at first because of the suspicion that something was wrong with the traditional scheme of things.

(The student is referred to the Preface and Chapter ix, especially, also Chapters ii, iii, vii and viii of "Ezra Studies," by Charles C. Torrey, 1910.)

Joel the prophet lived in this same general period. His book shows the priestly system in operation.

Priests and elders are the heads, not kings. The
state is a religious nation. The Greeks are mentioned which fact helps to indicate the period of history which we have reached.

We are given glimpses of the trials of agriculturists in those days. It is a diary of hard times
in Judah. The little province was struggling to
maintain itself and its temple service in the midst
of inhospitable natural conditions and petty neighborhood persecutions. There is alarm and panic
in Jerusalem because of unprecedented clouds of
destroying locusts. These, like an orderly army led
by Jehovah, swarm over every living thing. Most
graphically does the poet describe their invasion and
simulate with his rhythm their irresistible assault.
Yet even though the devastating swarms held possession of the land, had His people repented, God would
have mercifully spared them. More terrible did the
scourge become until everything that grew was de-
voured. The prophet mocked the voluptuaries whose
luxurious living was rendered impossible. He called
for mourning and a solemn penitential assembly. In
sackcloth and with fasting and cries unto God the
priests and people were called upon to bewail the
awful calamity.

During the late Persian and the early Greek periods of Palestinian history there is evidence of an
opposition to the rigors of the strict constructionists
who controlled the government. Such books as Ruth,
Jonah, Proverbs, Job and Ecclesiastes reveal the
keener thought of a loftier Judaism than that which
was dominant politically.

SUGGESTIONS FOR STUDY

1. What were the discouragements in Judah during the period of reconstruction?

2. Read Haggai, Zechariah and Malachi for a picture of life in the Persian province of Judah.

3. Read the Darius inscription at Behistun.

4. What indication of the relations of Hebrews and Edomites in Obadiah?

BOOK LIST

FOWLER: A History of the Literature of Ancient Israel.
KENT: Students' Old Testament.
MITCHELL: Ethics of the Old Testament.
SYKES: A History of Persia.

CHAPTER XIV

Palestine, To-day, Will Illuminate Many a Passage from the Bible.—But care must be used to separate between the more permanent and the changing features of the country and its life. It certainly will not do to suppose that everything oriental will illustrate Biblical history. The customs of India, for instance, are as different from those of Palestine as they are from those of China and Japan. Even Syria in its northern part is not to be compared with Palestine, where Jesus lived and where the prophets spoke. But present-day Palestine is eloquent of Biblical times from mountain and wilderness, plain and sea, and the paths that connect them. The seasons are the same as in ancient times, the early and the latter rains, the mists and drought, the wonderful Syrian sky and powerful rays of the sun, the dawn, the glowing noon, the waning afternoon, the inky night in the season of rain and the bejewelled sky of clear weather. There is the looming cliff, the scrub and thorn and flinty rock, the limestone chip flecking the brownish-red soil, the white wall, the clay paste when wet, the swirling lime-dust when dry, the foliage of the olive like a changeable fabric in the varying light, the foliage of the vineyards like a bath of green to thirsty eyes. There stand the gaunt hills, nature's bedawin, gaping caves, clambering terraces, feebly spouting springs, swiftly descending paths two feet wide over which human beings and flocks have gone

HILLS NEAR NAZARETH LOOKING SOUTH ACROSS THE PLAIN OF ESDRAELON

for many centuries. Seldom does one ever make them straight, kick a pebble out or remove a slippery rock from the course. Humanity goes as the other creatures do and all flow as a trickling stream to find the path and fulfil the days of their destiny.

By seeking an intimate knowledge of the physical lay of the land and its climatic features one will find a groundwork against which to display the lesser features. With Galilee, Jordan and the Dead Sea belong the wilderness of Judah, the mountains of Ephraim, the valleys running among the hills, the cry of the owl and the jackal, the thirst, the cooling stream, then the ways of the people, the gesture, inflexion, the rich gutturals, the credulity and passion of a present race akin to the ancient dwellers in the land.

In I Kings xvii, 7, where Elijah is pictured at the brook Cherith, we read, "And it came to pass after a while that the brook dried up because there was no rain in the land." In Job vi, 17, the more general statement concerning the brooks is found, "When it is hot they are consumed out of their place." Such passages illustrated by actual experience in the country to-day indicate a season of drought. Of the two things, sun and moisture, necessary for life, it is the moisture that is more likely to be lacking in Palestine. In wet countries the people look anxiously for the sun. But in dry, warm countries the anxiety is for moisture. Palestine is in the latter class of countries and feels especially grateful for rain.

Most of the water channels of Palestine are bone dry in summer. The two seasons are the dry, from

April to November, and the wet, from November to
April. It seems strange to hear a river bed called
by the name of a river when there is not a drop of
water in it. But there are a few streams that flow
the year through. Besides the two greater rivers,
the Jordan and the Aujeh, there are a few perennial
brooks fed by powerful springs. The dry season dis-
courages the wild growth in Palestine.

The two-fold nature of the year is emphasized in
the words of Gen. viii, 22, "Seedtime and harvest and
cold and heat and summer and winter and day and
night."

The synonymity of winter and rain appears in
Song ii, 11:

"For, lo, the winter is past,
The rain is over and gone."

Sometimes the weather will take days in getting
ready for a downpour. The gradual approach of
the rain and then its heavy fall are well described
in I Kings xviii, 43–45, where Elijah has his servant
report the progress of the oncoming storm.

The former rains which come some time near
December and the latter rains which come in or after
February are both very necessary. The former permit of plowing and sowing and the latter of accelerated growth and the filling out of the grain. In
Deut. xi, 14, it is said, "I will give the rain of your
land in its season, the former rain and the latter rain,
that thou mayest gather in thy grain and thy new wine
and thine oil." These are the three great harvests of
the year, the grain, grape, and olive harvest reaching
from April to October through the rainless part of the

year and they are greatly affected by the quantity of the last rains of the winter.

Through the long rainless season the winds are frequently from the eastern deserts and are named after their direction, sirocco. Their withering heat is frequently referred to in the Bible. Jer. xviii, 17, "I will scatter them as with an east wind before the enemy." Ezek. xvii, 10, "Shall it not utterly wither, when the east wind toucheth it?" Ezek. xix, 12 (of the nation Israel), "But it was plucked up in fury, it was cast down to the ground, and the east wind dried up its fruit." Hosea, xiii, 15, "Though he be fruitful among his brethren, an east wind shall come, the breath of Jehovah coming up from the wilderness, and his spring shall become dry and his fountain shall be dried up." Jonah iv, 8, says that "God prepared a sultry east wind, and the sun beat upon the head of Jonah that he fainted and requested for himself that he might die."

The most noteworthy thing about the character of the ground in Palestine is the limestone rock which determines the quality of the soil, the shapes of the hills, and the presence of thousands of caves of every size. This means that the country is porous and so, very much of the rainfall drains away from the surface into caverns and channels where it is not, under present methods, available except as cisterns, pits, and catch basins are provided for it. The many caves have been used for various purposes through the ages. Nowadays they are frequently used as shelters for sheep and goats.

(I Kings, xviii, 4) Obadiah, who was over Ahab's

household but feared Jehovah more than he did Jezebel, took an hundred prophets during the raging persecution and the great drought and hid them by fifty
in a cave, feeding them with bread and water. There
are caves where he could have housed the whole
hundred easily. When the Philistines afflicted the
Israelites in the days of Saul, the Hebrews are said
to have hidden in caves and holes and cisterns (I Sam.
xiii,6). There are hundreds of pits in all that country,
used formerly for water and grain. About Jebà one
can hear the hollow resonance as one rides over the
underground pits. In the valley of Michmash there
is a perpendicular cliff. Midway in the cliff there are
cave-rooms which seem to have no way of approach
unless one be swung past the openings by a rope.
Certainly no unwelcome person could force his way
into them.

Stones are so plentiful in most regions of the hill
country that they are the most obvious weapon in an
altercation. Stoning is frequently mentioned in both
testaments. In Deut. xxvii, 17, boundary markers are
mentioned. Stones were used for this purpose then
as now. Walls, towers, and huts are made of
loose stones which have to be reconstructed often, as
frost and rain make the loose structures unstable.

(Matt. v, 14.) The city set on a hill is a rule to
which there are occasional exceptions in Palestine.
The more wild the times and the smaller the village,
the more need that it be perched on an eminence
whence the inhabitants may detect the approach of
foes. There is usually a lofty dwelling in each of
these villages. It may be the head-man's house.

From the tower of Jezreel the watchman (II Kings ix, 17) espied Jehu as he rode from Ramoth-Gilead. Another continuing feature is the narrow entrance to the village, a mere lane between stone walls which makes it difficult for a crowd to surge into the settlement. In the story of Balaam (Num. xxii, 24) it is said, "Then the angel of Jehovah stood in a narrow path between the vineyards, a wall being on this side and a wall on that side."

To marry among one's kindred is both desirable and customary. (Gen. xxiv, 3, 4; Num. xxxvi, 8–11.) A large family, mostly boys, is hoped for. (Psa. cxxvii, 3–5; Gen. xxiv, 60; xxix, 34; xxx, 20.) In the struggle for existence male children are elements of success. One's daughters become merged in the family into which they marry. The custom is to marry off the older daughter before the younger. (Gen. xxix, 26.) Prayer and other religious observances, some of which may better be called superstitions, are resorted to by barren wives.

The guest room is still an adjunct of village life. (Mark 14:14.)

Names may be given to children to illustrate the parents' hopes, aspirations, fears, devotion, endearment, etc. (Ruth i, 20; cf. Ishbosheth.)

It would be easy to take up one's bed and walk off with it. (John v, 8, 9.)

Grass is mentioned in Matt. vi, 30, as fuel for the oven and is one of the kinds used for that purpose to-day. Usually the oven is housed in a little stone hut and several families use the same one.

Locusts are used as food in some parts of Palestine. (Matt. iii, 4.) Figs are still used as plasters. (II Kings xx, 7.) Parched wheat is a delicacy. (Josh. v, 11; Ru. ii, 14.) The common dish is usual among the peasantry. (Matt. xxvi, 23.)

Whitewashed sepulchres and shrines loom up among green trees and sometimes without them on hillsides. They are more wholesome looking at a distance than near by, which may also be said of many Palestinian structures.

The sower (Matt. xiii, 3) goes forth to sow and plows over the ground sown while the donkey, on whose back the seed-bag and plow were brought to the field, is turned loose to browse near the plowing oxen until needed on the homeward journey. (Job i, 14.)

Women work in the fields. (Ruth ii, 8, 9.) The animals eat chopped straw with their fodder. (Gen. xxiv, 25.) Tares are seen among the wheat. (Matt. xiii, 25–30.) At the threshing floor it is sometimes the custom to drive the animals over the grain in order to bruise the ears with their hoofs and sometimes sharp shod sledges are driven around over the heap. Contrary to Old Testament law, the animals are hitched together promiscuously and muzzled. (Harvest, Psa. cxxvi, 5, 6; Isa. ix, 3; threshing floors, Joel ii, 24; threshing, Hos. x, 11; Micah iv, 13 (hoof); Isa. xli, 15 (instruments); Deut. xxii, 10 (animals together); Deut. xxv, 4 (muzzling).

The sieve is used after the winnowing fork and the chaff is blown aside by the wind.

In the vineyards are huts or little towers where the caretakers and sometimes the family of the owners remain through the grape season. Olive trees are beaten with poles and the berries gathered from the ground. In lieu of banks, treasure is sometimes secreted in fields and many old tombs contain valuables. The hope of finding such treasure in the field is one of the dreams of the peasantry and often a theme of stories.

Bargaining of a kind like that common to-day in Palestine is evidenced in Old Testament records. (Gen. xxiii, 11–15.) The wasît is almost indispensable to-day as in olden times and has given rise to figures of spiritual intermediaries. (Job ix, 33; Gal. iii, 19; I Tim. ii, 5; Heb. viii, 6; ix, 15; xii, 24.)

Invitations are often delayed until the host is able to say "Come, for all things are now ready." (Matt. xxii, 3, 4.) Guests are over-urged to remain with the host. (Judges xix, 5–8.)

The artist who fashioned the exquisite book of Ruth had a taste for delineating the features of his land and the customs of his people. The result is an Israelite Arcadia which reads often like a transcript of present customs.

Even to-day natives of the region about Bethlehem-Judah have occasion to travel afoot or with donkeys across the Jordan valley to the field of Moab. Famine conditions threaten the people at times even in these days. Compound names in which the name for God appears are common as in the case of Eli-Melech. The name of his wife, Naomi, is common in its Arabic form. The wives of the two sons would, even to-day, live with the parents of the sons. When the father and the sons died, the three widows would have no tie of custom to hold them together any longer. The case of these three women was especially pitiable and destructive of any common interest, as there were no children among them. In these afflictions the hand of The Lord would be seen. At the parting of Naomi from her daughter-in-law the case of Orpah would excite no surprise while that of Ruth would seem as noteworthy now as then. The widow Naomi would have no penny's worth of claim in Moab, for she appertained to no man, neither husband nor son and, not being desirable in marriage, her case was one of hopeless poverty unless she could, perchance, find comfort among relatives in Bethlehem which was several days' journey afoot through the fiercest heat of all Palestine. As for Ruth, once away from Moab, she would be absolutely at the mercy of the love and honor of poor Naomi whose own chances would be of the slimmest. That one should marry Ruth and care for her in Moab might be likely, but in Bethlehem-Judah an improbable dream at the very best. It was more probable that she without a male relative would fall prey to attack as a helpless stranger. Even with a baby boy her chances would be better, but she was a helpless female, unblessed of man or God.

"And Ruth said, Entreat me not to leave thee, and to return from following after thee: for whither thou goest, I will go; and where thou lodgest, I will lodge: thy people shall be my people, and thy God my God: where thou diest, will I die, and there will I be buried: Jehovah do so to me, and more also, if aught but death part thee and me." (Ruth i, 16–17.)

"And it came to pass when they were come to

Bethlehem, that all the city was moved about them."
(Ruth i, 19.)

They came at the best time of the year, the barley
harvest. This is the beginning of the fruitful season
of harvests. Poor and hungry people could eat barley and there might be work, if not, then gleaning.
And if ever the peasants are disposed to be generous
it is after the anxiety and scarcity of the winter
season are over and they know themselves safely
through the terrors of famine and sickness and
arrived at the time of the first harvest. For after
the barley harvest comes the wheat harvest, then
the grape harvest, then figs, pomegranates, olives,
a succession of the fruits of the earth. During this
half of the year there is comparatively plenty to eat
and no danger of perishing with wet or cold.

It was at the beginning of this season that Naomi,
hungry, spent, and forlorn, came to Bethlehem-Judah
and remembered her wealthy kinsman. Would he
remember her? The imagination is dulled by food and
plenty. Ruth, with the energy of necessity, went out
to find her living in the society of harvesters. Boaz
came to his fields and servants and spoke the cour-
teous greeting, "The Lord be with you" (ii, 4), and
is answered as with one voice, "The Lord bless
thee." The eye of the oriental lighted upon the
fair damsel, and being answered as to her identity,
knew her story at once as who did not by this time
in all the place? Boaz had not called on Naomi. Only
the women of the kindred households would do that.
Possibly he would yet be appealed to in her dire
necessity. But he talked with the damsel. Our occi-

dental philosophy says, "if you want a thing done well, go, if not, send," but Naomi was not an occidental, fortunately for all concerned. She could have done no better, possibly, than to be represented in just such a meeting at just such a time by just such a girl. The idealism, the loyalty, the industry and the modesty of this Moabitess created an opportunity for the virtues of generous impulse to thrive under the auspices of a personal interest. Boaz is about as noble as men ought to be. Ruth is the choicest of Moab's country. The romance sweetens as it ripens. Around the harvester's common dish they are sitting, tearing off pieces from the sheets of spongy graham bread held on the knee, and dipping it, to give it a pleasant acid taste, in the huge bowl that sits on the ground in their midst. Then they have pulled some of the barley heads from the sheaves and have roasted them. It has the pleasant taste of the first of the season and the luxury of a dessert. Boaz, growingly kind, hands some of these to the girl, who is not lacking an out-of-door appetite. Probably Naomi at home is not dining to-day. Boaz connives with his servants so that the result of that day's gleaning for Ruth is surprising, an ephah of grain. (The Hebrew bushel.) Truly fortune was looking up. The good old woman at home might well be enthusiastic; here was plenty.

"And her mother-in-law said unto her, Where hast thou gleaned to-day? and where hast thou wrought? blessed be he that did take knowledge of thee. And she shewed her mother-in-law with whom she had wrought, and said, The man's name with whom

I wrought to-day is Boaz. And Naomi said unto her
daughter-in-law, Blessed be he of Jehovah, who hath
not left off his kindness to the living and to the dead.
And Naomi said unto her, The man is nigh of kin
to us, one of our near kinsmen.'' (Ruth ii, 19, 20.)
Yea, and better, ''Thou shalt keep fast by my young
men until they have ended all my harvest.'' (ii, 21.)
So, through two harvests, the barley and the wheat,
Ruth was to keep near her providence. (cf. iii, 15.)

The bodies of the aged may cease to strive in a
physical world, with youthful vigor, but their minds
may, with increment of years of wisdom and experience, devise good things.

''And Naomi, her mother-in-law, said unto her,
My daughter, shall I not seek rest for thee, that it
may be well with thee?'' (iii, 1.) And the good old
wise woman opens the view of her plan for Ruth and
for Boaz to the young woman's heart. Now Ruth
was not only energetic, she was also humble and could
learn. She could follow good leadership implicitly.
Her perfect submission to the wise outline of Naomi's
thought, to Naomi's knowledge both of the times
and country and of the character of the great man
whose riches were not yet complete nor whose heart
satisfied, led to one of the most idyllic scenes in all
chivalry. The man was revealed in all the hidden
possibilities of his great soul and he proved God-
fearing and clean.

When Ruth came back to report to Naomi, that
sleepless saint looked up with a quick glance and
with the heart-searching question, ''Who art thou,
my daughter?'' And she told her all. Then said

Naomi, "Sit still, my daughter, until thou know how the matter will fall: for the man will not rest, until he have finished the thing this day." (iii, 18.)

Now the gate of such a place as Bethlehem was several things in one. It was Town Hall, exchange, "the corner," the place to see the man you wished, arbitrate the case in hand, and do business.

" Boaz went up to the gate, and sat him down there." (Ruth iv, 1.) And there passed by a kinsman of Naomi of nearer degree than Boaz. Orientals are very accommodating with their time. Ten men were found without difficulty and these of the most important, the elders. They didn't know what the business was to be, but, so long as it was business and some one's affairs, they were filled with interest. The near kinsman was addressed before them all with a technical case of law and right. The question involved a property right which, on first hearing, the relative was glad to assume, but when Boaz went on skilfully to define the case more exactly and say that it meant for this relative to take a dead and childless kinsman's place, marry the widow and have children who should be known not as his but as the dead man's, the relative began to be appalled, at the complications of his own rights as a citizen, father, and property-holder, head of an independent household.

This case is one in which the modern custom of Palestine does not offer aid by resemblance and there is reason to believe that the custom was no longer in vogue in the days of the author of Ruth.

The practical result is that all hindrances are removed and Boaz follows heart and honor in one road to the door of Naomi and espouses the sweet heroine of the story. The story closes with the most delightful oriental success, a man-child.

SUGGESTIONS FOR STUDY

1. Study a physical map of Palestine and seek to imagine the progress of the seasons and the crops.

2. What is the latitude of Palestine and what countries does it resemble in climate, soil, crops, etc.?

3. From what point of view could Palestine be thought of as a land of abundance? Joshua v. 6.

4. Contrast the spirit of Ruth with that of Ezra and Nehemiah with reference to foreign marriage.

BOOK LIST

SMITH: The Historical Geography of the Holy Land.

PATON: Jerusalem in Bible Times.

BAEDEKER: Palestine and Syria.

WILD: Geographic Influences in Old Testament Masterpieces.

GRANT: The People of Palestine.

HUNTINGTON: The Transformation of Palestine.

CHAPTER XV

The Exile is considered by the more conservative writers to be the watershed of Hebrew thought and life. They follow the example of Josephus, who says that the people have been styled Jews from the time that they returned from Babylon. (Whiston's Josephus xi, 5.) There have been tendencies, as we have seen, to set the great turn in the tide of Hebrew affairs at a later period. At some time in the fifth or the following century a new ecclesiastical organization was born. A new Jewish nation arose markedly different from the ancient Hebrew kingdoms. Before that epochal change the people were seeking to establish a place for themselves among the nations. After that they cultivated a system of law and discipline of a more literary and liturgical nature. Before, they were immature, objective, frankly sensuous and idolatrous. After, they became more self-conscious, introspective and sternly monotheistic. The genius of a new people showed itself in the former state while in the latter period there is the doggedness of age and experience.

The coming of Alexander the Great brought a new world to Asia. The enthusiasm with which he was hailed by the Jews, when once they decided to follow his lead, was similar to the feeling aroused by Cyrus over two centuries previous. Judaism had become a people of a book. The tendency began in Hebrew times as far back as the days of Josiah at least. It was accelerated with every rebuff in the political world. The movement has never wholly ceased but revives with every scholastic impulse. Judaism developed a system of careful legal provision for every need of an educated person. With great patience and much subtlety a written constitution was made which would express the divine will concerning human life. Affairs, civil and criminal, public and private, political, ethical, etc., are included in the law. Such a written instrument cannot keep pace in particulars with the demands of a growing society, therefore there is an endless effort to adjust the old law to each novel case by interpretation. These interpretations become in turn an enormous tradition which in time engulfs the original code. A new codification and a fresh start is then needed. Thus the procession of the law continues through the centuries.

Whether this appeals to us or not depends partly on temperament and partly on training. In any case, we shall see that something like it is the fact in every civilized nation and that the disciplinary value of it has been high. Mental power has been quickened and refined and the ethics of the nation formulated. Too often the established order has seemed to forbid the prophetic voices of true religion. The words of an ancient prophet have been used against a new one, therefore any record may be employed wrongfully. The greater difficulty has been to distinguish between the true and false prophet.

Civil and Religious Control.—Although Judaism made an ecclesiastical state in which political and religious questions were often confused, as well as matters of ceremony and morals, yet there was always a recognition of the two functions of civil and priestly

rule. The civil and religious leaders in the days of
Haggai and Zechariah are mentioned. Both were
Hebrews. After that time there is a strong probability that the religious head will be a Jew and the
civil ruler a foreigner. There will surely be factions
in such a state. In Judah there was often a party
that cared little for political changes and affiliations
if they might be left alone in control of the religious
life of the people or allowed to worship according
to their wishes. The pious Jew who felt that the only
important thing in the world was the culture of religion and the true form of worship had little respect
for the more worldly Jew who wanted to develop
his country's interests economically and politically.
Those worldly-wise Jews who took the trend of the
times after Alexander's conquest were despised by
the puritanical Jews who resisted the Greek culture.
These latter were called the Hasidim or the Pious.
They found fault with the victorious Maccabees of the
Second Century because they seemed chiefly interested in the political salvation of the Jewish nation.
The descendants of the Pious would be the Pharisees
who were happiest when the ruler of the time, as a
Herod, gave the religious control into their care.

In many respects the religious party of the Jews
was most satisfactorily situated when its country
was ruled by a foreigner, as Persia, Macedonia, or
Rome, who would not meddle with the religious and
ecclesiastical prerogatives. This has been a common
experience with religious communities in the East
in modern times. In fact, they control who have the
people with them, and wherever the genius of a

people is primarily religious the native leaders will prefer the religious sceptre if they must choose.

The religious party among the Jews grew more influential because of its freedom from political responsibilities and territorial boundaries. It went throughout the world wherever Jews were to be found and ruled them from its spiritual capitals, Jerusalem, Babylon and Alexandria. Jerusalem was the head city of the faith as long as it stood. The antithesis of the church and the world had its rise among the Jewish doctors and priests ruling in a Graeco-Roman world. At the opening of the Christian era the moral triumphs of the Mosaic system were very plain to a Jew wherever he went. Converts were made from the Gentiles and the sacred law was read and studied.

The synagogue was a useful institution which instructed as it bound in one the Jewish people in many parts of the world. In spite of the law which centralized the religious life in one holy temple at Jerusalem, we know that other places of worship existed. There was the temple at Elephantine (p. 312) and places of assembly for prayer were a necessity. So hundreds of these arose. The temple at Jerusalem continued to be the one legal place of sacrifice for strict Jews. But in the thousand places of prayer the people were educated in morals and religion. It is clear that many social and racial interests would centre in the synagogue and that the Christian Church would derive much from it. The charm of this holy fellowship of worshippers of an austere but adorable deity attracted many an earnest pagan.

Proselytes or converts were made in considerable numbers. The cultural value of such a system of worship upon individuals must have been great and the fellowship was independent of political changes in the secular Roman world.

The class of experts known as the scribes were laymen who became so necessary as to outvie the priest in practical importance. Priests were comparatively few and localized at the temple. With the fall of the temple their vocation was in abeyance. The scribal explainers of the law and the rabbis who succeeded them outlasted temple and priests and have performed a service for the Jews not unlike that of Ezekiel after the fall of the first temple.

The work of the scribes included the service of the letter, even the writing out in fair copy of the Holy Scripture, the exposition of its significance and the decision of cases by it.

They were the lords of the only learning worth while, the knowledge of God, preserved in written record and oral tradition. They magnified their office and the genius of the Jewish people joined with them to establish this law as the dearest possession. The servants of the law, the rabbinical masters became, in Jewish esteem, the greatest of human beings. Before the exile the religious groups were prophetic and priestly, with the latter tending to outstrip the former. After the founding of the new Jewish state, the division was between priests and scribes, with the tendency favoring the scribes.

The religious literature of the Jews went on accumulating beyond the contents of the Bible. The Law was given a new setting in the Mishna; the teachings of the learned doctors of the Law, at first purely oral, were gathered in the Talmuds of Jerusalem and Babylon. The Jewish scriptures were translated into the popular dialects of the Targums and the many studies and notes were collected in the Midrashim and the Massorah. This development continued through the Middle Ages into modern times. In a very similar way the Christians continued writing, explaining, translating and discussing after the close of the New Testament. The Fathers, the Versions, the Commentaries and the succeeding Christian literature to date offers many analogies to the development of the Jewish literature.

Groups and Parties.—From the time of Nebuchadrezzar Hebrews may be thought of in two grand divisions, those who lived in Palestine and those who lived abroad. The foreign group consisted of those who had gone as captives from the home-land or voluntarily as traders and travelers. After the time of Alexander the Great the distinction was a sharper one. The home Jews were much more conservative than the Jews of the Diaspora. The foreign Jews were naturally affected by their surroundings. The Palestinian Jews continued using the Hebrew tongue until it was displaced by the Aramaic. The Jews in the Greek-speaking world learned that cultivated language and largely forgot Hebrew. Judaism, even in Palestine, was not one harmonious fellowship. The East with its intense fervor begets sects. In the New Testament period these may be illustrated by five of the party groups, Sadducees, Pharisees,

Essenes, the early followers of John the Baptist and the companions of Jesus. These arose in the order named. The Sadducees and the Pharisees existed as hostile parties long before the New Testament time. The Sadducees were modern Zadokites, descendants of the ancient priesthood of Jerusalem. They formed an aristocratic group keenly interested in the temple and city and little likely to favor any innovation in doctrine or practice. They were powerful politically during much of the Hasmonean history. The Pharisees are looked upon as the historical successors of The Pious or party of the Hasidim who were an outgrowth of the scribal fellowship. They specialized in religious interpretation and grew in favor with the ordinary Jews throughout Palestine. They became a stronger influence than the Sadducees.

The Essenes are sometimes explained as ultra-Pharisees. They were strict in their discipline. Most of them were agriculturists who renounced trade since it led to covetousness, disapproved of war and slavery and lived in a celibate brotherhood with brother-houses where they admitted their traveling members. They had rules of admission to the Essene fellowship, grades of membership, a costume and ritual. The Essenes were revered for their holy living and generosity. They remind us in many ways of the Shakers.

The Holy City.—Jerusalem is a sacred city to Jews, Christians and Moslems. It is the centre of interest for travelers to Palestine. Its history is known for 3400 years. Many ancient cities in Syria and Palestine have continued to be populated sites down to modern times. Such are Damascus, Beirut, Tyre, Sidon, Nazareth, Shechem, Hebron, Joppa, Gaza, Bethlehem and Jerusalem. This means that the natural conditions which led to their selection have continued to be influential in making those places human homes. The original Jerusalem was built on a little plateau overlooking the confluence of the valleys Hinnom and Kidron. North and west of this spot the increasing city spread along the two valleys. The earliest known ruler of the city was Abdi-khepa, who wrote letters to the Egyptian pharaoh, which show that Jerusalem was then a vassal of Egypt. Jerusalem must have been an old city even then. It was a natural, easily defended outpost of civilization against marauders from the region of the Dead Sea and the South. The place would be walled on the north at all times, where the hilly eminence connects with the larger plateau on which the present city is built. It afforded a protected market for nearby villagers as it does to-day. Jerusalem was able to hold out against the Hebrew invaders for two hundred years.

At the summit of the hill overlooking the Kidron valley is a rock outcrop about fifty feet square. This place has been the centre of a sanctuary for ages. It held the temples built in the days of Solomon, Darius and Herod and the present Moslem shrines popularly known as the Mosque of Omar and the Mosque el-Aksa.

Jewish soldiers served in the Greek and Roman armies and probably in considerable numbers in the

Persian army. In the Fifth Century a community of Jews lived at Elephantine, Egypt, near the First Cataract of the Nile. It included soldiers and had a temple that had been in existence for several generations. One reads in Jeremiah, forty-third and forty-fourth chapters, how after the destruction of Jerusalem and the murder of Gedaliah, the governor of the remnant, Jeremiah was forced to follow Hebrew refugees to Egypt. Doubtless the Hebrews at that time set up the necessary aids to worship in the localities where they settled. At Elephantine the temple was destroyed by persecutors and the authorities in Palestine were implored to rebuild it. The Persian governor was more encouraging than the Jerusalem religious leaders and orders were given to restore the place of worship. Perhaps these Egyptian Hebrews were nearer to what might later be called the Samaritan rite.

From the Persian day to the Turkish rule in modern times Jerusalem was usually under the aristocratic control of certain leading families of Jews, wealthy and often priestly in affiliations. The Persians like the Turks were clumsy controllers of the Mediterranean, they used the Phenician navies for their sea-faring.

The present city covers portions of seven little hills which may be viewed as parts of two large ones. The lines of ancient walls are traceable within and without the present defences, which are more picturesque than military.

In the New Testament Times the most prominent building in the city was the great temple rebuilt by

MOSLEM AT PRAYER
(Photograph by H.G. Mitchell)

MOSLEMS IN THE MOSQUE AREA AT FRIDAY PRAYERS

Herod. It was in the large Sacred Area (The Haram) near the site of the present Mosque of Omar. There was a military castle at the northwest corner of the compound which was connected with the area by a bridge. Herod's palace, a theatre, a forum, and a hippodrome with other structures suggestive of the worldly dominance of European powers were west and southwest of the temple area.*

SUGGESTIONS FOR STUDY

1. What evidence is there of any political ambition in Judah between the mention of Zerubbabel, in Zechariah, and the rise of the Maccabees?

2. Any similarities between Alexander and Cyrus?

3. Why did not the synagogue contravene the law against places of worship other than the temple?

4. What Jewish writings continued the succession of the Scripture outside the canon?

5. Trace the dispersed Jews to the different parts of the world. Acts ii. 5–11.

6. Which of the hills of Jerusalem was the original Zion?

BOOK LIST

I MACCABEES, DANIEL.
BEVAN: The House of Seleucus.
BEVAN: Jerusalem under the High Priests.
OESTERLEY and BOX: Religion and Worship of the Synagogue.
FAIRWEATHER: Background of the Gospels.
MATHEWS: A History of New Testament Times.
G. A. SMITH: History of Jerusalem.
Articles in Bible Dictionaries on Pharisees, Sadducees, Herod, Synagogue, etc.
DEUTSCH: The Talmud.
MERRILL: Galilee in the Time of Christ.
MASTERMAN: Studies in Galilee.
THE APOCRYPHA.
SCHÜRER: History of the Jewish People in the Time of Christ.
MONTGOMERY: The Samaritans.
ANGUS: The Environment of Early Christianity.

* See Paton's " Jerusalem in Bible Times."

CHAPTER XVI

The Conquest and Division of the East.—Persia was a quivering body politic before Alexander dealt his decisive blows in 334–331 B.C. Satraps rebelled, cities broke away from the authority of the Great King, kingdoms were carved from the amorphous Persian so greatly changed since the days of the greater Achaemenians. Bithynia, Pontus, Cappadocia set up independent governments in Asia Minor during the first half of the Fourth Century. In the second half of that century Alexander was a lad under the instruction of Aristotle, a conqueror at Granicus, Issus, Tyre and Arbela. In 323 he died in Babylon at the age of thirty-three years. Alexander's little son, born after the father's death, and his incompetent half-brother, were heirs to the best of the known world, but they disappeared before the factious field-marshals of the Great Conqueror.

The generals of Alexander and their successors ruled the lesser empires into which his conquests were divided. They fought great battles by land and sea, seeking to excel each other in extent of authority until the Roman was able to subdue the old Alexandrian world.

The Greek Empires of Syria and Egypt.—Shortly after the battle of Ipsus (301) when Antigonus was killed, Seleucus, who had been a general ruler under Alexander, controlled a large part of western Asia and built Antioch. This city became the chief Syrian capital. The extreme eastern and western parts of the empire were governed from Seleucia on the Tigris and Sardes, Croesus' old capital, respectively.

The two parts of Alexander's domain most interesting to us are these new kingdoms or empires north and south of Palestine. Syria on the north was ruled by the House of Seleucus and Egypt on the south was ruled by the House of Ptolemy. Both ruling families were Macedonian Greek. Hellenism, that is, Greek thought and feeling and way of life, spread far and wide in the East, but the oriental religions held their own and later permeated much of the West. The city of Alexandria became the great eastern centre of light and learning. Among the leading scholars of those days were prominent Jewish citizens of that Greco-Egyptian city.

It was not long before flourishing Greek cities were to be found throughout Syria. The culture of Europe mingled with the classical tendencies of Asia. Greek exercising schools, gymnasiums, baths, theatres, race-courses and talk were soon present as enlivening forces in the Semitic East. The luxury-loving Easterner seized upon the softer features of life and manners thus introduced but did not so often acquire the hardness of head or of physique of the Greeks. Yet trained athletic champions upholding the tradition of European sports went about from city to city exhibiting, winning prizes and popularity. In due time noted scholars arose in the East who adorned the pages of Church History.

Ecclesiasticus, with its sage, old-fashioned counsels (about 185 B.C.), reveals to us the puritanical firmness of orthodox Hebrew homes of those days.

Antiochus I, the successor of Seleucus, received his title Soter because he saved the Empire from an invasion of the Gauls. These European barbarians afterwards slew Antiochus and eventually settled a kingdom in Asia Minor. Their name stands in one of Paul's most important letters, To the Galatians.

The Hebrew Scriptures Published in Greek.—In the reign of Ptolemy Philadelphus of Egypt the Septuagint or Greek version of the Old Testament was begun. This translation from Hebrew into Greek was destined to be one of the most influential in history. Naturally it was more widely read than the Hebrew Bible by Jews and Christians and from it other important translations were made.

Josephus tells us a pleasing story of Ptolemy Philadelphus, who was the second successor of Alexander to rule Egypt. This ruler was a patron of the Jews and is said to have liberated 120,000 Jewish slaves who were serving in the army and in civilian occupations in Egypt. The same Ptolemy encouraged the collection of books for the great library in Alexandria, and, as his librarian recommended the translation of the Jewish legal writings for the library, sent word to Eleazar, high priest at Jerusalem, and invited him to provide six elderly scholars from every Jewish tribe to render the translation from Hebrew to Greek. With the request the king sent most persuasive words and gifts, furniture for the temple and offerings for the sacrifices. Josephus refers to the total number of translators as seventy instead of seventy-two, and naively says that he forbears to give their names but does record the royal

gifts as showing "how great a regard the king had
for God." Josephus continues to say that the old
men reached Egypt with their presents of courtesy
and "the parchments upon which they had their
laws written in golden letters." Ptolemy, after in-
terchanges of conversation, met the devout praises of
the delegates with "tears from excess of pleasure,
it being natural to men to show the same emotion in
great joy that they do in sorrow."

Josephus' tale of the royal reception, the consideration for the dietary of the scrupulous
strangers, the honor given to the God of Israel, the
philosophical questions asked, the policies of government discussed, the quiet scholar's retreat by the
sea to which the translators were taken to pursue
their task, the early morning call on royalty, the sea
baths, the studious labor until 3 P.M. of each day,
the ample provision of food and recreation, the completion of the translation in 72 days, the careful readings and revisions, in all this we see the scholarly
and cultural ideals of the days as well as if it were
all strictly historical.

Ptolemy wished to know why these excellent laws
had not been studied for the world's edification before, and the pious answer was that they were so holy
as to be practically taboo so "that no one had ven-
tured to touch upon the description of those laws
because they were divine and venerable and because
some that had attempted it had been afflicted by
God." One man who even contemplated the subject
had suffered temporary insanity of a month's
duration. A poet who wished to mention certain

things in the sacred books was afflicted with a disease
of the eyes which did not leave him until he desisted
from his purpose.

Ptolemy Philadelphus' precautions and great
good fortune can be appreciated in view of such
stories. The king was most appreciative and was
lavish in gifts to his aides. The Jews were grateful
for such a royal friend. Josephus loved to dilate
upon the traditional favor of kings to the Jewish
people, citing kindnesses and special privileges from
Seleucus, Nicator, Antiochus the Great, Vespasian
and Titus, and Marcus Agrippa.

In the wars between Syria and Egypt, Palestine
always suffered whichever side won. Antiochus the
Great overcame the Egyptian general Scopas in a
great battle at Banias, by the springs of the Jordan.
The Jews helped provision the victor's army and
received favor and remittance of taxes.

Whenever the Macedonian kings of Asia weakened, or even at times when they were fairly strong,
the Greek cities of the East developed a quasi-inde-
pendence, doing many sovereign acts for themselves.
The trade of soldier was a common one, as many a
local dynast and the greater emperors had occasion
to hire mercenaries. For the youthful and daring
citizens the adventure of soldiering must have been
very attractive and the control and provisioning of
armies must have been fairly satisfactory to have
drawn so many into the service. Because the Jews
made such loyal friends and subjects Antiochus took
two thousand Jewish families from Babylonia and
Mesopotamia to colonize disaffected regions of Lydia
and Phrygia.

Antiochus gave his daughter Cleopatra, an earlier possessor of the name than the famous Cleopatra in the time of Antony, to the ruling Ptolemy (V. Epiphanes, 205–181 B.C.). Judæa was included in the dowry.

The mischievous method of farming out the taxes that has done so much harm to the East in recent Turkish times was in vogue then. The influential men paid the government or guaranteed the payment of the sums required in tribute and in return gained the privilege of collecting taxes pretty much as they deemed fit. By the same method these chief collectors farmed out the privileges in smaller portions of their own right to under-collectors. The expense through waste and oppression was very great and the system odious to all but the absentee beneficiaries.

A brilliant and resourceful young Syrian by the name of Joseph was evidently a prince of tax-collectors, type of those who were dear to kings' hearts. He scented danger to his country and opportunity for himself in the unwillingness of his uncle the high priest Onias to meet the demands of the Suzerain, Egypt, in the collection of tribute. Joseph, by large gifts and courtly persuasions, secured the right over all bidders to the Judean tax collections. His competitors were old hands at the business. He offered to double their offer which he accused them of scaling down for selfish profit and he promised further to send to Egypt all the property seized from those who refused to pay. In order to carry out this latter promise he took with him two thousand soldiers on his return from Egypt and exhibited his prowess

at the city of Ascalon. There the people laughed at
his demands for taxes. Joseph executed a score of
prominent citizens and sent the treasure realized
from their confiscated estates to Ptolemy, who was
pleased and gave him carte blanche. Joseph thus
encouraged was able to show the age a new thing in
efficient tax collection throughout his field. He lived
thus twenty-two years a great man of the East and
was the father of eight sons, the youngest one of
whom, Hyrcanus, outdid his father in quick wit and
ready resource. Of this lad stories are told that
remind us of fairy lore. The elder sons were lazy
and inefficient and at every test Hyrcanus shone in
distinction above them. One test put upon him was
that he was sent to distant fields to plow with a large
number of oxen but no harness. He promptly slew
enough oxen for harness leather and to supply food
for his servants and with the live animals plowed
his stint. This young Hercules went on a visit to
represent his father at the Egyptian court, where by
his impudent cleverness he amazed the indulgent
monarch and returned home to become a great man
in the country east of Jordan. There to-day the
ruins of his sumptuous provisions for life, war and
defence are seen at Arak el-Emir. This adventurous
emir died in the reign of Antiochus IV, whose reign
was marked by further wars between Syria and
Egypt, to the great distress of Palestine.

Syria Afflicts the Jews in Palestine.—As of old, there
were partisans of both Egypt and Syria among the
citizens of Jerusalem. In 170 B.C., when Antiochus
came to Jerusalem, his partisans let him in. He

looted the city and executed many of his opponents. Antiochus seized the city again two years later after another Egyptian expedition and stripped it of treasure. He forbade the sacrifices and left the Jews in great wailing over the apparent wreckage of their habitation and their religious privileges. He built a citadel in Jerusalem from which he might overawe the town. Such Jews as became subservient to him made themselves hateful to the pious party.

Antiochus defiled the great altar at Jerusalem with swine's flesh and built a smaller altar upon it. He forced similar sacrifices throughout the country. The Jewish ritual and scriptures were banned on pain of death. Many Jews gave way under the severities of the persecution. Many resolute Jews were martyred. Some were beaten and torn to fragments. Others were crucified. The little children who had been subjected to the Jewish ritual were strangled upon the dying bodies of the mothers.

Josephus charged the Samaritans with a readiness to claim connection with the Jews when the latter were in favor with the powerful but with treachery toward the Jews when in trouble. The double descent of the Samaritans from former Israelites and from those colonists of the East whom the Assyrians brought to Palestine made it possible for them to claim either line they chose. Antiochus received the professions of the Samaritans that they were willing to live according to the Greek customs. They were designated as "the Sidonians who live at Shechem."

While Ptolemy Philometor was king of Egypt

21

(181–146 B.C.), Onias, the son of Onias, built a Jewish temple at Leontopolis, in the district of Heliopolis.

Rome was a growing influence in eastern politics. War broke out between Macedonia and Rome about 200 B.C., just about the time that Palestine was acknowledged as a Syrian rather than an Egyptian province. Asia Minor had been taken away from Syria. Armenia had broken its allegiance to Antioch. Such was the general situation when Antiochus IV came to the Syrian throne. Although the domain of Antiochus, who was called Epiphanes, was a small one, it was compact and offered a fair field for a good ruler.

The Suffering of the Jews Under Antiochus.—But the new king was the worst of his line. His fixed idea was to convert the Jews to the Greek way of religion. He was not satisfied to let the new order proceed normally. The high priest Onias III, the head of the puritans, was set aside and his brother Jason, who favored the Hellenist party of Jews, was made high priest.

A Greek gymnasium was erected at Jerusalem and Greek games introduced in which even priests are said to have become enthusiastic. The office of high priest was next coveted by Menelaus, a worse man than Jason. Bitter struggles led to petty civil war. This angered the Syrian king, who was at the time on an expedition in Egypt. He visited Jerusalem, as mentioned on page 320, and directed a terrible massacre of the population. The temple riches were plundered at the same time. The altar of incense, the seven-branched candlestick, and the table of shewbread were carried away by the king to Antioch.

Two years later (168 B.C.) worse things happened to the Jews. Antiochus went again to Egypt and there met with severe disappointment. In a frenzy of rage he turned upon Jerusalem and instituted a war of extermination against those who held to the Jewish religion. (Dan. xi, 30 f.) Strangers were brought into Jerusalem to colonize and fill the places of those destroyed or driven away. Jerusalem bade fair to become, as the Syrian king intended, a Greek city. The city walls were partially demolished and the old city of David was made a strongly fortified place where a Syrian garrison could keep the population in control.

What was begun in the city was continued in all the country roundabout. The expectation was that the Jewish religion would be rooted out. Officers were sent everywhere to see that the new requirements were fulfilled. A monthly search was made for signs of disobedience. By passive resistance, and then by open revolt, the Jews contested the power of the oppressor. One day at the town of Modin when the king's officer had sought to enforce the observance of heathen sacrifice, a priest by the name of Mattathias and his five sons—John, Simon, Judas, Eleazar and Jonathan—resisted the attempt and even slew on the very altar a Jew who was consenting to offer the required sacrifice. The king's officer was killed also and the altar destroyed by these rebels who then fled into the hills. Many joined the patriotic band so that it was able to go up and down through the country, destroying the heathen altars, killing renegades and encouraging the faithful.

All this seemed like a rash revolt, little likely to succeed against the great power of the Syrian king. The aged Mattathias died soon after and bequeathed the struggle to his sons, recommending that Simon be the counsellor of the enterprise and Judas the military leader. Judas was the practical leader, as most of the activity was to be fighting for a long time. His genius, intrepidity and generous devotion made him an ideal patriotic warrior. He won victory after victory, sometimes in the face of great discouragements and greatly superior numbers. The Jewish worship was re-installed at Jerusalem. The Syrian king sent a large army to quell the Jewish rebellion. So sure of victory did the Syrian army seem that it was accompanied by many foreign merchants who wished to be on hand to purchase the captured Jews as slaves.

By this time Judas, whose surname was Maccabeus, had drilled his bands of enthusiastic patriots into an army, the veteran of victorious encounters. The armies came near to each other in the province of Emmaus, west of Jerusalem, at the entrance of the hill country. The Syrians under Gorgias divided, leaving the main part in camp while the smaller went out to force Judas Maccabeus and his army to fight. Judas, well-informed, knew of the tactics and managed to place his army between the camp and the detachment which was distant with its general. He thrilled his small army with his courage, with the result that they threw themselves on the camp and main part of the army, utterly routing the Syrians and setting fire to the camp. About this time the scouting party under the general Gorgias returned and found an already victorious army prepared for them. The Syrians in dismay refused battle and fled into the old Philistine territory.

The next year Lysias led a still larger army into the Jews' country. This time he entered through the south country and reached a point about twenty miles or less south of Jerusalem on the Hebron road. Here at Beth-zur the armies met and a decisive victory for Judas and the patriots resulted. Lysias went back to Antioch to muster larger forces. Judas Maccabeus repaired the temple and rebuilt the altar, purifying all the places polluted by the Syrian persecutors. Everything was made clean and the temple was reconsecrated with a great feast to celebrate the occasion December, 165 B.C., just three years to a day after the pollution of the altar by heathen sacrifices. The festivities lasted eight days and it was resolved to keep the memorial by the Feast of Dedication each year thereafter. (See John x, 22.)

The first book of Maccabees is a good historical source ranking with our books of Kings in the Old Testament. During the Syrian persecutions the Apocalypse Daniel was flung from the agonized heart of a faithful Jew who sought to inspire his suffering nation with hope. Judas Maccabeus, the military genius of the family, died in 161 B.C. He fell fighting the Syrian foe.

Jonathan was the brother who succeeded Judas. From being the leader of the little band of patriots

remaining with the Maccabean cause after the defeat
of Judas he proceeded by most adroit skill and watch-
ful care to a position as the head of an all but independent nation (161–143 B.C.).

Actual independence, however, was not secured
until the administration of the next Maccabean
brother, Simon (143–135), or as some prefer to say,
not until the days of John Hyrcanus. All offices and
honors of headship were united in the titles conferred
on Simon. He was high priest and ethnarch, as well
as military governor of the country, and was recognized by the Syrian empire in the North. But though
Syria claimed nominal control over Palestine, the
real influence from the outside was being absorbed
by Rome.

Doubtless the successes of both Jonathan and
Simon depended partly upon the popular support
which the Hasidim were able now and then to throw
into the scale in favor of the Maccabean family.

The Hasidim emerge in the politics of the
time of the next Jewish ruler, John Hyrcanus
(135–105 B.C.), as an opposition party and are definitely called the Pharisees. Synchronous with the
rise of the Pharisees we may note the probable
naming of their opponents, the government party,
as the Sadducees.

John Hyrcanus ruled thirty years at least and
brought about full Jewish independence. He forced
the Idumeans (Edomites) to become converts to
Judaism. This event was fraught with consequences
of unforeseen importance to the future of the race
and dynasty of John Hyrcanus. He brought a bloody

end for the time being to the strife between Jews and Samaritans, destroying the cities of the latter.

Aristobulus (Judas), the son of John, was left to share the power with his mother, whom he imprisoned along with several brothers and associated with himself a favorite brother Antigonus. This brother died a victim to the suspicions of Aristobulus, who himself lived only a year after his accession.

Mahaffy comments on the frequency in that day with which queen-mothers were in positions of power in the different parts of Alexander's world. Hellenism and feminism were not infrequently joined.

Aristobulus left no children. His wife Salome released the imprisoned brothers and married the oldest, Alexander (Jonathan or Jannæus), making him both king and high priest. He became thus the first to enjoy the actual title of king. A coarse but successful warrior, he greatly extended the kingdom until it was as large as at any time in the olden days of the Hebrews. Alexander employed foreign mercenaries in his army and was supported by the party of the Sadducees. But the rank and file of the populace was against him. Led by the Pharisees they reviled him for holding in his bloody control the office of high-priest. The stories are familiar how, when they were asked by this king what would please them, the people answered that his own death would gratify them most, also how once they pelted Alexander with citrons as he officiated at the altar, whereupon he avenged himself savagely upon them. Civil war ensued in which Syria sided with the rebels. The Jewish state was brought to the verge of destruction, but Alexander was victorious, and before his death had regained most of his losses. He died about 78 B.C.

Salome was again widowed and in sole power. She committed herself definitely to the party of the Pharisees, made her son Hyrcanus II the high-priest with the result that the Sadducees were systematically persecuted in Jerusalem. The Jerusalem council was in the power of the Pharisees. The scribes were very influential. The religious party at Jerusalem was headed by Simon ben Shetach, brother of Salome. He was assisted by Judah ben Tabbai, an expert legalist from Alexandria in Egypt. Every Jew in the world above the age of twenty years was liable to an assessment of a half-shekel, annually, which went for the support of the temple-worship at Jerusalem.

Another son of Salome was named Aristobulus (II). His warlike character was in contrast with that of his weaker brother, the high priest. Moreover, he was hostile to the dominant Pharisees. So when Salome died and the opposition wished a leader, it found Aristobulus most available. Civil war followed in which the Romans manipulated the strife so as to get control of the politics of Palestine. Aristobulus defeated his brother in a battle at Jericho and succeeded for a short time to the chief power.

Just at this time the famous Idumean house, later known as the Herods, came into prominence. A very able member of the family was Antipater, the father of Herod the Great. Antipater's grandfather of the

same name had been governor of Idumea during the
reign of Alexander (Jannæus). This young Antipater threw his abilities to the side of Hyrcanus and
brought about a compact between him and Aretas,
the Arabian king of Petra. The combination was a
serious menace to Aristobulus. Pompey, the Roman,
was in the East, and through his delegate, Scaurus,
favored Aristobulus' side at first. Later, Pompey
approved Hyrcanus and the Pharisees and so brought
an end to the large importance of the Sadducean
party. Aristobulus and many other captive Jews
appeared in Pompey's triumph in Rome in September
of the year 61 B.C. This may be the beginning of the
Jewish synagogue in Rome from which the earliest
Christian society in that city may have separated.
But it is more probable that large numbers of Jews
had reached Rome before Pompey's time.

The tables were turned by Pharisaic Judaism
upon Hellenism and heavy blows were directed
against certain Greek cities. The weakening of Hel-
lenistic power in Syria let in the tides of Arabian
barbarism to the disruption of order in parts not
actually controlled by the zealous Jews. Hyrcanus,
left in nominal control of Palestine, had a secondary
power, in reality, to the ambitious Antipater.

Although Antipater had favored Pompey in his
quarrel with Cæsar the astute Idumean was able to
gain the good will of Cæsar after the latter's victory
over Pompey. Antipater was rewarded for his new
zeal for Cæsar's cause by the grant of Roman citi-
zenship, immunity from taxation, and the office of
procurator of Judea, Samaria, and Galilee. He now

overshadowed the mere ecclesiastical position of
Hyrcanus. His son Phasael was made governor of
Jerusalem and another son Herod was appointed
governor of Galilee. Several new privileges were
accorded the Jews. The mighty Cæsar fell a victim
to the Roman conspirators. After the defeat of
Brutus and Cassius, Herod secured the favor of
Antony. Herod had, for brilliant activity in his
office, been rewarded with the governorship of Cœle-
Syria. Antony, who was an old friend of their father,
appointed Phasael and Herod tetrarchs of Judea.
Meanwhile the last of the line of the Hasmoneans,
Antigonus, son of Aristobulus II, aided by Sadducees,
Parthians, Ptolemy Menneus of Chalcis, Marion of
Tyre, got the better of the Idumeans, captured Phasael, who then committed suicide. Antigonus was
king and high priest. Herod escaped to Rome and
was declared king of Judea by the Roman Senate.
He returned to take forcible possession of his kingdom. Backed by his Roman friends he was able
to do this, capturing Jerusalem 37 B.C. Antigonus
was executed and with him the Hasmonean House
went out of power. The Idumeans were secure in
authority under the Romans. Before his final success Herod had married Mariamne, who was doubly
related to the Hasmonean family, being a grand-
daughter of both Hyrcanus II and Aristobulus II, and
thus uniting in herself the opposing branches of the
Maccabean House.

Herod the Great is one of the most interesting
persons in history. One is amazed at his industry,
vigor and versatility, sickened by his cruelties, and

amused by his adroit gift in politics. He ruled the
hardest dependency of Rome in the most difficult
times imaginable. He had the polish of a Roman and
the savage heart of an Edomite. His family history
during his long reign was woefully tragical. When
he died he divided his domains among three sons:
Judea to Archelaus the king, Galilee and Perea to
Herod Antipas as tetrarch, and the northeastern
districts as a tetrarchy to Philip.

After the death of Herod the Great (4 B.C.) disorders broke forth in both Judea and Galilee, which
put in jeopardy the rights of the heirs under the will.
The three sons went to Rome to look after their
interests. Augustus sustained their claims for the
most part in spite of the strong protests of the Pharisees, who sent delegates to the Imperial City.
Serious uprisings and bloody contests had taken
place in Judea and Galilee. A fanatical religious
party called the Zealots, of similar interests to those
of the Pharisees but pursuing them by the most violent methods, came into prominence. They looked
for the immediate appearance of a Messiah and flung
themselves in anticipation of such help into a hopeless
contest with authority. In A.D. 6 Archelaus was dis-
graced and sent into exile by the emperor. Judea,
along with Samaria and Idumea, was organized into
a province under the Romans.

In the days of Jesus, Galilee was still controlled
by Herod Antipas, the slayer of John the Baptist.
Judea was under the procurators of Syria. Their
headquarters were at Cæsarea. Pontius Pilate was
procurator for ten years. He has been pilloried

for historic time because while on a visit to Jerusalem his day of judgment came.

With the establishment of the Roman procuratorship the old strife between Pharisees and Sadducees awoke in Jerusalem. First one party and then the other triumphed. The fiery Zealots developed an extreme section which became famous as the Assassins or Sicarii. (See Acts xxi, 38.) When the Sadducees called these violent fanatics to their aid they brought in a force that at last destroyed its employers. The country seethed with religious passion and bloodthirsty patriotism. Eventually, after several Romans had failed to control the situation, severer measures were used by Vespasian and Titus. Jerusalem was conquered after a terrible siege and its walls and buildings were destroyed in A.D. 70.

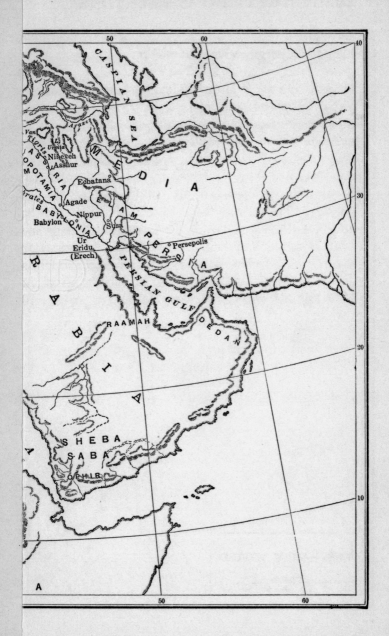

CASPIAN SEA

MEDIA

Araxes

Van
L.
Urmia
Tigris
Nineveh
Asshur
ASSYRIA
MESOPOTAMIA

Euphrates
Ecbatana

BABYLONIA
Agade
Nippur
Babylon
ELAM
Etam
Susa
Ur
Eridu
(Erech)

PERSIA

°Persepolis

ARABIA

PERSIAN GULF

RAAMAH

DEDAN

SHEBA

SABA

OPHIR

A

THE EARLY WORLD

SCALE OF MILES

INDEX